Sarah Tytler

Six Royal Ladies of the House of Hannover

Sarah Tytler

Six Royal Ladies of the House of Hannover

ISBN/EAN: 9783744650021

Printed in Europe, USA, Canada, Australia, Japan

Cover: Foto ©ninafisch / pixelio.de

More available books at **www.hansebooks.com**

Six Royal Ladies

of

The House of Hanover

CAROLINE OF BRUNSWICK, WIFE OF GEORGE IV. (WHEN SHE CAME TO ENGLAND AS A BRIDE).

Six Royal Ladies

of

The House of Hanover

By
SARAH TYTLER

Author of "The Tudor Queens," "Life of Marie Antoinette,"
"Life of Queen Victoria," etc.

With Portraits

London
Hutchinson & Co.
Paternoster Row
1898

PREFACE.

The compiler of the life-stories of the "Six Royal Ladies of the House of Hanover," apologises for what may seem to the reader instances of repetition. But in a series of lives which succeed and dove-tail into each other, where the same incidents, the same figures, under varying lights, appear and re-appear, a certain amount of repetition is inevitable. To avoid it would be to strip the different sketches of many of their characteristic touches, and to furnish inadequate representations of the times and of the individuals with whom the surroundings have to do.

CONTENTS.

I.

THE ELECTRESS SOPHIA.

	PAGE
CHAP. I. THE PRINCESS SOPHIA	3
,, II. A VISIT AND A MARRIAGE	15
,, III. THE DUCHESS	25
,, IV. COURT MATCH-MAKING	40
,, V. THE ELECTRESS	57

II.

SOPHIA DOROTHEA OF ZELL, WIFE OF GEORGE I.

,, I. SOPHIA DOROTHEA OF ZELL, WIFE OF GEORGE I.	75
,, II. KÖNIGSMARK'S DEATH	89

III.

CAROLINE OF ANSPACH, WIFE OF GEORGE II., AND HER DAUGHTERS.

,, I. THE ELECTORAL PRINCESS OF HANOVER AND PRINCESS OF WALES	109
,, II. AT LEICESTER HOUSE AND AT ST. JAMES'S	119
,, III. THE QUEEN	130

Contents

IV.

CHARLOTTE OF MECKLENBURG-STRELITZ, WIFE OF GEORGE III.

	PAGE
CHAP. I. A YOUNG QUEEN-CONSORT	169
„ II. A ROYAL WIFE AND MOTHER	199
„ III. AN AGING AND AGED QUEEN	222

V.

CAROLINE OF BRUNSWICK, WIFE OF GEORGE IV.

„ I. A ROYAL BRIDE	255
„ II. A CONTENTIOUS COUPLE	267
„ III. A WANDERING PRINCESS AND REPUDIATED WIFE	290

VI.

ADELAIDE OF SAXE-MEININGEN, WIFE OF WILLIAM IV.

„ I. THE DUCHESS	311
„ II. THE QUEEN	320

I.
THE ELECTRESS SOPHIA.

AUTHORITIES:

Memoirs of the Electress Sophia (1630–1680), *translated by H. Forrester; Memorien der Herzogin Sophie nachmals kurfürstin von Hannover, herausgegeben von Adolf Kocher; Letters of Charlotte Elizabeth, Duchess of Orleans;* Thackeray's *Four Georges.*

THE ELECTRESS SOPHIA (THE WORTHY LINK BETWEEN THE ROYAL HOUSES OF STUART AND HANOVER).

CHAPTER I.

THE PRINCESS SOPHIA.

When the Queen and the Prince Consort visited Germany in 1858 they made a brief halt at Hanover on their way to Potsdam, and drove out to Herrenhausen, the country palace of the old Electors and Dukes. The halt was not without its significance, for Hanover was the cradle of her Majesty's race on the German side, and Herrenhausen was long the home of the Electress Sophia (the connecting link, through her mother the Queen of Bohemia, between the royal houses of Stewart and Hanover), by whom the crown passed in the Protestant line to George I. and his successors. Not only so; the Electress was a power in herself, a gifted woman of strong mind and original character, who, though her immediate descendants did not inherit many of her individual traits, certainly left her impress on her successors. By her spirit and sagacity, not less than by her ambition, the great inheritance of the throne of England was secured to her children's children; and doubtless it was from her that her son, George I., derived the prudence and moderation which, in spite of many far from creditable or lovable qualities, served to seat him firmly on that throne.

But in course of time the wise and witty Electress has merged into a vague figure in the popular mind. Even when some sense of her capability and energy has lingered in men's memories, the most erroneous conception of the princess and woman have prevailed. This is partly due to the fact that her picture has been frequently drawn by foes as well as by friends, and oftener by her enemies than by her allies, in consequence of the number of Jacobite refugees in Germany, Holland, and France in her day. These ladies and gentlemen, from political bias and personal partiality to the Stewarts, were more or less ready to sketch their sovereign's rival unfavourably, and to transmit in their home correspondence all the hostile gossip and scandal regarding her and her Court. Under the circumstances, it is a testimony to Sophia's honest and upright life that the darker shades with which the writers felt justified in loading the likenesses of her son and grandson could not be applied to her. The detractors were compelled to limit their censures to representing the Electress as a harsh-tempered, worldly-minded, scheming little woman, who showed no feeling where feeling is most called for, whose sole aim was the aggrandisement of herself and her family, whose Protestant religion was a mere cloak for her sceptical philosophy. Her own nimbleness of tongue and readiness in sarcasm have also had something to do with these wholesale charges, which even the supporters of her dynasty, living in another country and not coming into personal contact with her, inadvertently adopted and handed down to the next generation. Her graphic, most entertaining autobiography was needed to correct the error. She wrote it in French; and while it is said that she was a law to herself as regards grammar and spelling, so vigorous and lifelike is her composition that her friend, the all-accomplished Leibnitz, said of it, in his unqualified admiration, that "by sheer force of creative originality she produced not only her own style, but her own French also." The Memoir was written to enliven the tedium of her husband's long absences from Herrenhausen, and to supply an occupation for her lively faculties. It is much to be regretted that the autobiography, which shows what a caricature of the real woman survived in England, was not continued to the end of her life. The narrow-souled plotter, the stern, cruel mother-in-law, the cynic and scoffer, which the Electress Sophia has been represented, was not the woman of whom Thackeray could write that she was "one of the handsomest, the most cheerful, sensible, the shrewdest, the most accomplished, of women"; not the woman to whom her plain-spoken, warm-hearted niece, Charlotte Elizabeth, Duchess of Orleans, could refer with cordial respect and tender affection to the close of her days; not the woman who was the intimate friend and "kind patroness" of the great Christian philosopher Leibnitz, the "Serena" of his letters, whom he held in the highest esteem.

The Electress Sophia was ambitious beyond question, for her children still more than for herself. She was, like her niece, Madame d'Orleans, what many people would call "brutally" matter-of-fact in her opinions, and unvarnished in her statements. She lived in a coarse, licentious generation, when every Court in Germany was deeply tinged with the vices still more than with the splendours of the Court of the great Louis. Her moral sense was not finer or keener than that of her neighbours. Her religion was exhibited more in her acts than in her professions. She was somewhat of a *moqueuse*, tempted to laugh at most things. Handsome and witty from youth to age; not only capable of winning and retaining affection, but endowed with the power of compelling admiration, she yet lacked the natural charm of her mother, the Queen of Bohemia and the Queen of Hearts—that facile charm of the Stewarts which is more frequently found in alliance with brilliant shallowness and reckless impulsiveness than with solid sense and calm wisdom.

But withal, the Electress Sophia was a woman of much worth and stability of nature, true to her obligations, a loyal wife, an attached mother, a faithful friend, a good mistress, respected, loved, and mourned most by those who knew and understood her best.

On October 14th, 1630, there was born at the Hague a little girl, who, humanly speaking, seemed little wanted in the world into which she had come. She was all but the last of the troop of children born to Elizabeth, daughter of James I. of England, and Frederick, the Prince Palatine of the Rhenish provinces. His acceptance, at the urgent instigation of his wife, of the crown offered him by the Protestants of Bohemia —which the couple enjoyed for but one winter—was followed by the loss of the battle of Prague, fought by the Catholic forces under his Emperor. It cost Frederick not only his newly-made kingdom, but the Palatinate also. From that date the landless pair were wanderers from European Court to Court, urging their claims on royal relatives, and beseeching help to win back Bohemia and the Rhine lands. In vain Frederick pressed on his neighbours his rights. In vain Elizabeth pawned her jewels in order to obtain the sinews of war, or employed all the fascinations of her beauty and misfortunes to attract adherents to a vanquished cause. Not till the Peace of Westphalia, after the death of Frederick, was the Palatinate restored to his eldest surviving son. In the meantime, after useless pilgrimages in search of money and soldiers, the couple, rich only in children, made their headquarters in Holland, where they strove to keep up in their poverty that most piteous of shadowy pretensions—a Court without a kingdom.

Sophia was the youngest of five sisters—Elizabeth,

Louise, Charlotte, and Henriette-Maria—who were kept in countenance by a still more formidable file of brothers—Henry, Charles Louis, Frederick, Edward, Philip, Rupert, and Maurice—conspicuous figures in the Civil War in England; and little Gustav, who was a year younger than Sophia. He was born at the time of their father's death, was a pretty, sickly boy, and died at the age of six years; sister Charlotte also died in childhood, and brother Henry did not survive his first youth; but the remaining ten reached the full estate of men and women.

So many of the family had come into the world before Sophia, that there was some difficulty in furnishing her with a name and providing her with the necessary complement of god-parents. It was by casting lots that her friends' choice fell on the Christian name "Sophia," and her sponsors had of necessity to be of lower rank than the magnates who had filled the same office at the christening of her elder brothers and sisters. Who could have guessed that, out of all the strong phalanx of goodly sons and fair daughters, little Sophia, too sharp and eager to have even any pretensions to childish beauty, would live to be the chosen representative of a great cause and creed, the member of the family in whom the hopes of the English Protestants and Whigs centred when the main branch of the Stewart line failed, either by death without heirs, or by the forfeiture of its responsibilities and privileges, and when all Elizabeth Stewart's elder children had either passed away and left no children in like manner, or had in their turn sold their birthright for a mass?

According to the vigorous, animated narrative with which the Electress Sophia occupied her leisure hours in middle age, she was removed when an infant, as soon as it was safe for her to perform the journey, from the Hague to Leyden, where she was brought up, in company with the brothers and sisters near her in age, under the care of an exemplary old lady who had reared the children's father. (The fact is mentioned as an indication of her advanced years. However, she was assisted in her duties by her two daughters, who were, as their pupil remarks in her naïve way, "older than their mother.") The reason of this banishment of the younger members of the household the writer explains with the perfect frankness which is occasionally somewhat startling to the reader. The Queen their mother preferred the company of her monkeys and dogs to that of her children. The poor Queen of Hearts believed herself born to preside over a Court, and much of her life was spent in endless machinations to recover her position. Her social charm has never been denied, but she does not seem to have been distinguished by the possession of the purely domestic virtues. Indeed, in her dealings with her sons and daughters, "the Queen," as they always termed her, in tenacious reference to her brief sovereignty, was more of a sovereign than of a mother. She even suffered herself to indulge in partialities and prejudices where her children were concerned, which were hardly calculated to promote family harmony.

The ladies to whom the children were entrusted were scrupulously conscientious in the fulfilment of their task. The little Sophia of early days recalls them in later years with gratitude and respect, though by no means without amusement at their homely looks and odd ways. She says they taught her "to love God and fear the devil," and brought her up in the good doctrines of Calvin.

There is an amusing account of one of those youthful days which bears witness, among other things, to the strictness of German discipline and the rigorousness of German etiquette. The bright, small pupil went at seven o'clock in *déshabille* to one of madame's daughters, who read the Bible and prayed with the child. Then Sophia learned by heart a portion of a popular code of German precepts or proverbs while her governess brushed her teeth, her grimaces in the process making an indelible impression on the clear, terribly observant eyes. Next the child was dressed and prepared by half-past eight for regular lessons, which continued till ten, when the dancing-master—always welcome—arrived. He gave "the exercise" till eleven—the dinner-hour for a meal of ceremony. It was served at a long table, before which the Princess's brothers "were drawn up, with their governors and gentlemen behind them." She made first a low curtsy to the Princes, and a slighter one to the others; another low curtsy in placing herself opposite her brothers; another slight one to her governess, who on entering the room with her daughters curtsied very low to the little Princess. She curtsied again in handing her gloves to her ladies; yet again in drawing near the table; again when the gentlemen brought her a large basin in which to wash her hands; again (as a form of "Amen") after grace was said; and for the last and ninth time, on seating herself at table. The food was appointed by rule for each day in the week. On Sundays and Wednesdays improving conversation was provided for the royal young people by the presence of a couple of divines or professors from the neighbouring university. There was "rest" till two, when lessons were resumed; at six there was supper, and at half-past eight bed, after reading in the Bible and prayers.

Princess Sophia led this diligent, monotonous life till she was nine years of age. In her second year she was left fatherless. Her brothers and sisters grew up. The Princes finished their education by travelling, or by entering the Emperor's army. The Princesses went to the Hague, to appear at the Court of the Princess of Orange, and at their mother's Court (by courtesy), where they could push their fortunes in the only way open to them. The little brother Gustav was dead, and it was held undesirable to keep up the establishment at Leyden for the Princess Sophia alone. She was taken to the Hague, to her great joy; for discipline and lessons were considerably relaxed, and the lively child was delighted with her share of the stir and bustle of the great world. Her cleverness and vivacity were acceptable in turn to the more formal and duller grown-up members of the household. Even the Queen allowed herself to be amused by the young girl's merry sallies, and granted to them a considerable amount of indulgence, to the pleased surprise, as it reads, of the recipient of the favour.

The Princess describes minutely her elder sisters—who were thenceforth her instructresses—the Princesses Elizabeth, Louise, and Henriette. According to their chronicler, they were all her superiors in personal attractions, and, in the case of the two elder sisters, in learning and accomplishments. Elizabeth was the greatest scholar, and had a philosophic and scientific bent. She corresponded with Descartes, then settled in Holland, and this may be the origin of the assertion—which does not seem to rest on any other foundation—that Sophia herself was the pupil of the French philosopher. Elizabeth had been partly brought up by her German grandmother, the Prince Palatine's mother, and was under the impression that the Queen, her own mother, had little love for her. In fact, Elizabeth was, to some extent, *une femme incomprise*—not in harmony with her surroundings. She desired to lead a single life, and in order to secure her independence became eventually Abbess of Herford. Louise also ended her life as an abbess—the Abbess of Maubisson ; but hers was a genuine perversion to Roman Catholicism. She was better fitted for society, was spirited and agreeable. She painted well, and Sophia's youthful admiration for her sister's work throws light on her subsequent interest in art. The third Princess, Henriette, was very fair and blooming. Her talents, we are told, lay in the direction of embroidery and cookery, and it sounds natural that she should be the first to marry. Her bridegroom was reckoned beneath her in rank, since he was only the lord of Siebenbürgen. The poor bride did not live long enough to question the wisdom of the step she had taken, for she died the year of her marriage, 1651.

Before Princess Sophia was in her teens, the Court at the Hague was excited by a visit from Henrietta-Maria of England. She came ostensibly to bring her little daughter, already married to the young Prince William of Orange, that she might be brought up in the States over which her husband was to rule. The Queen of England's real errand was to raise money, and procure weapons and recruits to assist her husband Charles I., then engaged in the Civil War. She was Sophia's aunt by marriage, and was then seen by the Princess for the first time. She gives, with her usual candour and animation, the impression produced upon her by Vandyck's beautiful Queen, the heroine of the devotion of the extreme Royalist party. Sophia was surprised to find her much-praised kinswoman a little woman, with long, thin arms, shoulders which did not match each other, and teeth projecting from her mouth like " guns from a fort." However, the unsparing critic acknowledges that the Queen had " beautiful eyes, a well-shaped nose, and an admirable complexion " ; so that our faith in Vandyck's veracity as an artist is not altogether shaken.

Mary Stewart, Princess William of Orange, was only ten years of age—a little younger than her cousin Sophia ; and it is half pathetic, half comical, to hear of the two as " playfellows."

As time passed, and the Civil War in England became more and more hopeless so far as the King's success was concerned, many English, Scotch, and Irish refugees thronged to the Hague, where the Prince of Wales (Charles II.) had taken refuge. Inevitably the titular Queen of Bohemia, herself an English princess and the Prince of Wales's aunt, with her family, occupied a prominent position in the strange scene. Princess Sophia at seventeen evidently enjoyed it, though, as she says in her expressive way, the family, in their chronic poverty, "had often nothing to eat save pearls and diamonds." She tells little of her own looks, except that she had light brown curling hair, gay, easy manners, a good though not a tall figure, and "the air of a Princess." In Thackeray's *Four Georges* there are two sketches of the Electress Sophia from contemporary prints. The sketch which represents her in youth is that of a pretty, slender girl, with long curls falling on her neck.

Because of suitability in age, perhaps quite as much as because of her beauty and bright wit, Sophia was regarded as eligible for the hand of her cousin, the Prince of Wales, who was a year her senior. The other aspirant was a daughter of the elder Princess of Orange. Factions of the emigrants ranged themselves on the different sides. That which advocated the claims of Sophia was headed by the Marquis of Montrose, while the Dukes of Hamilton and Lauderdale supported the pretensions of the other Princess. One can hardly imagine a situation more trying, or more likely to be injurious to a girl, than that which Princess Sophia then occupied, with all the petty strife and mean artifices which it implied. But she seems to have encountered it with her usual sound sense and clear-headedness, and to have sustained no damage from the encounter. She does not appear to have been particularly elated by any attentions which the Prince of Wales paid her. She saw through, to some extent, his extremely selfish and frivolous nature, which was early developed. She distrusted his extravagant compliments, attributing them, correctly on one occasion, to an attempt to make use of her in procuring money from Lord Craven for Charles and his friends. Lord Craven, son of a Lord Mayor of London, is well known for his chivalrous adherence to the Queen of Bohemia's interests, to which he devoted his life. Having attended her all through her chequered career, when she at last withdrew to London, in the reign of her nephew Charles II., and occupied, according to tradition, a house in Kensington Square, he hired the next house and dwelt in it, that he might still be in her immediate vicinity and at her service. Princess Sophia, in her Memoirs, merely mentions him as "an old Englishman," who took an interest in her and was in possession of money—a rare commodity among the English at the Hague in those days. He was evidently a person of consequence and trust in her mother's service; but the daughter does not drop a word which can give any colour to the common report that he was privately married to the Queen of Hearts, as it was said later that Harry Jermyn was married to Henrietta-Maria. Like her niece, the Duchess of Orleans, the Electress Sophia, in her frankness and simplicity, strenuously maintained the dignity of her birthright, and on that side was a rigid supporter of etiquette, so that no admission which might be regarded as impugning the family credit was to be expected from her.

The Princess's mother was more bent on the English alliance than was the daughter. Probably, in her keen, youthful penetration, she saw plainly the innumerable obstacles to its fulfilment. She refers to the Queen's having reproached her angrily for not having joined the promenade at Vorhoeit, when the Prince of Wales would have walked with her. The excuse brought forward by Princess Sophia was, it might be advisedly, of a ludicrously humdrum and prosaic description. It would have sounded better on the lips of a clumsy Dutch peasant than in the mouth of an elegant Princess. The delinquent protested she was prevented from walking by a corn on her foot. What would Horace Walpole have said to a Princess with corns?

CHAPTER II.

A VISIT AND A MARRIAGE.

PRINCESS SOPHIA's elder brother, Charles Louis, to whom the Palatinate had been given back, was thirteen years her senior, and was, as she said, more like a father than a brother to her. On his marriage to a Princess of Hesse-Cassel, he invited his youngest sister to pay him and his Princess a visit—an invitation which, in those non-travelling times, meant a prolonged sojourn of the guest with her entertainers. Sophia was nothing loth; change and variety are attractions in themselves at her age. She was glad to escape from the cabals and intrigues of the Hague; while the Queen her mother was persuaded that the transference of residence and guardianship was not necessarily a barrier to the match with the Prince of Wales. Sophia, whose every inclination for England and the English was to be encouraged at this date, was allowed to take with her a young English girl, named Carey, to whom the Princess had taken a great fancy, together with the girl's recently married sister and her brother-in-law. They were escorted by Lord Craven; and as the journey from the Hague to Heidelberg was a considerable undertaking for an inexperienced traveller who had never gone from home before, except for a day or two's sail in a canal-boat, a pinnace was borrowed, in which the little party went up the Rhine, with more state and much less expense and fatigue than would have been incurred had the journey been made by land.

On entering each principality belonging to her brother's neighbours, the reigning Duke or Prince hailed the distinguished traveller, and carried off her and her companions to the different residences, where the guests spent a night or a day, and were treated with all the splendour and hospitality which could be got up at a moment's notice. Not a word does Princess Sophia say of the charmingly picturesque scenery, which must have been a revelation to her after the lowlands of Holland. There was little love of primitive Nature in that generation, and no pretence at the admiration which did not arise spontaneously. But the traveller has piquant notices, very much to the point, of the homely magnificence of the castles she entered, where the tapestries were fine, but the less said of the chairs and beds the better; while the life of royalty, viewed behind the scenes, displayed a decidedly seamy side.

Even on beautiful Heidelberg, which had been her father and mother's, and was now her brother's capital, the wandering Princess makes no further remark than that the castle was partly ruinous—a result of the Thirty Years' War—so that the Elector Palatine and the Electress were living in a house in the town, called the Commissariat House.

Princess Sophia continued on excellent terms with her brother; but she could feel little regard for her sister-in-law, a strange young woman, full of airs and affectations, with a moody temper. She made not the slightest disguise of the circumstance that she had married the Elector Palatine—who in the beginning was enslaved by her beauty—against her will, while her heart was given to a Prince of Würtemberg. Her tastes were card-playing, and especially hunting, and for neither of these pursuits had Sophia much inclination. The family life was not improved by the arrival of another of the Queen of Bohemia's daughters, Princess Elizabeth, the *femme incomprise*, who made common cause with the other misunderstood woman the Electress, and formed a party against Princess Sophia and the Elector Palatine. Sophia did not think her elder sister had gained in wisdom as she had gained in years. At the same time, in retrospect, she allows honestly that she ought to have taken her sister's advice and yielded to her authority. There is no corroboration of what follows in the Princess's autobiography, but from information derived from another source it appears that she had an official position in her brother's household as governess to his children. Doubtless it was as State governess, and the appointment, apart from its salary, was little more than nominal; but the commencement of the connection between the aunt and her niece Charlotte Elizabeth, afterwards Duchess of Orleans, was thus laid, though it had a more solid superstructure when the little girl joined her kinswoman, after her marriage in Hanover, and was carefully brought up by her there till she had reached the age of twelve years.

It is easy to guess how the unhappy *ménage* at Heidelberg must have sharpened Princess Sophia's anxiety to attain for herself the only provision possible for her—an independent establishment by marriage. In those plain-speaking days, ladies, even not royal, made no secret of the strong obligation which rested upon them to fulfil their destiny in this respect. They must marry in order to retain their position, or even, in extreme cases, to preserve for themselves the bare necessaries of life. Accordingly, matrimonial prospects were discussed by the ladies and their relatives with the greatest openness and *sang froid*. Years were passing for Princess Sophia. In 1652 she suffered from the common scourge, small-pox, which in her opinion impaired her good looks. Domestic affairs at Heidelberg did not improve. Indeed, the Elector Charles Louis now openly announced his intention of divorcing the Princess of Hesse-Cassel on the ground of her contumacious temper, and of marrying, after the manner of Henry VIII. of England, one of her maids-of-honour, Mademoiselle von Hagen. The wretched Electress saw too late the result of her folly. The Elector's passionate love, which his sister Sophia had predicted was too violent to last, had changed to a rooted aversion, and nothing the Electress could do would propitiate him or turn him from his intention.

There was no lack of suitors for Princess Sophia's hand; but it became more and more an urgent duty to make a wise selection from them. Her future husband had already crossed her path more than once. She had known Ernest Augustus of Brunswick when he was in Holland as a lad. He appeared again at Heidelberg on his way home from the gaieties of Venice, with which he and his brother Duke George were entranced. He figures in Thackeray's essays as one of the "jovial Brunswick Princes" who had succeeded their pious fathers, the supporters of Luther. Sophia says complacently he was much admired, but as a younger son he was out of the question in the light of a *parti* for a penniless Princess who, at the same time, never lost sight of her illustrious descent and what was due to it. However, the young couple played the guitar together, which served the gentleman as an opportunity for the display of what the lady, moved to enthusiasm, calls " his exquisite hands." As she also records that he excelled in dancing, no doubt the pair were partners at the Court balls. After his departure he began a correspondence in reference to guitar music; which Sophia states she stopped, lest it should be misinterpreted.

A likely suitor turned up in the person of a widowed

Prince Adolf, brother to the King of Sweden. The Princess notes that he had a fine figure, and then qualifies the word of approval by one of those telling quizzical touches which occur often in her animated narrative. He had a long chin, "like a shoe-horn" (who does not see the chin?). A more serious objection than that of the long chin came to her ears in the rumour that he had beaten his first wife; therefore the Princess would have nothing to say to him, and without doubt was confirmed in her disinclination by the conviction that her sister-in-law—not yet set aside—was his vehement champion in order to get rid of Princess Sophia.

Duke George William of Brunswick, the elder brother of Ernest Augustus, was the next applicant for the Princess's hand. Though he appreciated her personal and mental qualities he was but a lukewarm lover. He had at that date an utter distaste to marriage. He was still more a man of pleasure and of the world than his younger brother had shown himself. Duke George was only consenting to marry because of the pressure put upon him on this point by his subjects. He had come to Heidelberg in company with his favourite brother Ernest Augustus, on the road to their beloved Venice. George went so far as to ask Princess Sophia's hand in marriage—a proposal to which she immediately said "Yes," as she frankly announces; for she considered him decidedly preferable as a suitor to Prince Adolf of Sweden. The fact that Duke George was a jovial Prince did not assume alarming proportions in eyes too early enlightened and not over-fastidious. The marriage contract was drawn up and signed, with the single proviso that it was to be kept secret for a time. Sophia does not hint at the slightest exception on Ernest Augustus's part, save on the grounds that he disliked the idea of his elder brother's marriage, lest it should impair the close friendship which had existed between the two.

The deed done, the bridegroom-elect, instead of deciding to tarry at Heidelberg and cultivate the society of his promised bride, as she possibly expected, went on with Ernest Augustus to Italy, there to eat, drink, and be merry; while Princess Sophia remained with her brother, experiencing the awkwardness of an unacknowledged engagement. It left her to be pestered by the advances of the persistent Prince Adolf, who arrived with a sister, the Margravine of Baden, to help him to plead his cause. As for the Elector Palatine, he had to temporise in the matter, in order to escape the danger of provoking the hostility of the King of Sweden, who might be sensitive with regard to the injury to his kinsman's feelings.

A third wooer, who wooed by proxy—the proxy being a Roman Catholic priest, fired with the hope of converting Sophia to the Roman Catholic Church—was the Prince of Parma.

In the interval Duke George, plunged in dissipation in Venice, was more and more unwilling to fulfil his pledge. He hit upon the plan of getting his easy-minded, compliant brother Ernest to be his substitute. There were four Brunswick brothers—Christian, George William, John Frederick, and Ernest Augustus—among whom their father's possessions had been divided at his death. Christian and John Frederick (who went over to the Roman Catholic Church) were then without heirs. Duke George undertook to surrender the chief of his revenues to Ernest Augustus and bound himself not to marry, so that if Princess Sophia would consent to accept Ernest in the room of George she would be the first lady in Hanover, the mother of its future Dukes if God gave her children, "the mother to the family and the country."

With regard to this extraordinary suggestion, her brother, the Elector Palatine, wrote to the Princess that, for his part, he preferred Duke Ernest, as more amiable and sensible than Duke George—an opinion in which she agreed; while she volunteered the scathing remark on her own account, that "a good establishment was all she cared for, and that if this was secured by the younger brother the change was a matter of indifference." This cool speech of the Princess's has been often used in evidence of her lack of proper feeling and common delicacy; but before condemning her many things must be thought of. She was, as she owns, piqued by Duke George's desertion. Her very language betrays that she was smarting keenly under the mortification, so as to be prompted to employ the most scornful, careless words which came to her lips.

On the other hand, it is necessary to remember the exceedingly mercenary light in which the marriages, not of royal personages alone, but even of squires' daughters, were viewed in the seventeenth century. Lady Verney, in her delightful chronicle of the family history of the Verneys, has pointed out the truth, that while faithful, attached wives and devoted mothers were to be found as readily then as now, there was actually hardly a vestige of proof that love between young men and maidens existed as an inducement to marriage. Men and women married—often in very early youth—at the instigation of relatives and friends, to better the worldly position of bridegrooms and brides, to establish themselves creditably in life, and not to gratify personal affection. The letters of the Verney girls amply bear out the conclusion. They clamour to have their matrimonial chances, and weigh the income and expectations of the gentlemen suggested to them as husbands—frequently on the slightest acquaintance—with all the acumen of the most worldly of matrons. Lady Verney quotes another example of this unblushing regard of the means to the end which the candidates were not ashamed to proclaim. A young lady writes to a suitor, who has given her the liberty to inquire into his worldly estate, that she can hear of no estate, and that without one she will not enter on the question. There is no pretence at less material sentiment, no blinking of the main point at issue.

Princess Sophia was not a rare example of mercenariness, and it must be admitted that she was in considerable straits. She was twenty-seven years of age; she would soon be *passée*. Her position in her brother's family was getting more and more untenable in the light of his proposed divorce of the Electress and marriage with her maid-of-honour. There seems to have been no question of Sophia's return to her mother's care, while a Princess of those days could not dig, and to beg she was ashamed. The only apparent solution of the difficulty was that she should marry Ernest Augustus, or another Prince, perhaps less to her mind. She accepted the situation composedly, as was her nature—a little sardonically, if you will—and, having accepted it, she determined to make the best of it, and to do her duty according to her light in all its relations.

In Duke George's thankfulness at his escape from matrimony, he was willing to save the Elector Palatine all the expense and trouble of the wedding, which the Duke would have had celebrated with state and splendour in Hanover. But Charles Louis exhibited some dignity in declining to accept the proposal. He said that Duke Ernest might come privately to Heidelberg if he would, but Princess Sophia should be married there. So it was settled. In the September of 1658 Ernest Augustus arrived at Heidelberg with a small retinue.

In recording the event, the Princess announces cheerfully : " I, being resolved to love him, was delighted to find how amiable " (in the French sense, " pleasing ") " he was."

On her marriage-day the bride was dressed, German fashion, in white silver brocade. Her flowing hair was surmounted by " a large crown of family diamonds." The little lady's train was of enormous length, and was borne by four maids-of-honour. She was escorted to church by her brothers, the Elector and Prince Edward. Duke Ernest was supported by the little Electoral Prince and the Duc de Deux-Ponts. Twenty-four gentlemen marched in front, bearing lighted torches, decked with ribbons of the bride and bridegroom's colours—blue and white for the Princess, red and yellow for the Duke. Cannon fired salutes while the procession wended its way. After the ceremony the bridal couple stood opposite each other while the canopy was held over their heads during the singing of the " Te Deum." The company returned to the royal apartments, where Sophia formally renounced her claim to the Palatinate.

When supper was served at an oval table, Duke Ernest and his Duchess sat in the centre, with the Elector on their right and his young son on their left. Beyond them sat the Princesses, the small Charlotte Elizabeth (Madame d'Orleans), and the Duchesse de Deux-Ponts. After supper there was dancing, the Princes bearing lighted torches and dancing before and behind the bride.

In the course of a few days Ernest Augustus returned to Hanover by post to prepare for his wife's reception. " He went just as he came," she writes ; and then she adds, with proud satisfaction, " except that his feelings towards me had undergone a total and unexpected change." From these words one is led to suppose that Duke Ernest, though he had politely relieved his brother from an oppressive obligation, was equally unwilling to marry; and that, instead of regarding the Princess with partiality, he had been latterly prejudiced against her. A key to the alteration in his feelings may be found in her succeeding declaration that her affection for him far exceeded her former esteem, and that she now felt for him "all that true love could inspire."

CHAPTER III.

THE DUCHESS.

DUKE ERNEST, in his new regard for his wife, hastened to send a state coach in which she might journey to Hanover. But she seems to have been still more impressed by the fact of her brother the Elector's escort as far as Weinheim. She records the circumstance that she shed some tears in parting from him —tears which were lessened by the hope of seeing him again, and of being honoured with his letters. The circumstantial mention of the tears leads to the conclusion that they were a comparatively rare indulgence with the warm-hearted but sensible Sophia. Here was no whimpering, childish girl, no half-weak, half-cunning woman, unable to restrain her feelings, and prepared to give way to emotion on the slightest provocation, as a natural and graceful resource—her ever present defence when she was found in fault, whether the fault were trifling or heinous.

The progress to Hanover, like the earlier journey from the Hague to Heidelberg, was through a succession of friendly states, the rulers of which were not seldom family connections, either of the Princess or of her husband. She was treated with even more honour and ceremony than before, for was she not a wedded wife and a Duchess, instead of a maiden Princess? Sophia had in the midst of her sagacity and frankness, like her niece, Charlotte Elizabeth of Orleans, perhaps as an element of her wisdom and straight-forwardness, a true German's strong sense of the propriety of etiquette. She would say and do unconventional things; she could even laugh at Court forms; but she was never inclined to abate one jot of the homage due to her as a Princess. At Darmstadt the fireworks which were given to celebrate the occasion were the work of the young Landgrave. In the Landgravine's room the visitor saw what was an unaccustomed proof of luxury and refinement—a sideboard laid out with glass and china. This lady danced in a ballet with her children in the course of the evening, in order to entertain her guest. Possibly Sophia showed that she regarded this as unbending too far, for she adds she was bidden not to be surprised, since the Landgravine's mother had been accustomed to practise the same condescension.

Near the town of Hanover the young Duchess was met in state by the four ducal brothers—Christian, George William, John Frederick, and Ernest Augustus. No *arrière pensée* which had to do with her brief betrothal to the roving brother, Duke George, was suffered to mar the harmony of the party when all the four entered Duchess Ernest's carriage. She is particular in telling that she entered the town to the sound of cannon, and that when she alighted she was received by four Duchesses of royal rank; the first being her mother-in-law, the Duchess-Dowager of Hanover. Her husband, Duke Ernest, led her to the handsome room which had been specially prepared for her, while the rest of the fine company followed the bride and bridegroom. On the third day the newcomer took her place as the mistress of the establishment, and surely no royal bride ever did the honours with greater dignity and tact than did the pretty high-spirited little woman who was to be at the head of a Court. It was not a mock Court like that of

her mother, the Queen of Bohemia ; not even a
Court in the future like that great Court of England,
which was eventually dangled before Sophia's longing
eyes. It was a solid, not unprosperous Court of the
present. It was somewhat dull and heavy, perhaps ;
for if its *Ritter-saal* was all its own, its terrace and
gardens, pinnacled pavilions and gorgeous theatre
and opera house, were second-hand importations to
the sandy plains of the north of the *chefs-d'œuvre* of
French art and magnificence which studded the green
wooded belt round Paris. Such imitations are apt to
lose much of the spirit and grace of the originals, but
to those who know no better the borrowed lacquer
and tinsel are quite satisfactory. Certainly Ernest
Augustus spent in the course of his reign large sums
of money on extravagant display and lavish excess.
He raised the necessary funds partly by equipping and
selling the services of regiments of his subjects, trained
to be foreign mercenaries and destined to water the
battle-fields of Europe with their blood. But his
practice was the way of the Continental world then,
and was regarded as perfectly legitimate.

Sophia enjoyed heartily her first experience of comparative independence, state, and bounty. But it is
evident her chief gratification was derived from the
hold she had acquired over her husband's esteem
and affection. She owns she was proud even of
his jealousy of his elder brother Duke George, whose
privilege it was to "hand" the little lady every day
to her noontide dinner. She valued the jealousy,
inconvenient as it was in the light in which a less
wise woman might have been tempted to regard it.
It was a testimony to Duke Ernest's recently kindled
passion for her. She was guileless of unworthy
coquetry ; she was careful to give no ground for the
jealousy ; so much so, that she would hardly let her

eyes rest on Duke George when he was acting, for months and years on end, the part of her appointed cavalier. It was not her fault that he had the inconceivable impertinence to express to her his regret that he had relinquished her to his brother, and occasionally to pester her with his unwelcome attentions.

Without a crumb of food to nourish it, her husband's unreasonable doubt of her regard died a natural death. While it had pleased her in one sense, in another it had drawn from her some of her seldom-shed tears. With the jealousy, as might have been expected in the shallow, showy, man, died all the romance and fervour of his earlier love. There was nothing left for her save the abiding friendship, which was richly earned and could not well be withdrawn.

Sophia makes no statement to this effect, utters no complaint of her husband, has scarcely a word to say of him which is not full of praise of his princely qualities and of her affection for him. There can be no doubt that she was sincerely, even fondly, attached to her Duke, little as he deserved it in some lights; while he gave her all that such a man had to give in the respect and confidence, to which even he could see she was amply entitled. He did not bestow on her an undivided heart, an unwavering constancy. He did not make her glad by his preference for her and her society before that of other associates, even if they had been creditable instead of discreditable. He had no single-hearted, manly devotion in return for her tenderness. In fact, he was light-minded and faithless, steeped to the lips in the coarse vices of the time in the midst of his lazy good-nature and unthinking generosity. Sophia had known him to be what he was from the beginning, and yet she could learn to love him, and could love him really and truly to the end. This was not merely for the sake of appearances, or in the light of self-interest—motives which have been liberally attributed to her; while she has received many a taunt for her apparent lack of feeling where Ernest Augustus's conspicuous failings were concerned. Neither was it because love is blinding—she was not the woman to be so blinded; it was rather because her standard of men and princes was low. I have already written that the Electress Sophia, with all her abilities and virtues, was not more delicate-minded and higher-souled in reference to the morality of her time than were the mass of her contemporaries. This is evident from her Memoirs and letters. Hers was not one of those noble natures which are laws to themselves in accordance with the Divine law and testimony, which stand out like beacons, dispensing purest rays of heavenly light to generations otherwise corrupt and benighted; still she and the women who most resembled her—Sophia's beloved niece the Duchess of Orleans; her granddaughter by marriage, Caroline of Anspach; even the great Maria Theresa—had much in them and in their relations to their husbands and children which can be cordially commended. The virtue of the wives was beyond question. They were loyal, forbearing, even affectionate to husbands who were far from deserving such allegiance. As mothers these Princesses were for the most part excellent. They played the parts which fell to their share according to their lights, honourably and for the general good of the community. Each country and Court with which the women had to do was more or less the better for them.

It is a little difficult to understand how they did it, and the only rational explanation which can be found is, that hard experience had imparted to them early no very exalted opinion of men and the marriage state.

Duchess Sophia relates that Duke Christian was "given to drinking"; and adds, "it was well-nigh his only *fault*," quite as if it was as minor an evil as it was a common offence at the German Courts.

The Princesses in question accepted men and the married condition as they found them, without any great effort or hope to improve them. The wives, in their high estate, were content and thankful for the respect which did not fail them, and for the portion of consideration and kindness which fell to their lot. They never dreamt of themselves as injured victims; they simply saw themselves as undergoing the ordinary fate of women and princesses. They succeeded in being indulgent, even tender, to the foibles of the husbands who tried them most severely. Madame d'Orleans was possibly the hardest beset as she was the most plain-spoken of the group, since she was married to a man who, in addition to all the attributes of a vicious fool, was a fantastic mountebank. He appropriated and wore with exultation his first wife's jewels without regard to the two daughters whom she left behind. He not only rouged himself, he rouged, against her will, the cheeks of his second wife, so honest in her homeliness. Yet even Madame, while candidly summing up her husband's little peculiarities, not only bore with them patiently, but cared for him in spite of them and of his peevish protest that she bored him with her wifely duty and affection.

Duke Ernest's fleeting passion for his wife, and his vexation that she should ever have been betrothed to Duke George William, did not wean him from his close alliance with his elder brother and his undesirable resorts to Italy in Duke George's company. When the two proposed to set out as usual very shortly after Duke Ernest's marriage, Sophia intrepidly consented to accompany them. But as the long journey was to be made—it might be not unadvisedly on the gentlemen's part—in an open carriage in the depth of winter, she had to relinquish the attempt at the end of the first stage. She confesses she cried again from loneliness and want of congenial company after she returned alone to the capital, while the two Dukes proceeded without her.

During all the years which had passed since Sophia had quitted the Hague, she had kept with her, as a proof of the strength of her friendship, the young English girl named Carey, and her married and now widowed sister. But after the Duchess's marriage, she says, naïvely enough, that, as her heart was "given up to the Duke," she cared only for what he liked; she therefore allowed the widow to return to the Hague, and "consented" to the marriage to Baron de Bonstett of Mistress Carey, who was no longer young and feared the name of an old maid.

On her husband's next visit to Italy with his brother, Duchess Sophia went to her mother at the Hague and passed a pleasant time there. The Queen welcomed the daughter who had done well for herself, who brought with her the Queen's grand-daughter—the only grandchild she had seen—Charlotte Elizabeth, of the Rhenish lands, already in her young aunt the Duchess's care. It must have been during this sojourn at the Hague that the incident took place which Madame d'Orléans afterwards described in the bright fashion not far removed from her aunt's style.

The Queen and the little Princess Palatine went, unaccompanied by the Duchess, for some unexplained reason, to pay a visit of ceremony to the reigning Princess of Orange—the same Princess William of Orange who had come as a bride of ten years, accompanied by her mother, Henrietta-Maria, from England, when the child-wife and the young Princess Sophia, her cousin, were playfellows.

"Before starting," writes Madame d'Orleans, "my aunt said to me, 'Lisette, do not behave in your usual flighty manner. Follow the Queen step by step, so as not to cause her to wait for you.'

"I answered, 'Oh, my honoured aunt will hear how well I have comported myself.'

"When we arrived at the Princess Royal's" (Princess Royal of England, Princess of Orange of Holland), "I found her son" (afterwards William III. of England, by a second Orange marriage with a second Mary Stewart), "with whom I had often played. After gazing at his mother for a long time—for I did not know her in the least—I turned round to the Prince of Orange, and said, 'Tell me, I pray you, the name of that woman with so strange a nose.'

"He burst out laughing, and replied, 'It is the Princess Royal, my mother.'

"I was astonished, and remained stupefied. To console me, Frau von Heyde took myself and the Prince of Orange into the Princess Royal's bedchamber, where we played at many games. I had asked to be informed when the Queen" (her grandmother) "was about to leave. We were rolling together on a Turkey carpet when I was called. I jumped up and ran into the hall, but the Queen was already in the ante-chamber; so, having always been a bold child, I pulled the Princess Royal" (her father's cousin) "by the gown, made her a pretty curtsy, and followed the Queen step by step to the coach. Every one was laughing—I knew not why. When we arrived at home the Queen went straight to my aunt and sat down on her bed; then, bursting out laughing, she exclaimed, 'Lisette has made a fine visit,' and told her what had passed. Our dear Electress laughed even more heartily than the Queen and said, 'Well done, Lisette! You have revenged us on the haughty

Princess.'" A speech which implies that Charles I.'s tragic end had not broken the spirit of his daughter. We too laugh across the centuries as her own narrative brings before us *l'enfant terrible* making rude remarks on a Princess Royal's nose to the Princess Royal's son, and walking too late, in her mincing, prim, child's fashion, "step by step" after the Queen, her grandmother.

In the month of June, 1660, Duchess Sophia's first child was born. To the great joy of all it was a son, who was named George Louis after two of his uncles.

On the next visit of the ducal brothers to Italy, the Duchess spent the time with her brother at Heidelberg. When her husband and brother-in-law came to fetch her home she sailed with them down the Rhine to Rotterdam. There she found her mother on the point of embarking for her native country. Elizabeth Stewart found her last refuge in England during the reign of her nephew Charles II. But the poor Queen of Hearts was not destined to be long a pensioner on the bounty of her royal kinsman. She ended her storm-tossed life a year afterwards.

Sophia's second son was born, and then a change took place in Duke Ernest's fortunes. On the death of the Bishop of Osnabrück—a prince-bishop and a lay ruler—the lay bishopric which belonged to the House of Hanover fell to Duke Ernest, and he and his wife went to stay in Osnabrück, the castle of Ibourg being their residence.

"The bonds of holy matrimony had not changed the Duke's gay nature," Sophia writes calmly of her husband's love of dissipation and delight in Italy. But he at last made up his mind to take her there, or, rather, to let her follow him after he had left her to winter again at Heidelberg. She had a great train, though she travelled *incognito*; even a band of musicians was not wanting. Her ladies (with whose Northern fairness and beauty the Duke designed to dazzle the Southerns) and women " occupied four carriages, the gentlemen rode, and the servants went in carts." With this cumbrous cavalcade she passed through Southern Germany and the Tyrol, and crossed the Alps—no light undertaking in those days. The overturning of a carriage was so common an occurrence that the Duchess was carried in a litter, and two of her ladies either walked or rode on horseback the whole way.

At last the wandering Duke met the party and escorted them by Verona and Vicenza to his beloved Venice. The Duchess, who in 1665 was in her thirty-fifth year, full of life and spirit, gives an animated account of what struck her in the novelty of the surroundings. She admired the gardens and *corsos*; she praised the wit of the Italian ladies and the gallantry of their cavaliers; she tried to accommodate her reasonable soul to the gaudy show and giddy whirl—approaching riot—of frivolous amusement in which the Duke delighted; she danced in the open air with him and her ladies; she went with her companions, "dressed out like actresses in gold and silver brocade and quantities of feathers," to witness mock tilting on the Lido. But nature would have its way; she found Venice " extremely melancholy." She herself grew sad in an atmosphere of folly, while her health suffered. " It may be imagined," she writes, " how strange a German felt in a country where nothing is thought of but love, and where a lady would consider herself disgraced were she without admirers. I had always learned to look on coquetry as a crime, but according to Italian morality it was a virtue."

On the evening of the Duke and Duchess's arrival

at Milan she was persuaded to attend a masked ball, and when pressed to unmask on account of the heat, did it philosophically, in spite of the unpleasantness of exposing herself to the splendid throng in travelling costume and morning cap; for, as she explains, " comfort always carried the day " with her.

When she accounts for not feeling the long carriage journey to Rome tedious because a table was set in the carriage, at which she played cards all the way with two Venetian noblemen, we call to mind two things—the general, well-nigh universal, indifference in her generation to natural scenery, unless it was improved upon (?) by art ; and the fact that the young girl who, when she first came to Heidelberg, had no predilection for cards or hunting, had changed to some extent with the flight of time. In the monotony of Court life she had accommodated herself to what, in the seventeenth century, was, with few exceptions, the established rule, of card-playing in all circles, royal, social, and domestic.

At Piacenza, where the travellers were entertained by a deputy from the Duke of Parma, much merriment was occasioned by the fact that, while they were splendidly lodged, they were half starved. Duchess Sophia remembered after an interval of years the supper served to the hungry guests who had waited long for the scanty meal—" a very small salad dressed with currants, six fresh eggs, at which everybody snatched, and an eel pie."

At Parma the Duchess-Dowager, who had in former days coveted Sophia for a daughter-in-law, desired to make her acquaintance, and paid her many attentions.

At Rome the party were lodged in a palace by the Duke of Tuscany, where Sophia passed but a dull time, since she remained *incognito*, and ostensibly received no visitors ; her husband in the meanwhile spent his evenings playing basset with Madame Colonna, a niece of Cardinal Mazarin's. Curiosity led the Duchess to make use of the privilege of her rank in order to pay an impromptu visit to the once famous beauty, and join in a game of the perpetual basset. Madame Colonna was discovered lying on a bed dressed in a blue and silver silk dressing-gown tied with flame-coloured ribbon; on her head a point lace cap, which was drawn over the forehead without touching the ears. The Duchess failed to recognise the personal attractions which had once bewitched the French Court. The daughter of kings avoided giving the Cardinal's niece the hand which she thought fit to claim at future meetings. Even on Sophia's palace staircase she could not resist taking precedence of her encroaching visitor. Madame Colonna had a scheme for the perversion of the staunch little Protestant Princess. If it had been effectual, it would have changed the destinies of the House of Hanover, of England, and of Europe.

The Pope, Alexander VII., would have received Sophia *incognito*; but she declined the concession because of what she considered had been a slight to the pretensions of her brother-in-law, Duke John Frederick, in spite of his having professed Roman Catholicism. To her regret she missed seeing the clever, eccentric Christina of Sweden, who was then in Rome.

Duchess Sophia's great pleasures were walking in the exquisite gardens and paying daily visits to the fine statues and pictures which served to recall the art-loving Princess Louise, Abbess of Maubisson, whose work at the Hague had been the admiration of her little sister.

The Duchess was deeply impressed by St. Peter's, and there she saw the Pope without being seen by him, and was not edified by his behaviour.

At the Church of Maria della Vittoria she came

across a curious memento which had not an agreeable significance for her. It was the crown and sceptre of the Emperor Ferdinand, sent by him as an offering to a little picture of the Virgin, which had, as he believed, enabled him to defeat Sophia's father, the so-called King of Bohemia, in the battle of Prague. When the monk who exhibited the trophies suggested that so great a Princess ought to add to them, she replied dryly, with her ready wit, "Yes; if the Virgin had been on the other side."

Duchess Sophia was home-sick, and longing to be with her two little sons. She was thankful when her husband gave the word for their return, though, as was his wont, he did not travel with her, but allowed her to start in advance. The roads were so bad in Tuscany that the carriage containing the Duchess's maids-of-honour was upset nine times in one day, while her waiting-women's mules broke down, and they had to mount on post-horses and ride *en croupe* with two gentlemen of the suite, a postilion sounding his horn before them.

Florence charmed Duchess Sophia. She "greatly admired" the Pitti Palace, its gardens and pictures. At a convent in Bologna her strong sense of humour was tickled by the spectacle of "the great beards of the old nuns, which made them look like the husbands of the young ones."

The travellers were in Venice again for the Carnival, the freedom of which was to the Duchess's mind, though the cold caused her to walk about "like a noble Venetian," wrapped in a fur-trimmed robe. In the midst of the merry-making she showed that in spite of her respect for etiquette the love of frolic could get the better of her. She agreed joyfully to travel post with the Duke to Milan, while her ladies either preceded or followed her. She was dressed for the expedition in "a long tight cloak and wig," and occupied a *vetturino*, while Duke Ernest, an Italian count, and a valet rode by her carriage. She was thankful, however, when her identity escaped recognition, and she was not seen in her disguise by the nobility, who had prepared a public reception for the couple. The ladies of the town came in state to see her, and she received them, as she recounts comically, "with a fainting fit." They were greatly distressed, undressed her, and put her to bed, loading her with caressing epithets. Yet they kept her dancing day and night for a fortnight!

The Duke and Duchess went back to Germany by Switzerland and the St. Gothard Pass. It is one of the signs of the change which has passed over the public taste to find a woman at once so bright and thoughtful as the Duchess Sophia having little to say of the land of the mountain and the flood beyond dwelling on the "frightful precipices" and the "nasty sledges" drawn by bullocks. At Bâsle Sophia's native Rhine was reached, and she and her husband sailed down the river to the Palatinate. At Gemersheim, of which Mistress Carey's husband, Baron de Bonstett, was high bailiff, the old friends had the joy of meeting again.

But bad news awaited the Duke and Duchess farther on. Their brother, Duke Christian of Zell (whose only fault was that of being given to drink), had died during their absence. Duke George William, who ought by his father's will to have been Duke Christian's successor in Zell, though sent for to his dying brother, had not troubled himself to obey the summons, while the Roman Catholic brother, John Frederick, had made hay while the sun shone by taking possession of the territory. After some difficulty he was induced to make a compromise, and resign Zell to Duke George. This Duke had long entertained a great admiration for a French lady named Eleanore d'Olbrense, who was in the suite of the Princess of Tarrente. He now overcame his objection to matrimony so far as to marry Eleanore d'Olbrense morganatically—a contract by which she became his wife but not his Duchess. His family gave their consent to the contract, which was signed both by Duke Ernest and Duchess Sophia, with the express understanding that it did not invalidate Duke George's earlier pledge to constitute his brother Duke Ernest, with his children, his legal heirs.

To please her husband and brother-in-law, the Duchess had treated Mademoiselle d'Olbrense with consideration and attention, but she neither liked nor trusted her. Sophia had been told that Mademoiselle was gay and giddy, indulging in playfully beating and pinching her friends as part of her charming artillery. On the contrary, the Duchess found the lady grave and dignified. The readiness with which she makes this admission, and records the first favourable impression made on her, goes far to contradict a common impression that mere pique at encountering and being compelled to acknowledge her successor in Duke George's light affections had much to do with the future relations which existed between Sophia and the Zell family.

The agreeable impression was only temporary; the Duchess had soon good reason to suspect Mademoiselle d'Olbrense—or Madame de Harburg, by the title which her husband gave her—of scheming, craft, and dissimulation.

CHAPTER IV.

COURT MATCH-MAKING.

OTHER children were born to Duchess Sophia. Like the Queen of Hearts, she was the mother of many sons, seven in number. One, a twin boy, died in early infancy; six grew up to man's estate, for her tribulation rather than her rejoicing. She had one dearly-loved daughter. It was of this girl when she was thirteen that the Duchess is reputed to have said, in reply to the question of an agent of the French King, that she was of no religion as yet. Her friends were waiting to ascertain who was to be her husband before they decided in what Church she should be brought up. Many severe animadversions have been passed on the lack of principle and heart in this speech. Is it possible that everybody does not recognise the mocking tongue of the Duchess in an answer addressed to Gourville—himself a pervert from Protestantism—who was seeking to reconcile the Duke and Duchess to the Roman Catholic creed? The jest was as transparent as the frequently-repeated assertion which deceived the Duchess of Orleans—that she (Duchess Sophia) was very fond of the Turks, and thought them very good people. Those were still the palmy days of Turkish valour; but it is easy to read in the pointed praise the under-current of sarcasm. The followers of the Crescent were quite as good, even when they were guilty of those practices for which they were most condemned, as some of the so-called followers of the Cross whom

Sophia had known. No attempt seems to have been made to find out whether the witty Duchess was in jest or in earnest, whether her quick tongue ran away with her, as on former occasions, while she sought to administer a characteristic rebuke to the inquisitive interloper—a chameleon in his own person. Nobody appears to have taken the trouble of ascertaining whether the woman who built a church for French Protestant refugees, who declined to allow the Church of England service to supersede the Lutheran or the Calvinistic services in her chapel, lest people should say she had been of no religion before the Bill of Succession appointed her heir to the English throne—the woman who was the confidential friend of the Christian philosopher Leibnitz—had a practice at all in keeping with the scandalous worldliness of the assertion attributed to her in sober earnest. So far as can be gathered from the letters of Madame d'Orleans, the Duchess's niece, brought up by her aunt till she was twelve years of age, the reverse was the truth. Charlotte Elizabeth notes after she was an elderly woman the careful training she received, the Catechism she was made to know by heart, containing those very doctrines which she, in her maturer years, emphatically styles "good." Madame d'Orleans put the utmost value on a child's being trained in the way it should go. She attributes the follies and misfortunes of the wretched Sophia Dorothea of Zell to the absence of proper instruction in her youth from the mother whom Charlotte Elizabeth had known in *her* youth and in the honesty of her heart had always heartily disliked. Such criminal neglect of the first principles of religion and morality in dealing with her children the Duchess of Orleans was very far from ascribing to her beloved Electress.

Another almost ludicrous misconception which is

still current is that the Court of Hanover in the Electress Sophia's day was dull and illiterate, so that the French airs and graces and superficial accomplishments of an Eleanore d'Olbrense and her wrong-headed, ill-fated daughter afforded a brilliant contrast to the general moroseness and stupidity. Why, the Duchess Sophia, the kind, sympathetic patroness of scholars and of all strangers of " parts " who came to Hanover, the fluent speaker of five languages, the skilled embroidress, the brilliant hostess, was a tower of strength in her own little person. Her daughter, Sophia Charlotte, was in her time beautiful, learned, and wise. The grand-daughters by birth and by marriage, the fourth Sophia and Caroline of Anspach, were equally distinguished by the good fairies' gifts. Caroline had been badly educated in her childhood, so that she had to teach herself spelling, according to Madame d'Orleans ; but her strength and originality of character, together with the later training she had from the Queen of Prussia, enabled her to overcome all difficulties. The Court of Hanover in the circle of the Princesses was second to no European Court of the time in feminine intellect and culture.

In 1670 the Duchess tried her hand at a little match-making. Duke Ernest's sister, the Queen of Denmark, came with her husband and family to Glückstadt, where her relatives visited her. The Duchess liked the Queen, her sister-in-law, and admired her daughters, especially the youngest, Princess Wilhelmine. The Duke and Duchess agreed that the Princess his niece would be a very fit wife for Sophia's nephew, her brother the Prince Palatine's eldest son. The delicate negotiations were all successful ; even to the bridegroom-elect's inspection of the proposed bride's miniature, and his visit to Osnabrück to meet her. The marriage did not take place till 1671, when the Duchess Sophia was the *chaperon* selected to meet the Queen of Denmark, who travelled as far as Altona with her daughter and to conduct the Princess to Heidelberg, where the marriage was to be celebrated. Eleanore d'Olbrense, Madame de Harburg, was also at Altona with her Duke, a brother of the Queen's and an uncle of the bride-elect's. When the Queen of Denmark declined to kiss Madame de Harburg, she revenged herself by making invidious remarks on the dishes at table; on which Sophia utters the lofty commentary that Madame's mind was "too base" to understand that the great ones of this earth are "sustained by higher things than *ragoûts*."

Before the friendly Duchess had quite completed her mission, while the shy, silent Princess Wilhelmine was still detained at Weinheim till all was ready for her state entrance into her husband's future capital, her aunt was obliged to leave her. She went on in advance to Heidelberg, supped with her brother the Elector, and on the following morning her son, Prince Christian, was born. The Elector, sending to ask when she would go with him to meet the Princess, received the answer that she was otherwise engaged; on which he hastened to offer his congratulations. Sophia missed seeing the magnificence of the marriage ceremony, which might have reminded her of her own wedding in the same place.

Duke Ernest went off as usual to Venice while his wife paid the young couple a happy visit at Weinheim. There she took part in the preparations for another marriage—that of her dear niece Charlotte Elizabeth with Louis XIV.'s brother, "Monsieur" the Duke of Orleans, whose first wife had been Princess Henrietta Anne, youngest daughter of Charles I. The splendour of the alliance dazzled all eyes save those of the eminently sensible young Princess chiefly concerned.

She demurred, though it was said to be at the bridegroom's Roman Catholic creed, and not at the current though unfounded rumour that he was privy to his first wife's death by poison.

Charlotte Elizabeth's scruples were overcome; she was assured of freedom in her religion (three French bishops tried in vain to bring her round to their opinions). The marriage treaty was signed, and the second bride started immediately, under the escort of another aunt, for France. There, during the many years of her exile, she wrote diligently, without pausing to ascertain whether the missives always reached their destination, and without waiting too exactingly for replies, those sagacious, half-resigned, alas! coarse letters to her kindred in Germany, letters a portion of which has been made public for the information (and sometimes the disgust) of later generations. Madame wrote for forty years, twice a week without fail, a long confidential letter to her aunt. The single break in the correspondence was when Sophia went to France, and dwelt, a much-honoured guest, in the house of Madame. The correspondence ceased only with the lamented death of the aged Electress.

In 1674 the talk of a marriage between a Prince of Wolfenbüttel and "the little Sophia of Zell," the only child of Duke George and Madame de Harburg, precipitated a step which had long been dreaded. The child would succeed, partly by the instrumentality of her uncle, Duke Ernest, to her father's large fortune; but she could not take royal rank unless the morganatic marriage between the father and mother was converted into a royal marriage. This was not done immediately, nor till various compromises had been tried. In the meantime the two Dukes, as if there was no bone of contention between them, went to war against the French, and defeated Marshal de Créqui. Sophia's eldest son, George Louis, was with his father, and never quitted his side. She gives in her Memoirs the letter which the Duke wrote to her to announce the German victory. He winds up his praise of the Prince by calling him "a son worthy of his mother." Little wonder that the wife and mother's heart was proud, and small credit to the manœuvring Eleanore d'Olbrense, who sought to make mischief out of the letter (which was impulsively shown to her) by pointing out that it contained no mention of Duke George, and but slighting reference to the soldiers from Zell.

The estrangement between the brothers, once so closely united, became confirmed, and the announcement of a marriage between Duke George and Madame de Harburg, which would raise her to his rank and make her his Duchess, grew more and more imminent, to the indignation and disappointment of Duke Ernest and Duchess Sophia ; because, in the event of a son's being born to Duke George, his former pledge would go for nothing—Zell would be lost to the younger branch of the House of Hanover.

Friends of the family, in striving to reconcile the brothers, suggested what was destined to be the disastrous expedient of a marriage between the eldest son of the one and the only daughter of the other, thus uniting hostile claims. Duchess Sophia says nothing of her own feelings, but records what she believed to be her husband's reluctance to a conclusion which he felt was a degradation to the family, and his deliberate demand for a great dowry, while he protracted the negotiations in the hope that they might fall through without any fault of his. This statement is in direct opposition to the assertion of the Zell party, their mouthpiece being the newly-made Duchess of Hanover, as quoted by Dr. Doran. The version given by the very dubious lady, of whom

Duchess Sophia notes incidentally that she never spoke the truth, is as follows. The Duchess Sophia was bent on the marriage in order to secure her niece's large fortune for her (Sophia's) son. In order to compass her ends she paid Duke George a private visit, arriving so early in the morning that he was still in his dressing-room, into which she insisted on intruding, taking a seat there, and plying her specious arguments for the marriage, unconscious and reckless of the fact that they were perfectly audible to the future bride's mother in the adjacent bedroom. Such conduct is not at all in keeping with the ordinary behaviour of the little woman, whose liveliness included a strong sense of the ridiculous, and might balance, but did not by any means overthrow, her respect for the *bienséances*.

The next great event in Duchess Sophia's life was her visit to France in 1679, when she was in her fiftieth year. It was a matter of more moment to her, and excited in her a keener interest, than her journey to Italy had done. Its ostensible purpose was to visit her sister, Princess Louise, Abbess of Maubisson, whom the Duchess had not seen for thirty years, and her niece, almost her adopted child, Madame d'Orleans, who had now been married eight years and was the mother of two children, while, like most royal brides of these days, she did not return to her native country. But there were other less openly-expressed motives at work, which the Duchess acknowledged in her Memoirs. The Duke had been led to nourish an ambitious dream in connection with the visit to which he had been brought to consent. His only daughter, Sophia Charlotte, who was to accompany her mother, was fair to see, as well as gifted with wit and learning. Toland, describing her at a later date, calls her "the most beautiful Princess of her time." He says she was not very tall and rather too plump, with regular features, fair complexion, blue eyes, and "cole black hair."[1] He commends her philosophy and wit and mentions, in connection with her passionate love of music, that she "played to perfection on the harpsichord, and sang finely." Why should not this paragon take the fancy of the Dauphin, who was still unmarried, win the approval of the great Louis, which was of more consequence, and achieve the greatest match in Europe? The prospect was even more dazzling than the overtures for the Duchess of Orleans' marriage had been to her interested relatives. Would there be liberty to follow the Protestant religion accorded in this case also? Or was the temptation so great that there was danger of the stipulation being neglected or given up?

The Duke did not go with his wife and daughter—he only escorted them as far as Holland. There the Duchess had the satisfaction of meeting and greeting warmly one of the English friends of her youth, the elder Mistress Carey, long a widow. Sophia was travelling *incognito*, as she had travelled formerly. She was, as it were, introduced into the new region by the Duchess of Mecklenburg-Schwerin, a lady of the great French house of Montmorency. Her familiarity with the manners and customs of her native country was a benefit to the traveller; but the benefit was counterbalanced by her superciliousness, and by the amount of care and attention which her beauty was supposed to require. However, the caustic comment was qualified by the cordial admission on the part of the critic (always ready to see and reckon up redeeming qualities where these existed) of the general worth and friendliness of the Franco-German Duchess.

---

[1] Lady Mary Wortley Montagu, in referring to the beauty of the Hanoverian women, remarks on their dark hair and eyes and fair complexion.

With a pen as vigorous and graphic as ever Sophia describes what strikes her in France—the dirtiness of the inns, the excellence of the cookery, the politeness of the officials, her joy at seeing her sister (who laughed with her aside over Court forms and ceremonies), her delight when she found herself embraced by her old charge, Madame, who was awaiting the Duchess's arrival, and " ran " to meet her.

The Duchess Sophia's descriptions of the French Court are inimitable; one sees every strongly suggestive and picturesque figure. Yonder is the magnificent Louis, who is the soul of politeness, yet does not forget that Duke Ernest and Duke George of Brunswick have beaten the French soldiers under Créqui. Here is the amiable nonentity the Queen, who confines herself to "dressing and eating," the vocations for which she is fit, and keeps saying how well the King loves her, and that she is much obliged to him. There is the silent and awkward Dauphin, with whom Sophia seeks intrepidly, but in vain, to make conversation, doubtless not without an ulterior reference to her charming young Princess, on whose beauty and wit the King compliments the mother in courtly phrase, but with no sign of desiring an alliance between France and Hanover. Here again is fussy, fantastic Monsieur, the King's brother, who is exceedingly courteous to the Duchess, as a host is bound to be to the guest he desires to honour. He is annoyed at being caught *en famille* in his night-cap tied with flame-coloured ribbons. He is constantly exhibiting his beloved jewels. Honest, homely Madame, his second wife, is an old acquaintance of the reader's. Not so the victim ready to be sacrificed, whom her kind-hearted stepmother loved dearly— poor Marie Louise, daughter of Henrietta of England, whose untimely death resembled closely that of her mother. Duchess Sophia witnessed Marie Louise's betrothal and marriage by proxy to the King of Spain. She records the passionate grief of the Princess at quitting France, and mentions how, in showing the bridegroom's unattractive miniature — unattractive though set with brilliants—the girl permitted herself to remark, with what bitterness may be guessed, that she believed he was thought to resemble "that ugly baboon the Duke of Wolfenbüttel." State necessities are great, for Sophia, excellent woman though she was, and herself the mother of a young and fondly cherished daughter, does not utter the ghost of a protest against the sacrifice.

It is matter of regret that we cannot give more of the Duchess's lively experiences, while we sympathise with her independent spirit and German patriotism in declining to kiss the gown of the Queen of France, or to take a *tabouret* (the stool allotted to Duchesses of inferior rank), after she had been thought worthy of a chair in the presence of her own Empress. Questions of etiquette were continually arising and were sufficiently perplexing even to adepts in what was little short of a science. Madame d'Orleans, by her marriage to the King of France's brother, was raised a step in rank above her aunt, Duchess Sophia, to whom, nevertheless, she gave the precedence, on account, as she explains of the affection she bore her kinswoman. This tribute of regard was not accomplished without many elaborate manœuvres, feints of staying behind, eating meals in private together, etc. The new Queen of Spain was still farther in advance of both her stepmother and the Duchess Sophia. As one result, she had to sup alone with her father, Monsieur, who in France was second only to the King and the Dauphin; while the two elder ladies, who would otherwise have had to yield the *pas* to their junior, ate their meals apart.

The gardens of Versailles and St. Cloud afforded supreme delight to Sophia. Their artificial stateliness and splendour, their terraces, groves, fountains, statues, represented cultivated adorned nature, the beau-ideal of such rural tastes as the generation possessed. But from the superbness of Court gaieties, and the supposed elegance of princely alleys and arbours, Sophia was fain to retreat to what she called her " harbour of refuge," the Convent of Maubisson, where the sisters, who were congenial spirits, enjoyed their brief reunion.

The Duchess of Orleans had been eager to promote a marriage between her cousin of Brunswick and the Dauphin ; but before parting from her aunt she had to announce that the preliminaries of his marriage with a Bavarian Princess were settled, so that in one respect the visit was fruitless. By the Moselle and the Rhine the travellers made their way north, the Duchess pushing on in her eagerness to rejoin her Duke. " Words," she says, " fail to describe my joy at seeing the Duke once more." He on his part was " well pleased " (as he well might be) with all her proceedings, and thought she had " come off with great honour and credit."

But troubles on every side awaited Duchess Sophia. The Duke was in haste to be off to Italy. The project of a marriage between her son George and his cousin of Zell was again broached. It is scarcely possible to read the Duchess's few restrained words on the subject without being of the opinion of the editor and the translator of her fragment of autobiography, that the alliance, though she yielded at last to it, was extremely repugnant to her. It is hard to understand how impartial English writers can revive the idle, slanderous gossip of her enemies, which represents her as urgently advocating the union to secure Sophia of Zell's fortune for George. Duke Ernest's father's will had been a strange one in this respect, that he left to his sons in succession, according to their seniority, as they survived each other, and without reference to their heirs, the territories of Zell and Hanover, so that if Duke Ernest died before his remaining brothers, Duke George William and Duke John Frederick, his children would be deprived of their patrimony.

Another cause of anxiety and sorrow was the fatal illness of Sophia's eldest sister, Princess Elizabeth, Abbess of Herford. In her last days affection revived, and she craved earnestly for her sister's society. The Duchess repaired to the convent and stayed with the dying woman, striving to support and cheer her till she was summoned home by the startling news of the sudden death of Duke John Frederick at Augsburg. He had been bound for Italy, like his brother, but died on the road; and Duke Ernest, who in the midst of his joviality had a due regard for his material interests, was recalled forthwith to take possession of his late brother's inheritance of Hanover, irrespective of the fact that Duke John was married and the father of several daughters.

A visit to the Duke's sister and Sophia's friend, the Queen of Denmark, at her palace of Nicoping, afforded a consoling break in those multitudinous griefs and worries; but no sooner had the Duchess returned to Hanover than the tidings reached her, during one of the chronic absences of her husband, that death had caused her another heavy loss in the person of her favourite brother and constant friend and correspondent, the half father of her girlish days—the Elector Palatine, Charles Louis. This last blow went far to prostrate the woman, who was as strong and faithful in her attachments as she was high-spirited and resolute in her actions. For the first time her spirits flag.

She allows herself to complain of that mysterious, all-prevalent malady of the century, which seems to have belonged more to the mind than the body—"the spleen." She anticipates following speedily her brother and sister, yet with fresh-springing courage and cheerfulness hopes that her Duke's return from his inveterate roving will give her back health of body and mind.

Here, alas! ends the Duchess's vivid chronicle of her history. We have to depend for the rest of her life on public events, side-lights, and the notices of her contemporaries. It was not till twenty years after she laid aside her Memoirs that the prospect of her succession to the throne of England assumed anything like a definite shape, or could have appeared to so shrewd an observer and reasoner more than the merest shadow of a chance. In the meantime a suggestion of marrying George of Hanover to Princess Anne of England was mooted. He went to the English Court on the strength of it; but the proposal was dropped, and he was recalled by his father that he might enter into fresh negotiations in connection with the ill-starred marriage between him and Sophia of Zell, which took place in the following year, 1682. This conclusion was accomplished in spite of what we believe was Duchess Sophia's hearty dislike to the arrangement, and rooted distrust of it. It appeared to be a satisfactory family compromise, which would unite Hanover and Zell without further trouble. In the end the two Dukes, George William and Ernest Augustus, had set their hearts upon it—more or less. Sophia gave way to necessity, as she had always known how to give way with dignity when nothing else could be done. The story of this miserable marriage, unwelcome alike to bridegroom and bride, will find its fitting place on another page of the domestic annals of the Royal House of Hanover. It is sufficient to say here that the most vehement partisan of the erring Sophia Dorothea of Zell has not ventured to accuse her mother-in-law of any direct participation in the tragedy. The offences charged against the elder Sophia are limited to cold alienation *after* the younger Sophia had shown herself, by her reckless folly and misconduct, unworthy of all confidence and esteem, and of unwomanly passiveness at a crisis when it would have been in all probability as useless as it was distasteful to the Duchess to interfere. It has not been denied that on Sophia Dorothea's first arrival in Hanover, during the brief period when she behaved as if she felt disposed to acknowledge her responsibilities and do credit to her position, she was kindly received and treated with consideration by her husband's kindred.[1] Her beauty and grace found favour in their eyes, though her beauty was her mother's, and her grace was a Frenchwoman's grace—one of those Frenchwomen who had so branded their countrywomen that the emphatic answer of a contemporary German Prince when a French Princess had been proposed to him as a wife, and a hundred advantages from the alliance urged upon him, was, "No Frenchwoman."

Without doubt there must have been, in addition to the natural antipathy to the scheming and deceitful mother who had reached the position of Duchess of Hanover by scantily honourable means, an utter lack of harmony and sympathy between the honest, upright, self-controlled Duchess, and her unprincipled, passion-ridden daughter-in-law, who counted virtue, reputation, her husband's honour, and her children's affection—all that good women hold most dear—well lost for the insolent,

---

[1] Poellnitz describes the Electress as kind to and careful of her daughter-in-law in illness, even after Sophia Dorothea's quarrels with Prince George were notorious.

lawless love of a man of whom Thackeray could write, "a greater scamp does not walk the history of the seventeenth century." It would offer small excuse in Duchess Sophia's eyes that her niece Sophia Dorothea had come an unwilling bride to Hanover, or that the culprit's husband and cousin, after the shortest effort to do the best for her and himself, had been guilty of the grossest sins against her, and had further displayed a complete want of courtesy and forbearance where she was concerned. A faithless, even a brutal husband, did not, in the Duchess Sophia's code, go far to justify a disloyal and defiant wife. The woman and mother would only see, in the wife's retaliation on her husband, the wreck of any not very brilliant promise the young man had ever displayed. George was brave and manly enough, as he had early proved. He had served his Emperor with credit, if not distinction, "on the Danube, against the Turks, at the siege of Vienna, in Italy, and on the Rhine." He was not without sense and prudence, after his surly, selfish fashion. He was not without a heart—for his country if for nothing else. Such a wife as his mother had been to his father, such a wife as Caroline of Anspach was to George's son, the second George, might have done something to redeem his not too shining or heroic qualities from waste and degradation. It must be said, however, that the silent, loutish Prince, though he was a Prince, was destitute of his father's easy geniality and lavish joviality, which dazzled even Duchess Sophia's clear eyes and caused her to view her pleasure-loving Duke as a splendid paladin. But a mother's eye cannot be expected to spy out every imperfection in her child. The Duchess stood by her son, her first-born, the lad of whose youthful valour she had been so proud throughout his career, always zealous for his interest, always striving to see whatever merit he could claim, while her niece Madame d'Orleans was remarking indignantly on his lack of consideration for the mother whose chief care was for him.[1]

In 1684 Duchess Sophia had a great source of congratulation, though it involved a separation from her only daughter. Two years after Prince George's unpromising marriage (for which the Duchess had one consolation in the birth of a grandson, an heir to Hanover and Zell, and to a still greater inheritance, as yet only faintly foreshadowed), Sophia Charlotte of Brunswick married the Elector of Brandenburg, who became in time the first King of Prussia. He was eleven years her senior, and already a widower, the father of a son; but these were trifles in the sum of his recommendations. She was the first Queen of Prussia, and the grandmother of Frederick the Great. Her famous grandson said of her: "She had the genius of a great, and the knowledge of a learned man . . . she loved and sought truth as her husband loved splendour." Toland writes that she was so liberal in her ideas of Government she was called throughout Germany "the republican Queen."

None of the Duchess's six sons achieved much honour save George through his English inheritance. They were soldiers, like their elder brother, and led the armies their father sent out to fight in the European wars. The dangers they encountered and their adverse fates must have sorely wrung the heart of the woman who recorded, "I am a fool with my children." In 1690 Duchess Sophia fell ill; so ill that her niece, Madame d'Orleans, was in anxious fear for the life dear to her. Little wonder that the Duchess sickened, for in that disastrous year two of her sons—Prince

---

[1] George I. was the Duchess of Orleans' *bête noire*, and there was no love lost between them. Their feud began at a very early date, when the future Duchess was a child at play. Hiding behind the door of her aunt's room the day George was born, she rushed forward to see the newly-born infant, and narrowly escaped a whipping for her pains.

Augustus and Prince Charles [1]—fell in Transylvania, fighting against the Turks. Augustus was her second son—"the poor Gus" whose prodigal ways had got him into trouble with his father, so that he was "thrust out of the parent nest, and had no more keep." "I laugh in the day and cry all night about it," admits the poor, brave, distracted wife and mother.

Another son, Prince Maximilian, was a yet more heinous offender. When his father decided that there should be no division of his territories among his children, that he would leave them intact to his eldest son George, Maximilian broke out into open rebellion. The Prince was put under arrest, and one of the subordinates who aided and abetted him, a Hanoverian count bearing the now historical name of Molcke, or Moltke, suffered capital punishment for the offence. On Maximilian's release and nominal forgiveness he repaired to Rome, and adopted the Roman Catholic religion, after the fashion of his uncle, Duke John. He ended his career an officer in the Emperor's service and a declared Jacobite, in opposition to his mother's and brother's claims to the succession to the throne of England, while his name was a forbidden word, as may well be imagined, in the old Hanover residency.

[1] Poellnitz calls Prince Charles his mother's favourite son.

CHAPTER V.

THE ELECTRESS.

In 1692 Duke Ernest received the coveted rank of Elector, reserved for a select number of German Princes; and the titles Duke of Brunswick, or lay Bishop of Osnabrück, and Duchess of Brunswick, are henceforth merged in the higher titles of Elector and Electress. It was said the promotion was the payment of the transference of a section of Ernest Augustus's troops from the service of France to that of the Emperor. Be that as it may, Ernest's devoted wife was certain to look on the step as no more than his due. It did not pass without being contested in Germany, and just when the dispute was settled in Ernest Augustus's favour in 1698, his death was the heaviest of Sophia's many bereavements. She had attributed a host of shining qualities to her Duke and Elector to atone for his deficiencies in the more solid virtues. Whatever were his faults—and they were many and flagrant, both as a man and a husband—he had never failed in treating her with the respect and deference which belonged to the Princess, to the faithful, life-long ally, to the mother of his children. In her widowed state, though she still presided over her son's Court, her position was different from what it had been in the lifetime of her husband. She was ready to be the first to give her allegiance to the new Elector; but George was incapable of showing any graciousness in the acceptance of the allegiance from the mother always ready to make excuses for him. In some respects her position was thenceforth one of sufferance; and though succeeding events lent it a fresh importance, they bred also additional difficulties between the Electress and her son. It was reported that she was jealous of his interference in her English concerns. It might be said, with more propriety, that he was jealous both of her and of his son (George II.), and that the idea that she or he might eclipse the Elector in the eyes of their English partisans rendered him positively hostile to their advances. This passed with superficial observers for singular high-mindedness and disinterestedness on the part of the Elector; but he was not by any means too high-minded and disinterested to take the good things which were offered to him; and had he been actuated by motives of policy alone, he could not have pursued a wiser course than that of the assumed reluctance and indifference with which he met his great destiny. Neither was the attitude altogether assumed; it was the result of his sluggishness, doggedness, and ungraciousness to his family, quite as much as of his cool craft.

A great resource and interest to the Electress, in those days of loss and mourning, was the education of her grandchildren, the son and daughter of the Elector George, who, on the disgrace and imprisonment of their mother, passed into the Electress Sophia's keeping. Unfortunately, the boy grew up very much a repetition of his unprepossessing father, brave, cautious, callous, selfish, indulging freely in the vice around him, while the Electress did not bestow on him the unrequited affection she had lavished on his father. In the quarrels between father and son, which rent the residency into two factions, she invariably took the father's part. The Electress's grand-daughter, a fourth Sophia and a second Sophia Dorothea, better repaid her training. Under the Electress's care she grew up with a greater resemblance to her aunt, the Queen of Prussia, than to her unhappy mother. Sophia Dorothea the second was intellectual, upright, full of sense and good humour. She was tall, with light-brown hair and lively blue eyes, which redeemed the irregularity of her features.

In 1701, while William of Orange still reigned in England, the last of Princess Anne's sickly children, the young Duke of Gloucester, died; and a patriotic English Parliament, dreading the return of Roman Catholicism and despotism in England with the recall of the exiled Stewarts, voted the Bill of Succession, by which the inheritance of the English crown was settled on the Electress Sophia and her children, as the nearest Protestant heirs in the royal line. In doing so, the Parliament passed over the son and daughter of James II. at St. Germain; the children of that rueful young Queen of Spain (the grand-daughter of Charles I.), at whose marriage the Electress Sophia had assisted during her visit to France, and the Duchess of Savoy, the Queen of Spain's sister, with her children, in addition to the surviving descendants of Sophia's brothers. All these persons had disqualified themselves from succeeding to the throne of England by their profession of the Roman Catholic religion.

The Bill of Succession was great news for Hanover, and was followed by grand doings there. Till then the prospect of inheriting England had been very dim and uncertain; even yet it was insecure; and George I. is believed never to have regarded the English crown as resting firmly on his head. But if George was unfit to be more than an Elector, there was a queenly spirit behind him which age could not tame or sorrow break. The Electress Sophia was then seventy years old, but it could be said of her, as of

the great lawgiver, that her eye was not dim or her
natural strength abated. Her heart was fired by the
glorious vista opening out before her, the magnificent
prospect for her children's children ; and surely she
herself was fit to reign, not in a mock sovereignty
over a foreign country such as her mother had clung
to, but in the right of that mother over the three
kingdoms of her ancestors. " If I can but die Queen
of England, I will be content," she said ; and her
ambition was neither unworthy nor unnatural.

In 1701 the Earl of Macclesfield, accompanied by
Lord Say and Sele, Lord Tunbridge, and Lord Mohun,
went to Hanover in order to deliver the Act of
Succession to the Electress. Lord Macclesfield, it is
said vaguely, " bore a relation to the Queen of
Bohemia," so that Sophia might have had some previous acquaintance with him when he was in her
mother's service, a distinct recommendation to the office
with which he was entrusted. Luckily, in addition
to the noblemen who accompanied him, he had, in
the person of a private gentleman named Toland, a
lively chronicler of what passed. If his account is
stripped of its laudatory verbiage, it remains a graphic
commentary on scene and circumstances. Thrifty
Hanover in Elector George's day blossomed into
lavish expenditure for the occasion. There was feasting everywhere at the Government's expense. No
Englishman present in the town was suffered to pay
for his entertainment. Balls, plays, and operas followed
each other in rapid succession. But the crowning
performances were the delivery to Sophia of the Act
of Succession, the great ball on the evening of the
day, to celebrate the event, and the investiture of
Elector George with the Order of the Garter. The
Electress presented Macclesfield with her picture
surmounted by a diamond crown. The Elector's

offering to the peer was a gold ewer. Dr. Sandys, Lord Macclesfield's chaplain, preached and read the Common Prayers of the Church of England before the Electress, who had been brought up a Calvinist, while her son was a Lutheran. She was ready to listen to the service in her ante-chamber, and uttered the responses " as punctually as if she had made them all her life and was well acquainted with the Liturgy"; but she would not consent to have it set up in her chapel. It was the English form of Protestantism, she said, but it was only a form—one of many—and she did not desire that in which she had been reared to be eclipsed and thrust out of sight, as though it were not Christianity. Here is Toland's description of the Electress at the age of seventy-three; it is a fitting pendant to the piquant sketches she furnishes of herself as the young Princess at the Hague and at Heidelberg, and as the young Duchess of her Italian adventures. She was of " a vigorous and cheerful countenance." Her step was as firm and her bearing as erect as that of any young lady. There was not one wrinkle in her face, which was still very agreeable (she was a handsome old woman, as she had been a pretty girl). There was not one tooth out of her head, and she read without spectacles, as Toland often saw her do, letters of a small character, in the dusk of the evening. She was as great a worker as the late Queen Mary (Anne's sister); a visitor could not turn himself in the palace without meeting monuments of her industry. All the chairs in the privy-chamber were wrought by her hand; so were the ornaments of the altar in the Electoral chapel. She was the most constant and indefatigable walker Toland had ever known; never missing a day, if the weather were fine, for one or two hours, and often more, in the fine gardens of Herrenhausen (the country house of the Dukes and Electors, a mile and a half from the town). She had read a prodigious quantity, and spoke four or five different languages.[1] She was adored for her goodness and affability. Toland was the first to kiss her hand after the Bill of Succession was read; when she said to him that she was afraid the nation had already repented of their choice of an old woman, but she hoped none of her posterity would give the English cause to weary of them. Doubtless it was in reference to this admission of her age that Toland so dwells on her native vigour, and the absence of any sign in her of physical weakness and infirmity.

Sophia's intellect was far too acute to leave her unacquainted with the fact—which her son George fully recognised—that, in spite of the Act of Succession, it was still very doubtful whether Whig and Tory would agree at last to place her on the throne, whether there would not be a reaction in accordance with Queen Anne's well-known leaning to the claims of her nearest relations, which must end by restoring the exiled Stewarts to their forfeited rights. She was not a woman to be blinded by the most soaring ambition. It was in her son and grandson's interests, as well as in her own, that she watched as keenly as in the days of her youth every sign of the times, and counselled wise counsels, which helped to win the day.

It was a momentous period for all Europe when Charles XII. of Sweden blazed like a meteor across the political sky; when Peter the Great donned his carpenter's cap and converted old Muscovy into modern Russia; when the wars of the Spanish Succession raged

[1] Sophia must have appeared a prodigy of learning to Toland, contrasted with what he might have heard of the illiteracy of Queen Anne, and of the late Queen Mary, who was a thoughtful and intelligent woman; but even she could not write a letter in her mother-tongue without lapsing into lamentable spelling. There had been a great reaction from the classical culture of Elizabeth's reign where women were concerned. Their education had sunk to a low ebb.

in blood and fire far and near, and darkened the last days of the great Louis; when Marlborough's splendid fruitless victories of Blenheim, Ramillies, Malplaquet, etc., covered the English arms with glory. The Electress had a special interest in Malborough and his campaigns. Her youngest son, Prince Ernest, was in his camp. In addition, Marlborough was the great Whig leader, and sworn ally of the House of Brunswick, while his termagant of a wife could twist Sophia's second cousin, Anne, round her little finger. Still, the position was perilous. The Tories were formidable under Harley and St. John. Even Marlborough was to be profoundly distrusted. He had a fair face and a fair tongue, but his political creed could be manipulated to any extent to suit his interests. He had the most tempting means of making his peace at any time with the Stewarts through his sister-in-law, Frances, Lady Tyrconnel, and his nephew, the Duke of Berwick, and there is abundant proof that he availed himself of the means.

In 1703 Marlborough was employed by the Electress to procure for her a portrait of her cousin Anne. There was a resemblance between the cousins; both were stout, both were comely, with the same full face and double chin. But Anne's heavily good-humoured face was like a lamp without a kindling light within when we see it by the face of the Electress Sophia. Thackeray has supplied a sketch from a contemporary print of the Electress. Instead of the flowing curls of her youth, her head is crowned by a high structure of silk or lace in the fashion of the day, and this again surmounts the short locks of what may be a carefully arranged wig. The face is that of a fine-looking old lady, bright with intelligence and beaming with sense and kindliness, while "the air of a Princess" is as conspicuous as ever. Looking at Anne's stolid face,

Sophia might be pardoned for thinking that if her cousin's reign was called the Augustan Age of England, her own would be more deserving of the name; for was she not infinitely better qualified than Anne, with her dull wits and weak will, to enter with fullest sympathy into communion with those master spirits which were rendering the country and the period illustrious?

The years which followed still brought the same mingling of joy and sorrow that had been the burden of the years which went before them. In 1703 Sophia's son, Prince Christian, was slain in a battle on the Danube between the French and the Imperial troops. In 1704 his sister, the Queen of Prussia, died in the prime of life. Madame d'Orleans, in recording the death, says, "She was respected and liked by all who knew her." Yet she, according to the same trustworthy authority, failed a little, after the manner of her brothers, in what was due to her mother: "All her children—even the Queen of Prussia, whom she loved so—never treated her as they ought to have done." Alas! poor mother! who was "a fool about her children." It would seem as if Sophia's warm heart had not descended either to son or daughter, though the daughter inherited the mother's fine intellect.

The speech of the Queen of Prussia on her death-bed is a marvel of philosophy, strongly tinged with sarcasm rather than with reverent devotion or human tenderness. "Do not pity me," she said; "I go to satisfy my curiosity on subjects that Leibnitz has never been able to explain—space, eternity, being, and nothing; while in my funeral the King my husband will find a new opportunity of displaying his magnificence."

In 1705 the joint marriages of the Electress's two grandchildren, the Electoral Prince (George II.) and his sister Sophia Dorothea, were celebrated with all the splendour befitting the brilliant prospects of the House of Brunswick. The fourth Sophia married her cousin, the Crown Prince of Prussia, and was in her turn Queen of Prussia—no unworthy successor to the first Queen. "Three remarkable Englishmen," writes Dr. Doran, "were present at the marriage. These were Lord Halifax, Sir John Vanbrugh, and Joseph Addison." The statesman came with a Bill of naturalisation for the Electoral family, and with the Order of the Garter for the second George; the great architect and play-writer appeared in his official capacity as Clarencieux King-at-Arms; the great essayist was in the company by favour of Halifax.

Prince George married Caroline of Anspach, and here Sophia had her reward. Her grand-daughter by marriage was a congenial spirit, whose education, neglected in her youth at the Court of Saxony, had been so supplemented by the guidance and example of the Electress's daughter, into whose care Caroline passed, that she ended by being one of the best instructed and most accomplished women of her day. What is more to the purpose, she was wise and witty, like Sophia's self. She was the most dutiful, devoted of wives to a husband who was by no means respect-inspiring. She was a grand-daughter after the Electress's own heart. Nine years of Caroline's married life were spent at the Court of Hanover; and the elder members of her numerous family were born there. In them Sophia lived to see herself surrounded by her descendants of the third generation.

But the succession to the Crown of England was still hanging in the balance, and as time passed the plots and cabals in connection with it thickened and deepened. Neither was the Electoral family by any means united on that or on any other subject, for the quarrels of the two Georges were notorious. The Elector George professed a chilling indifference to the English succession. Sophia, to whom he was *her* Elector, was placed in a difficult position. She was bound to yield to him and to conciliate him. It was no less her policy than her pleasure to defer to his views, and veil her eager interest in the progress of events. She had a hard part to play. If she was induced, according to Marlborough's testimony, " repeatedly to disavow, both in public and private, her wish to visit England"—a step already mooted in Parliament—the awkwardness of the situation is some excuse for the dissimulation in a notably candid and honest woman. Sophia had been a great traveller for her day. She had visited Italy, Switzerland, many parts of Germany, Holland—the place of her birth— France. It would be strange if she was never to see England, her mother's country, and still more the country over which she might be called to reign.[1] Aged as she was, she was ready and willing to face the undertaking, and if it had been accomplished she could hardly have failed to win the golden opinions which her son and grandson were so little calculated to earn. But the opposition of the English Tories to Sophia's appearance on the scene was naturally strong. Anne was set against it; many of the Whigs themselves were cool on the point, dreading to advocate a step which would entirely compromise them, while it might bring division into their ranks. The Electress had the mortification, severe to a woman of her ardent spirit, to find herself held at arm's length as it were by a large proportion of those who should have been her warmest supporters. Another question in dispute was the propriety of the Electress's receiving from the English Government a pension befitting the heir

[1] In speaking to Lord Dartmouth during her husband's life, Sophia said she could not leave the Elector and her family, otherwise she would be glad to see her own country, as she called it, and would willingly have her bones laid by her mother's in Westminster Abbey.

to the throne. Never in the whole course of her career had Sophia affected to despise money or money's power. In her present ambiguous circumstances in relation to her discourteous son, whose subject she was, while she was likely soon to be his Queen, the practical independence which such a pension would give her rendered the suggestion doubly welcome. This question of a pension was used as a bait by both the great political factions, for the Tories dissembled, and approached the Electress with specious overtures. There were many English now in Hanover; several were in the Electress's household; and their presence certainly did not tend to allay the ferment of expectation, and the undercurrent of scheming and manœuvring which was for ever at work. "Such humours, such jealousies, such villainies in the Hanoverian Court," declared one of the baffled negotiators. The Electress listened to both Whigs and Tories, and tried to make friends with both, as the future sovereign who was to rule the entire nation. The object of the Tories is said to have been to secure from the Electoral family such expressions of satisfaction with the Tory Government as should help to keep them in office till the death of Anne and the proclamation of the Pretender. For this purpose they induced Anne, sorely against her will, to renew her expressions of goodwill to the Hanoverian House, while recognising them as her heirs. The Electoral Prince and Caroline of Anspach's eldest daughter was named Anne after the Queen of England, who consented to be her god-mother.

In 1706, George, the Electoral Prince, had been created by Queen Anne Duke of Cambridge, with the right to sit in the English House of Peers, and to take precedence of his fellow peers. But for eight years the creation remained in abeyance, and any proposal for the Prince to visit England or to take his seat in the Peers was strenuously opposed by the Tories, and was regarded with extreme disapproval by Anne, who dreaded a public demonstration in his favour. At the same time Harley sent a kinsman and namesake to Hanover to impose upon the Electress by renewed arrangements for her visiting England and for her receiving a pension. Marlborough, on his side, despatched his political agent, an Irish gentleman named Molyneux, to warn the Elector's secretary of the treachery of the Tories, and their determination to place the Pretender on the throne.

By a fresh ruse of the Tories, Baron Schutz arrived in Hanover with a writ summoning the Duke of Cambridge to take his seat in the House of Lords, and with letters from the Queen and her ministers, written in the friendliest terms, to the Electress and her son. When these letters failed to produce the effect they were intended to have, of drawing from the heads of the House of Hanover such expressions of confidence and regard as would help the Tories and displease the Whigs, the Government began to show their true colours, though the veil was not altogether withdrawn. Anne was made to write that the writ had been served without her authority; that while she was favourable to the Protestant settlement, she would suffer no diminution of her royal prerogatives, and that her intention was to oppose the Electoral Prince's visit to England and his taking his seat in her House of Peers, however fatal the consequences. At the same time her minister, Harley, wrote to Sophia, recommending her to rely implicitly on the friendship of the Queen (he was quite cognisant of its lukewarm nature) and dissuading her from identifying her interests with those of the Whigs.

The Electress's answer was to direct copies of the letters to be at once forwarded to Marlborough, as the

Whigs' ostensible representative. It is from Marlborough's agent, Molyneux, that we hear the sad result of the prolonged strife. His account is given with genuine regret and kindly feeling.

"The last post—I finished my letter about six in the evening [June 9th, 1714], not an hour after the post went. I went directly afterwards to Herrenhausen, the country house of the Court, and there the first thing I heard was that the good old Electress was fast dying in one of the public walks. I ran up there, and found her just expiring in the arms of the poor Electoral Princess amidst the tears of a great many of her servants, who endeavoured in vain to help her. I can give you no account of her illness, but that I believe the chagrin of those villainous letters— I sent you last—has been in a great measure the cause of it. The Rheingravine,[1] who has been with her these fifteen years, has told me she never knew anything make so deep an impression on her as the affair of the Prince's journey, which I am sure she had to the last degree at heart; and she has done me the honour to tell me so twenty times. In the midst of this concern those letters arrived, and those, I verily believe, have broken her heart and brought her with sorrow to the grave. The letters were delivered on Wednesday at noon. That evening when I came to Court she was at cards, but so full of these letters that she got up and ordered me to follow her into the garden, where she gave them to me to read, and walked and spoke a great deal in connection with them. I believe she walked three hours that night. The next morning, which was Thursday, I heard she was out of order; and on going immediately to Court, she ordered me to be called into her bedchamber. She gave me the letters I sent you to copy; she bid me

---

[1] A half-sister of Madame d'Orleans, and a niece of the Electress.

send them (the copies) the next post, and bring them (the originals) afterwards to her Court. That was on Thursday. In the morning of Friday she told me she was very well, but seemed very chagrined. She was dressed, and dined with the Elector as usual. About four she did me the honour to send me to town for some other copies of the same letters, and then she was still perfectly well. She worked and talked very heartily in the Orangerie;[1] after that, at about six, she went to walk in the garden, and was still very well. A shower of rain came on. As she was walking pretty fast to get to shelter, they told her they believed she walked a little too fast. She answered, 'I believe I do,' and dropped down in saying those words, which were her last. They raised her up, chafed her with spirits, tried to bleed her; but it was all in vain, and when I came up to her she was as dead as if she had been four days so. No Princess ever died more regretted, and I infinitely pity those servants that have known her a long time, when I, that have had the honour to know her but a month, can scarce refrain from tears in relating this."

When Madame d'Orleans heard of the death of the aunt for whom she had so great an affection, she quoted from a letter of the Electress's in which she had written that sudden death was best; that it might be painful to die in one's bed, having on one side the minister or priest, and on the other the doctor, "who can do nothing for you." Thus passed away in the manner she desired a brave, true woman, who had been early taught, what she had never forgotten, " to love God and fear the devil." The Electress Sophia had reached the age of eighty-four. Three out of her eight children survived her, the Elector George,

---

[1] Queen Anne's orangerie, a kind of magnified summer-house, is to be seen in the grounds of Kensington Palace.

Prince Maximilian the renegade, and Prince Ernest, the youngest born. The last was sufficiently trustworthy to be placed at the head of the Council, to which George entrusted the management of the affairs of Hanover when he left for England, taking with him the son with whom he was not on speaking terms for years at a time.

The Electress's wish was not granted, that "Sophia, Queen of Great Britain," should be inscribed on her tomb. Few Queens more deserving of the title ever reigned. The prize she coveted had been all but within her grasp. Sophia died in the month of June; two months afterwards, in the August of the same year, her second cousin, Anne, who had been ailing and failing for some time, died of dropsy. She was fifty years of age, and more than thirty years Sophia's junior.

II.

SOPHIA DOROTHEA OF ZELL, WIFE OF GEORGE I.

AUTHORITIES:

Histoire Secrète de la Duchesse d'Hanover, Epouse de George Premier, by the Baron von Poellnitz; *Memoirs of Sophia Dorothea,* from the secret archives of Hanover, Brunswick, Berlin, and Vienna; Dr. Doran's *Lives of the Queens of the House of Hanover;* Thackeray's *Four Georges.*

SOPHIA DOROTHEA OF ZELL, WIFE OF GEORGE I. (THE PRISONER OF AHLDEN).

CHAPTER I.

SOPHIA DOROTHEA OF ZELL, WIFE OF GEORGE I.

CELLE, or Zell, is described by Thackeray as "a little town of 10,000 people, that lies on the railway between Hamburg and Hanover, in the midst of great plains of sand upon the river Celle." It was the seat of one of the duchies into which the House of Brunswick and Hanover was divided, and it was the birthplace of the unhappy Sophia Dorothea. Her miserable fate has raised up for her—sometimes in quarters where one would least expect such advocates—zealous partisans, unreasoning and unreasonable in their partisanship, disposed, in order to clear their heroine, to sully recklessly the reputation of all who stood in opposition to her in her lifetime.

Sophia Dorothea, daughter of Duke George William of Brunswick, by his morganatic marriage with Eleanore d'Olbrense, was born at Zell in September, 1666. Her birth was the signal for her father's bestowal on her mother, to whom he had already accorded the style of Madame de Harburg, the additional title of Countess von Wilhelmsburg, endowing her with the island of Wilhelmsburg, on the Elbe, near Hamburg. The island was thickly stocked with game, which found a ready sale in Hamburg, so that it was a perquisite of some value. As time passed, and the other children born to the couple did not survive their infancy, the Duke, with the consent of his brother Duke Ernest, added to his settlements on his wife, and especially on his child, till the little girl became a great enough heiress to cause the fact that she was the child of a morganatic marriage, and that her mother was not of royal rank, to be in a measure overlooked. There were suitors for her hand even then, not only among the nobles, but among the minor Princes of Northern Germany. It was quite possible that at any time, by the Emperor's consent, Duke George's wife might be promoted to the rank of his Duchess. Duke Ernest and Duchess Sophia lived in dread of this contingency, which would seriously affect their children's interests. It was not likely to escape the attention, or to fail to enter into the calculations of the neighbouring magnates. All things considered, it was not probable that a handsome noble lad, in his early teens, who was at that time a page in the royal suite maintained at Zell, and a playfellow of the small seven-year-old Sophia, would have much chance of winning her hand when he was twenty-three and she was fourteen—the age fixed for her majority and her selection of a husband. It might be the distinctive audacity of the Königsmarks, the lad's family—destined to make Europe ring with questionable exploits—which originated the idea that was in existence in those early days. This lad, fated to be Sophia Dorothea's evil genius, was Philip Christopher von Königsmark. His family, one of note in Brandenburg, had settled in Sweden, where it produced men of more honourable renown than those descendants whose splendid vices and daring crimes electrified the civilised world.

A more promising bridegroom for the little beauty and heiress of Duke George William's Court offered himself, when she was still only nine years of age, in the person of Frederic, eldest son of the reigning Duke of Wolfenbüttel, her father's cousin. He was willing to waive—for the time, doubtless—the question of her not being of royal rank, and the young couple were formally betrothed; but the bridegroom-elect was slain the following year at the siege of Phillipsburg. Augustus of Wolfenbüttel, the Duke's second son, took the place of his elder brother; but in the meantime the Emperor's consent had been obtained, the Countess of Wilhelmsburg was recognised as the Duchess of Hanover, and Sophia Dorothea was, by Imperial decree, a Princess as well as her father's heiress. Her hand in marriage was more in request than ever, while her father was not favourable to the pretensions of the Prince of Wolfenbüttel. The excuse which Duke George gave was that he regarded the death of the elder brother as a bad omen. Probably the Duke was already hankering after a marriage for his daughter with Duke Ernest's eldest son Prince George, the marriage on which both brothers were eventually determined. It would keep the Brunswick possessions as much as possible united, and it would combine the rights of the cousins, supposing there should be an attempt to bring forward Prince George as a rival to Sophia Dorothea, on the ground of the pledge to Duke Ernest, before his marriage, that his children should inherit the duchy of Hanover. If the royal fathers desired the marriage of the cousins, the mothers—never on cordial terms—were both averse to it. We have already heard how long Duchess Sophia resisted the match, and persuaded herself that her Duke, whatever his policy in dealing with his brother on the matter, was equally opposed to it. Eleanore, Duchess of Hanover, had no reason to suppose, on her side, that her sister-in-law would treat her as an equal or a friend were the alliance completed. She inclined strongly to the Wolfenbüttel connection, since the reigning Duke had always supported her claims.

Duke George delayed the decision by putting off

his daughter's majority for two years, till she was sixteen instead of fourteen, while Prince George went to England to make overtures for the hand of Princess Anne. But always in the background there lurked the advisability of the marriage of George and Sophia Dorothea, with all its fatally specious recommendations.

Sophia Dorothea's admirers speak of her as at this time a beautiful, graceful, amiable young girl, excelling in many accomplishments. With regard to the beauty and grace, they may be taken for granted. She was the daughter of a beautiful mother, and one portrait of her, which survives, represents her in a straw hat and laced bodice—a fair, buxom young woman, with charms of a voluptuous type. Her eyes are half sleepy, half languishing, her square chin is cleft by a dimple.

In reference to her accomplishments, these are always judiciously generalised, and spoken of vaguely. The exception, which is emphatically insisted upon, is " her exquisite dancing, such as might have been expected from the daughter of a French mother." We may give entire credence to her exquisite dancing. Her garrulous, simple-minded champion, Baron von Poellnitz, mentions it particularly, when on the occasion of a ball given by Prince George the Princess " stood up " with Count von Königsmark, and the performance of the pair won the admiration of the assembled company.

The amiability of a poor little girl of sixteen who has never quitted her father's residency has not been severely tested. In the course of a very few years Sophia Dorothea's amiability developed into a violent and stubborn temper, with all the headstrong passions of an undisciplined nature.

The "careful education" given to the girl by her mother the Duchess, so frequently dwelt upon by poor Sophia Dorothea's adherents, sounds as apocryphal in the sequel as do "the virtues" largely ascribed to

Eleanore d'Olbrense, both before and after her marriage, by the same disingenuous commentators. The virtues appear to resolve themselves into the craft with which an ambitious woman procured her promotion, and the plausible propriety by which she took care to retain the advantages she had secured. So far from bringing up her only child with exceptional attention and devotion to principle, a trustworthy contemporary, the Duchess of Orleans, who, as a rule, is eminently truthful even when she is most prejudiced, gives as her deliberate opinion, which I have already had occasion to quote, that the Princess's errors and misfortunes were due in the first place to the wretchedly neglected education for which her mother was responsible.

The birthday, when Sophia Dorothea would attain the mature age of sixteen, was now at hand, and the question whether she was to marry Augustus of Wolfenbüttel or George of Hanover had to be settled without further loss of time. Then is said to occur the conversion of the Duchess Sophia to the two Dukes' secret wishes, and the odd nocturnal visit to Zell, in which one is not inclined to put much faith. Poellnitz records it, but in a very modified form. The Duchess arrived early, which seeing that she had only twenty miles to travel was not very wonderful. She had an interview with *both* her brother and sister-in-law, and offered her congratulations on their daughter's birthday. The only attempt—if it was an attempt—at concealing the main object of the visit from Duchess Eleanore was that Duchess Sophia spoke in German, the native tongue of herself and the Duke, which the accomplished lady who had been for seventeen years the wife of a German Duke, dwelling in a German duchy, was not supposed to understand. Granting that French was largely the language of European Courts at this date, this circumstance is in itself singular.

Poellnitz, unlike the other defenders of Sophia Dorothea, does not find it necessary to traduce the Electress Sophia in his attempt to make a cause for her unhappy daughter-in-law. He is perfectly fair to the elder lady, fully admitting her fine qualities and her general goodness and kindness. His censure is confined to the sharp sarcastic speeches which she addressed to Sophia Dorothea, in which we can easily believe, as in keeping with the speaker, and to her non-interference at the last crisis. His most severe reflection on the Electress is when he includes her in the list of Sophia Dorothea's enemies who were punished for their hostility to her, the Electress's punishment being that her wish to be Queen of Great Britain was not granted.

As an instance of the numerous inaccuracies and inconsistencies which are to be found in the accounts of the Duchess Sophia's alleged visit to Zell and its consequences, it was certainly made, if made at all, before Sophia Dorothea's birthday on September 15th, and it is expressly said that the journey was taken on one of the very hottest nights of the season; while it is added, without hesitation, that the inauspicious marriage thus brought about was pressed on with indecent haste, and was celebrated within a few days, at the most a few weeks. As it happened, Sophia Dorothea was not married till the following November (1682), fully two months after her birthday.

Whether or not there is any truth in the tradition, which still survives among the romance-loving maidens of Zell, that Sophia Dorothea had already given her heart to Prince Augustus of Wolfenbüttel (the son of " the ugly baboon," to whom Marie Louise of Orleans likened her unseen Spanish husband), it is beyond question that the unwilling bride had no heart for George of Hanover, though she wrote a formal letter of acquiescence in her parents' wishes to his parents. She is said to have fainted when she heard of his arrival in the character of an accepted bridegroom at the gate of the castle.

On the gloomy November day of wind and rain when the wedding took place she still clung to the friends of her youth, and shrank unconquerably from the twenty miles' journey which was to take her so far away, as it seemed to her inexperience in those days of bad roads and difficult locomotion. Above all, the parting was to commit her to the care of an unattractive, ungracious cousin and husband. Few young men could have been more repellent to a self-willed, frivolous girl than the ungainly, silent, gruff lad of twenty-two, who deserved some pity on his own account. Grievous as were his sins, he too was a victim to political expediency, since he was as utterly disinclined to the marriage as his young wife showed herself.

In spite of it all, the first two years of the pair's married life at Hanover seemed to give promise of a bright ending to a bad beginning. Princess George, as the Electoral Princess was familiarly called, behaved as if she had some sense of the duties as well as of the compensations of her lot, and had made up her mind to live up to them. She was so young, and personally so attractive, that good-natured people would have been ready to forgive a great deal to her if she had but continued to give any sign of doing her best. It is not denied on any hand that she was received at the Court of Hanover with all the cordiality and distinction to which the bride of the heir-apparent was entitled. Even Prince George thawed a little from the churlish and defiant attitude natural to him in all circumstances. She was a mother at seventeen, her son George Augustus (George II.)

being born in 1683, when there was the usual rejoicing over an heir, and the usual increase of importance and consideration for the young mother.

But very soon the horizon clouded over, never again to reveal a serene domestic sky. The Court of Hanover, then one of the most brilliant in Germany, was, even with the Electress Sophia at its head, no nursing-ground for the sanctity of home and the growth of home virtues. Its moral standard was of the lowest. Vice reigned triumphant in high places, as in other European Courts of the time. The Elector and his son were among the most flagrant offenders in the gross self-indulgence and open profligacy which prevailed. The Electress, according to the tenets of the women like her, wisely or unwisely ignored what she could not prevent, and pursued the even tenor of her way; honourable among the base, upright among the depraved, gathering around her a circle of like-minded men and women, and contenting herself with their respect and regard. For this apparent indifference to the conduct of her neighbours she has been loudly and persistently reproached; but it would be difficult to say how she could have improved the aspect of affairs by an undignified exhibition of furious resentment and open rebellion against her husband and sovereign. Sophia Dorothea writhed and raged under similar domestic injuries; she was ready to retaliate by showing herself far from beyond suspicion, and the result was not encouraging.

Hanover, on its dissolute side, was dominated by one wicked woman. She is held up, without reserve, to the detestation of her worthier contemporaries and of posterity as the Jezebel of her country and generation. She was one of two handsome unprincipled sisters named Meissenbach, who came with their father, a political adventurer, to the Hanoverian Court. These adventurers were very often soldiers of fortune or members of noble families, fallen into poverty, with their wives and daughters. The whole were apt to be the parasitical pests of the period. If the men were, as a rule, to be deprecated, the women were in equal measure to be detested.

The Fräulein von Meissenbach first appeared in public as shepherdesses in a Court pastoral, which was played to welcome back the two Princes George and Maximilian, arriving with their governors, from their foreign travels and campaigns. In proof of the success of the sisters, they married the two governors, and were from that time conspicuous figures at Court. One of the governors, Platen, became in time the Elector's Prime Minister, and was ennobled. His wife, thus made a Countess, possessed great political and social influence, still more from the Elector's favour than from the Count's position. As the wife of her husband's Prime Minister, and necessarily in this sense one of the first of the Court ladies, the Electress consented to treat the lady with all courtesy, while steadily refusing to regard her in any other light.

Sophia Dorothea adopted different tactics. She treated Madame von Platen and her sister with marked rudeness and contempt. A furious war raged henceforth between the contending parties in a rivalry which was as humiliating to Princess George as it was galling to the haughty favourite. Princess George was not without wit, though it was less silencing than that of her mother-in-law. She did not fail in scornful retorts and vindictive innuendoes.

Prince Maximilian's *embroglio* with his father occurred about this time. The Prince headed a small plot for the separation of Hanover and Zell, which the Elector desired to unite and preserve as his eldest son's inheritance. For this piece of insubordination Prince

Maximilian found it necessary to fly from Hanover. He took refuge, to begin with, at the Court of Wolfenbüttel, but was reconciled for a time to his family before he repaired to Italy and completed his treason by renouncing the Protestant religion and denying his mother's claim to the throne of England. His subordinate fellow-conspirator Molcke, possibly also his tempter, was, as has been already mentioned, arrested and suffered the extreme penalty of the law, being beheaded at Hanover.

Sophia Dorothea was so far implicated in the matter. Her partisans declare that an attempt was made to induce Molcke to criminate her by offering him his life in return for compromising evidence against the Princess, and that he gallantly refused, preferring to die. It must be remembered that such evidence referred to the treasonable withdrawal of Sophia Dorothea's native duchy of Zell from Hanover, and not to her subsequent follies and indiscretions; so that even her connection with the conspiracy, if it could have been proved, would not have subjected her to a heavier penalty than was at first inflicted on her brother-in-law. Poellnitz, in his rambling, gossiping little narrative, details a violent altercation Sophia Dorothea had with her husband on Prince Maximilian and Molcke's affair, when she reproached him bitterly for not exerting himself to vindicate her from the charge of conspiracy. The quarrels between husband and wife were now so inveterate that he, in his sullen moods, would not speak to her for two months on end, and only noticed her in public, while she revenged herself by biting taunts and gibes in private.

An illness of Sophia Dorothea's followed on these scenes, when Poellnitz asserts that the Electress Sophia went to her, and watched over her, never leaving her till the birth of the poor young creature's daughter— the second Sophia Dorothea—in 1688, when the mother was still only twenty-one years of age. On her recovery, while yet weak and low-spirited, the Electress carried her daughter-in-law with her to Herrenhausen, and there tried every means to cheer and entertain her.

Two years after the birth of the younger child of George and Sophia Dorothea, the feud between husband and wife having remained unhealed, an inopportune visitor arrived at the Court of Hanover in the person of the same Philip von Königsmark who had been the Princess's early acquaintance and playfellow at Zell. If the beautiful aspiring page had been fascinating to the thoughtless child, infinitely more attractive to the vain, shallow, reckless nature of the discontented woman and neglected wife was the man who, like her husband, was six years her senior. Königsmark was still beautiful, with the *beauté de diable* of an insolent, manly beauty. He was showily clever and brilliant, a lively talker, an apt mimic, a splendid spendthrift, a daring and dauntless soldier. He was considered so great an acquisition to the Court circle that the Elector immediately conferred on him the appointment of Colonel of the Hanoverian Guards. Sophia Dorothea was confirmed in her admiration of the newcomer by the sensation which Königsmark created at Court. Even the Princess's declared enemy, Madame von Platen, who united to the wiles of a skilful *intriguante* the vilest of coquetry, was eager to attract his attention and win his friendship, and he did not decline her overtures. Prince Charles, the Electress's best-loved son, was dazzled, lad-like, by the graces and *bons mots*, the adventures and escapades of the sorry-enough hero. Prince Charles had a liking for his wayward young sister-in-law and was in the habit of visiting her every day, when he carried with him his last fancy in the shape of a friend. The Prince even induced his mother to give Königsmark special invitations to Herrenhausen.

But when every allowance is made for the force of example, the general infatuation with which the magnificent stranger was greeted at Hanover, and the early associations which linked him with Sophia Dorothea's childhood at Zell, and seemed to constitute him her particular ally, it is impossible to overlook the deplorable lack of sense, the culpable indiscretion, of such an alliance between a Princess—situated as Sophia Dorothea was, on the terms on which she stood with her husband—and an avowed man of gallantry boasting of his conquests. In the interval since the two were parted Count Philip had been mixed up in one of the most ruffianly outrages which had scandalised a by no means sensitive generation. This was the story of his brother Carl Johann von Königsmark, who had come to England in his hunt for an heiress. Her fortune was to be won by his handsome person and desperate character, and was to serve as a substitute for the plunder no longer to be had for the taking by the bold robber-knights of the Middle Ages. He brought with him his boy-brother Philip, and established him in a school preparatory to sending him to Oxford.

Carl Johann decided that his prize should be the heiress of the Percies, who at thirteen years of age was the widow of Cavendish, Earl of Ogle, son of the Duke of Newcastle. When Königsmark made his suit to the lady's relatives, it was dismissed with scant ceremony, and she was prudently remarried to Thomas Thynne of Longleat, a young man whose wealth had procured for him the sobriquet of "Tom of Ten Thousand." The second marriage was no serious obstacle to his pursuit in the eyes of a Königsmark. He engaged and armed a group of foreign scoundrels who, mounted on horseback, waylaid and beset Thynne as he was driving in his coach in Pall Mall in the dusk of the evening. A shot from the blunderbuss of one of his assailants inflicted on the unfortunate man a wound of which he died shortly afterwards. The deed of violence was so wanton, apart from Königsmark's design, and so dastardly, it was committed in so public a place, that no man could feel secure of his life if the murder went unpunished. The perpetrators and the instigator of the assassination were arrested and tried. It would have gone hard with Königsmark had he not been helped by the favour shown to him by the King, Charles II. The merry monarch could not bear that so fine a gentleman should pay with the forfeit of his life for what his royal sponsor was pleased to regard as little more than a frolic. To his friends Königsmark insisted that his confederates had mistaken his intentions. These were only to force Thynne to fight a duel with him, which would have been a more legitimate and gentlemanlike way of disposing of the barrier to the Count's success. To the Court he lied without scruple, and caused his young brother to lie in roundly asserting that Carl Johann's sole business with his accomplices was the purchase of horses. The wretched tools in the crime were sacrificed without mercy, and received the full penalty of the law, while their employer was acquitted.

Sophia Dorothea could not have been ignorant of this wicked business, and though one brother was not answerable for the sin of another, it marked the stamp of men and women like the Königsmarks, who were the scourges of the society in which they moved.

To the earlier enmity between the Countess von Platen and Princess George was added the unseemly contest for Philip von Königsmark's favour, since he combined paying court to the silly Princess with taking care to stand high in the good graces of the wife of the Prime Minister.

The Court rang with idle invidious gossip, evilly flavoured slander and angry passages between the persons principally concerned. Now it was an embroidered glove of Sophia Dorothea's which her enemies said she dropped by accident when walking *tête-à-tête* with Königsmark and her friends alleged the Countess von Platen stole in order to leave it in Prince George's path and arouse his wrath against the Princess.

Again it was a trick of the incorrigible Prince Maximilian. He was for the moment back at Court, and seems from internal evidence to have been like his brother, Prince Charles, one of Sophia Dorothea's thoughtless ill-advised adherents. In a public assembly Prince Maximilian contrived to flirt a few drops of the water in which peas had been boiled into Madame von Platen's face, because peas-water was believed to be an infallible test for the exposure of the rouge with which she sought to repair the ravages of time on her once brilliant complexion.

All these petty wrangles and ugly scandals in connection with the wife of her eldest son must have been gall and wormwood to the proud self-respect of the Electress. Yet, according to Poellnitz, she stood by her daughter-in-law for a time, and even sought to show her confidence in her by permitting Prince Charles to bring his friend into the royal circle.

Königsmark accompanied Prince Charles—and this also may have been a well-meant arrangement of the Electress Sophia's—when the Prince went to fight the Turks on the Danube, where he fell in battle as two of his elder brothers had fallen before him. When the melancholy news reached Herrenhausen, Sophia Dorothea was with the Electress, and Madame von Platen was also in attendance. The rumour was that Königsmark had also fallen, and the sacred sorrow of the bereaved mother was broken in upon by the noisy unrestrained lamentations of two of her companions for their graceless cavalier.

CHAPTER II.

KÖNIGSMARK'S FLIGHT AND DEATH.

UNFORTUNATELY for all, as it reads, Count Philip was not slain then. He returned to work further and still more fatal mischief at the Court of Hanover. At last the jovial Elector interfered so far as to suggest to Königsmark strongly, but not in an altogether unfriendly spirit, the advisability of his quitting Hanover for a time at least. The Count had just sufficient prudence to see the judiciousness of the advice, and to take it. He set out on a visit to Augustus, King of Saxony, who was about the most licentious sovereign presiding over the most riotous Court at a period in history when such Courts were the rule rather than the exception in Northern Europe.

Sophia Dorothea was induced to consent to the separation from Königsmark, and in consideration of what was supposed to be the heart-broken misery of the man, she agreed to put the crowning touch to her inconceivable folly and wrong-doing by entering into an intimate correspondence with a renowned and abandoned *roué*. This much is admitted by her most zealous supporters, and attested with a certain amount of reservation by her lady-in-waiting and confidential friend, Fräulein von Knesebeck. Even without further confirmation it would be hard to believe in the perfect innocence of poor Sophia Dorothea after she had taken this deplorably compromising step. Thackeray was warranted in writing that he was "astonished" to find a writer like Dr. Doran acquit this most unfortunate lady. The explanation is that the credulity and wilful blindness of partisanship have no bounds. In order to rehabilitate the smirched and tarnished character of Sophia Dorothea, English writers continue, down to the present day, to assail with covert sneers the spotless reputation of the Electress Sophia, in whose side her daughter-in-law must have been a sharp thorn, and with whom Sophia Dorothea was not to be named in the same breath. These unhesitating detractors dwell with quite comical disgust on the Electress's learning and love of philosopy, as if these acquirements and tastes were so many reproaches in themselves, positive proofs of her unwomanliness and coldness of heart.

Königsmark, instead of pining in despair in his exile from Hanover, was one of the gayest and most dissipated revellers at the Court of Saxony. In a fit of drunken bragging he proclaimed his double conquest of Princess George and Madame von Platen, while he held up to ridicule the antiquated airs and graces of the elder lady. In all probability he corroborated his story by a display of the letters he had received—an insane act which sealed his doom.

Away in Hanover the quarrels between Prince George and his wife were progressing from words to blows, if Sophia Dorothea is to be believed. The unseemly result is not unlikely, when the two persons engaged in the perpetual disputes are considered, the grim enraged man and the hysterically violent woman. One day in answer to a privileged remonstrance, as her friends would describe it—Thackeray called it " her intolerable tongue "—George, according to Sophia Dorothea, sprang at her throat, and she was only saved from strangulation by the screams (which happily were not stifled) that brought to her aid Knesebeck and her other attendants. They bore her senseless to her room.

After this notable outbreak, Sophia Dorothea was naturally able to obtain from the Elector permission to pay a long-proposed visit to her parents at Zell. When one thinks that Zell was only twenty miles distant, even the rough roads and heavy coaches of the time do not appear to present a difficulty which a self-willed and rebellious wife and daughter-in-law could not have surmounted long before, if she had so chosen. One of the puzzling incongruities in Sophia Dorothea's history is the exceedingly small space—as we count space—in which all the events occurred. The two residencies and the fortress of Ahlden were all within a day or a day and a half's journey of each other even then, within a couple of hours by modern railways. It is like a grievous "storm in a teacup," in a different sense from that in which the phrase is generally used.

Sophia Dorothea met with a different reception at Zell from what she wished, though she might have easily foreseen it. Her mother is said to have greeted her affectionately, and to have been willing to grant a ready hearing and unlimited sympathy to the fluently told tale of her daughter's wrongs and sufferings. But the formerly attached father had been made acquainted beforehand, from more credible sources, with the Princess's conduct. He was gravely displeased, and absolutely refused to have anything to do with the suggestion—whether it proceeded from her mother or herself—that she should get a "separation" from Prince George. He insisted that she should return to her husband and children.

The explanation given by Sophia Dorothea's party of her father's condemnation is far-fetched and improbable. They say that the Duke's ears were poisoned, so that he turned against his own child, and that the chief agent in deceiving him and abusing his confidence was his minister Bernsdorf, who was in the pay of Hanover, and was also a tool of the ubiquitous Madame von Platen.

A man is rarely turned against his own flesh and blood, sole daughter of his house and heart, especially if her worst offences have been impulsiveness and imprudence. The statesman who is accused of having defamed her was her countryman who had seen her grow up from a child, if not into the paragon of excellence she has been fondly represented, at least into a light-hearted girl. It may well be supposed, without giving him great credit, that he had some kindly feeling for his master's daughter, some interest in his Princess, until these feelings were changed into resentment and mortification by the levity and perversity with which she was doing her best to bring to nothing the alliance between Zell and Hanover.

Princess George was compelled by her father to return to her detested husband and home. In the act of doing so she was guilty of a display of petulant defiance of her husband's family, and of the rules of common courtesy, not to say of Court etiquette, which, slight as it was, marks the insubordinate regardless nature of the woman. The road by which she travelled in her coach those twenty miles to Hanover took her close to the country palace of Herrenhausen, where the royal family were then staying. Her simple duty was to stop long enough to pay her respects to the Elector and Electress. The Elector had always been willing to befriend her, and if the Electress's forbearance had come to an end, it had stood Sophia Dorothea in good stead before now, and it might have been revived. Instead of alighting, Sophia Dorothea drove past without a sign, treating the heads of the house with marked rudeness, and indicating the position of opposition to their authority and disregard for their wishes which she intended to take up for the future.

The excuse made for the Princess is, that she saw

Madame von Platen watching for her approach from one of the windows ; but as Madame von Platen was not the mistress of Herrenhausen we fail to see that her presence, however exasperating, freed Sophia Dorothea from her obligations to be civil and respectful to her husband's parents, the sovereigns of the country.

Soon after Sophia Dorothea's return to Hanover, Count Philip von Königsmark reappeared there, it is said, with the intention of completing the arrangements by which he was to resign his colonelcy of the Hanoverian Guards, and to enter the service of the King of Saxony.

It was the summer of the year 1694. Sophia Dorothea was no longer an inexperienced girl, she was a woman of eight-and-twenty, the mother of a boy of ten and a girl of seven. Her husband was absent on a visit to his sister, the Queen of Prussia, at Berlin. When in Prussia (by Poellnitz's account), he was induced on the representations of his sister to write a conciliatory letter to his wife, which came too late.

On the night of July 1st Königsmark, in compliance with a note which had reached him, repaired to the residency. The note was written in pencil, in the name of the Princess George, and appointed him to meet her in her apartments. This note is said to have been a forgery of Madame von Platen's. It is certain she was early acquainted with the interview.

When the Count requested admission to the Princess he was received by the lady-in-waiting, Fräulein von Knesebeck, who in her subsequent declaration asserted she at once recognised that Königsmark had been imposed upon. But in spite of the recognition he was admitted into the Princess's rooms, and remained there for a couple of hours. It is not denied that he was then arranging the details of the flight for which her carriages and horses were in readiness. Königsmark was to be the Princess's escort either to Paris,[1] as he proposed, or to the Court of Wolfenbüttel (only forty miles distant), which Fräulein von Knesebeck maintained was the Princess's choice.

In the meantime Madame von Platen was informed of the meeting. Maddened by Königsmark's double treachery to her in Saxony, she carried her information to the Elector. He was incensed at the insolence of the assignation under his roof, and gave an order for the arrest of the Count, placing for the purpose several soldiers of the guard at the disposal of his informant; she had thus the opportunity of revenging herself at once on the Princess and on Königsmark.

Madame von Platen did not stint herself in her revenge—this much is known, though the manner in which the affair was hushed up has left it shrouded in mystery. Königsmark did not leave the residency alive, though he was not missed for some time. So far as can be gathered from the conflicting statements, Madame von Platen had the soldiers given to her placed in the shadow of the great stove in the *Rittersaal* through which the Count had to pass on his way from Sophia Dorothea's apartments. Though it was in the stillness of night, so silently and rapidly was the deed done that scarcely a sound made itself heard, unless it might be the barking of the Princess's little dog, which warned her and her attendant that there was some disturbance in the hall.

When Königsmark came within the shadow of the stove he was suddenly set upon by four armed men. He strove to defend himself, and succeeded in wounding more than one of the guards, but quickly fell mortally wounded. In the various records of the crime and in the vivid tradition which still preserves

---

[1] Sophia Dorothea is said to have entertained for some time the idea of escaping to Paris and becoming a Roman Catholic.

its outlines, the Countess, who had been lurking in the vicinity, is represented as coming forward to make assurance doubly sure, and to taunt the vanquished man on whom she had formerly lavished her ill-omened regard. He is said to have cursed her where she stood, and asserted the innocence of the Princess, when the infuriated woman stamped with her high-heeled shoe on the mouth from which the breath was passing.

How Königsmark's tell-tale body was disposed of has never been clearly ascertained. The Elector is reported to have been at his wit's end with alarm and vexation at the undreamt of severity with which his orders had been executed. He either caused the body to be at once burnt, or he had it immediately cast into a drain and covered with quicklime.

Another version of the story relates that many years afterwards, when most of the persons concerned in the tragedy were dead, on the second visit which George II. paid to Hanover, in the course of alterations made in the residency, Königsmark's skeleton was found beneath the flooring of Sophia Dorothea's dressing-room, where he had been strangled. Some of the tellers of the tale allege that the first tidings which Sophia Dorothea had of the Count's death were received from the Prime Minister, Count von Platen, who was sent to examine her on her guilt or innocence after Königsmark's papers had been seized.

There can be no question that Prince George was not implicated in Königsmark's murder. The Prince was still absent in Berlin. It is said that on his return to Hanover he expressed his displeasure at the act of violence which had been committed. He was annoyed by the publicity which had been given to the charge brought against the Princess, and only withdrew his objections after reading one of her letters to Königsmark.

Unutterably sad as Sophia Dorothea's fate was thenceforth, it is only her extreme partisans who will venture to say that she was treated with excessive harshness and deliberate cruelty. It ought to be borne in mind that her father was from first to last fully cognisant of the treatment complained of, and in entire accordance with it. Those persons who prefer to believe Duke George William an utterly unnatural parent, Sophia Dorothea an injured victim, and all the other actors in the drama her false accusers and persecutors, argue that the sole motive which actuated these quite different individuals, apart from their enmity to the Princess, with her piteously few allies, was the desire to insure the union of Hanover and Zell. For this purpose, it is alleged, and not from any humane and merciful desire to spare the unhappy woman, not from any honourable disinclination to expose a scandal which would bring disgrace on the whole House of Hanover, on the innocent children of the offender as well as on her culpable husband, the authorities adopted the course which has been found so open to censure.

For a time Sophia Dorothea remained in her own apartments and was said to be suffering from illness. She was visited and examined by statesmen, lawyers, and Lutheran ministers, in a vain endeavour to elicit the truth from her. A test was applied to her which savours to us of profanity. It was a relic of the ordeals of the Middle Ages, and was in keeping with the lingering superstition of the seventeenth century. She was required to take the sacrament in the presence of a gathering of officials and clergymen, but before doing so she was called upon to make a solemn statement of her innocence of any offence against her husband. The old belief was that the sacred symbols of bread and wine would choke the lying eater. Even when this conviction died out of the popular mind it was thought that the culprit would at least flinch and waver before the test. Sophia Dorothea surmounted it unfalteringly (with what mental reservations who can tell?). It is sufficient to show the spirit in which she played her part. She immediately turned tauntingly to Count von Platen, whom she believed to be listening incredulously, and asked him if his *excellent* wife could do the same? One is led to suppose that this performance of Sophia Dorothea's was one of " the prodigious falsehoods " which Thackeray attributes to her.

Fräulein von Knesebeck was arrested and examined. She gave her evidence in her mistress's favour; she declared that she had been present at every interview between the Princess and Königsmark, and that she was guiltless of all save indiscretion and an intention to flee from Hanover. But the Fräulein's single testimony, especially as she had by her own confession connived at the indiscretion and been a partner in the wrong-doing, went for little or nothing. There was enough blame attributed to her to cause her to be imprisoned in the castle of Schwartzfeld, in the Hartz district.

Sophia Dorothea's latter-day friends will still have it that her judges—the Elector and his ministers, her father and her husband—continued anxious to "patch up" a reconciliation between the ill-suited pair thus wrenched asunder, and that to every overture she gave only one reply—"If I am guilty I am unworthy of him: if I am innocent he is unworthy of me." The speech sounds heroic, but it is an equivocation after all, such an equivocation as a miserable woman standing at bay might very well take refuge in. The Consistory Court which finally dissolved the marriage, so far as George was concerned, did so merely on the grounds of incompatibility of temper and of the contumaciousness of the wife, not on any accusation in which Königsmark's name was mentioned. There was not even an implication that Sophia Dorothea had sinned against her marriage vow, in intent if not in deed.

The Princess had already been suffered to quit Hanover and repair to Lavenau, since there was no home for her at Zell. Her children, whom she had been willing to abandon, were removed from her keeping, and committed to the more trustworthy care of their grandmother, the Electress. In all further proceedings the Princess was treated with such punctilious respect and consideration as were consistent with her safety as a state prisoner. No doubt this was due in some degree to the near relationship of her father to the Elector, and to that father's acquiescence in the sentence of the Court. It is worthy of notice that Sophia Dorothea herself declined to impugn the sentence when it was pointed out to her by her counsel that she had legal grounds for protest. One of her biographers makes the comment that she declined " disdainfully," on account of the injustice with which she was treated. Yet a candid reader is left with the impression that in all likelihood the refusal to protest was the result of a consciousness that she had been more gently dealt with than she deserved, or had any reason to expect.

Sophia Dorothea had an ample income settled upon her, and she was allowed to manage her own affairs; she had the retinue of a woman of her rank appointed for her. She received the title of Duchess of Ahlden.

In the month of October, following the July in which Königsmark was slain (1694), Sophia Dorothea was conducted to Ahlden, a strong castle on the verge of one of the waste heaths of Northern Germany, and on the banks of the Aller, which flowed past her native Zell. Her captivity lasted, as no one could have foreseen, for the long period of thirty-two years, during which her "silent husband" never once uttered her name.

Sophia Dorothea in her castle prison still presided over a Court in miniature, held levees and was visited by the neighbouring country gentry and clergy. She occupied herself as time went on with the care of her property and the control of her household, down to the writing out of the daily *menu*; she conducted through her secretary a certain amount of correspondence under necessary restrictions; she also wrote a good deal privately—a practice which has caused a mass of fictitious papers, including her own story and that of her mother, told in high-flown dialogues, to be offered to the public in her name; she took an interest in the peasantry around, and conferred substantial benefits upon them. She made gifts to the parish church, though she only heard service in one of the rooms in the castle. She was not suffered to walk abroad, not even on the ramparts, but she could take carriage exercise daily. She was either driven in one of the ponderous coaches of the time, or she drove herself in a cabriolet with a coachman riding by her side. She was uniformly attended by a detachment of cavalry with drawn swords. For half a century after Sophia Dorothea's place was vacant at Ahlden, the peasants in the locality would talk with bated breath of the great lady who had tenanted the castle. The old men and women remembered for themselves, while the young men and women had been told by their fathers and mothers that her carriage would rumble or whirl past the labourers going to and from their work, when the hot haze of summer or the dark mists of winter lay on the heath. The prancing horses and gleaming weapons of her escort of soldiers would thunder and flash out of the obscurity on the chance wayfarer.

As the years went on there was some relaxation of the strictness of the imprisonment. The Princess's mother, the Duchess of Hanover, and her ladies were permitted to pay occasional visits to Ahlden. Poellnitz, in contradiction of the general theory, which represents the Elector Ernest Augustus as the most lenient of Sophia Dorothea's judges, gives the date of this concession as after Ernest's death, in which case the granting of the grace was owing either to the silent husband or to the Electress Sophia.

All the time Sophia Dorothea lived in tantalising nearness, both to Zell and to Hanover, where her children were growing up strangers to her. She had no intercourse with her son after his early boyhood, unless we accept the mythical story of the second George's single attempt to visit his mother. When hunting one day, not very far from Ahlden, so the tale runs, he rode away from his suite with the intention of fording the river Aller and seeking admittance to the little fortress. If there is any truth in the legend, he was overtaken and induced to relinquish his intention. With her daughter, the second Sophia Dorothea, the mother did have some correspondence subsequent to the daughter's marriage, and her portrait was suffered to reach Ahlden. The so-called treachery of the elder woman's secretary put a stop to the communications. The tide of events was flowing as briskly as ever outside the grey castle walls and beyond the dim monotony of the heath, while the solitary figure left stranded by her own deed was as untouched by them as if she had been already numbered with the dead. The glorious succession to the throne of England on which Sophia Dorothea would never sit as Queen-Consort, was settled on the House of Hanover. Her father, the pleasure-loving Duke George William, died an old man of seventy in August, 1705, not without some relenting and alterations of his will in favour of the daughter who had then been a prisoner for eleven years. He never saw her face, however, from the time when he cut short her visit to Zell and bade her return to her husband and children. Sophia Dorothea might almost have heard, with the wind in the proper direction, the tolling of his knell. The last echo of the ringing of the bells for the joint marriages of her son and daughter, which were celebrated the same year as that of the old Duke's death, might have come to her were it only in the vigorous clang of the uncouth bell of the parish church of Ahlden; but she had no share in the pompous ceremonies and joyous festivals. It might be that she had some hope from her daughter's removal to the Court of Prussia that there would be interference in that quarter on her behalf. If so, the hope was doomed to disappointment, beyond a little brief correspondence and the barest acknowledgment of the relationship, which some allege was merely accorded in order to secure to the daughter her share in her mother and grandmother's very considerable possessions. The most active step which the future Queen of Prussia took for her mother's benefit was to receive into her service Fräulein von Knesebeck, who had escaped from Schwartzfeld. It is hardly necessary to say that it is more than probable this act was a politic measure to hush up the story of Sophia Dorothea's disgrace rather than an expression of the daughter's gratitude to her mother's confidante, who forthwith drew up a fresh statement of Princess George's innocence.

The unfortunate Fräulein had undergone a good deal of hardship on her first mistress's account, ending in the serio-comic adventure of the escape from Schwartzfeld. This feat was accomplished by the instrumentality of a "tiler," or a friend of the lady's in the disguise of a tiler. Under the pretence of repairing that part of the castle in which she was detained, he made a hole in the roof through which she was drawn up under cloud of night. The governor of the castle was roused in time to witness the flight, which he did not prevent, because as he pled in his defence he believed it was that of two demons of the Hartz mountains engaged on an excursion through the air.

Nine more years and the good Electress had died, with her death closely followed by that of Queen Anne. George I. was called to reign in England, and departed with seeming unwillingness to take to himself his great inheritance, but without an apparent thought of the skeleton he left behind in his well-beloved Hanover. Two years afterwards George revisited his native country, where he was received with every sign of regard; but there was no token of remembrance of Sophia Dorothea, no amnesty where she was concerned. Four years later, in 1720, George was again in Germany for a season, his last visit there during the lifetime of the wife who had ceased to exist for him.

In the following year, 1721, the changeful life of Eleanore d'Olbrense, Duchess of Hanover, ended. She might not have been a wise guardian to her daughter in the days of her youth, but when the Duchess died a woman far on in years, with her perished the last friend who had a vital interest in Sophia Dorothea. We are told the English royal family went into mourning for the late Electress's old rival and enemy; if so, it was more than they did for Duchess Eleanore's unhappy daughter. Sophia Dorothea did not outlive her mother more than five years. In 1724, in the same dreary month of November which had seen the Princess's marriage more than forty years before, when the white fogs and mist wreaths were scudding like legions of sheeted ghosts across the desolate heath, the gradual failure of the Princess's health culminated in a sudden and violent illness which induced unconsciousness. She died quietly, with her suite the sole watchers and mourners by her death-bed. She was a rapidly aging woman approaching her sixtieth year. She had entered on that living death of imprisonment a young wife and mother, still in her blooming prime. Her son (George II.), the boy of ten she had left behind her, was the Prince of Wales nearly forty years of age, the father of a numerous family. Her daughter, the little girl of seven, was the Queen of Prussia, and was enduring the brutal treatment of a husband compared to whom the Prince George of old, unloving, surly and dissipated, was a paragon. Sophia Dorothea's grandson, Frederic the Great, was already a boy of strange eccentric promise.

Sophia Dorothea was not buried at Ahlden; her body was removed to Zell, where it rests with the dust of her father's race. Not only was there no mourning for her at her husband's Court, but he is said to have resented the fact that the Court of Prussia paid the small compliment to the memory of the dead woman. This complacency on the part of Prussia was unquestionably occasioned by the circumstance that the Queen was to a large extent her mother's heir.

A tradition existed throughout Germany that an unknown woman had uttered in the hearing of George I. the sardonic prophecy that he had better take care of the health of his wife since he would not survive her a year. Another version of the same story was that Sophia Dorothea, on her death-bed, cited her husband to meet her before the judgment-seat of God within a year and a day. The citation was reported to be contained in a letter written by the dying woman to her husband. It did not reach him till he was on his next, and as it proved his last, visit to Hanover. His excesses had left him an old and infirm man at sixty-seven. Before embarking he had taken leave of his son and daughter-in-law with quite unusual marks of affection and regret, saying he knew he should never see them again. Between Dolden (where he had eaten heartily of a late supper, the materials for which included part of a melon) and Lender, to which he was travelling by night, he is reported to have received in some mysterious manner Sophia Dorothea's letter. He was much agitated on reading it, and complained of illness, for which he was bled, according to the universal panacea for disease in past centuries, while he still journeyed to Hanover. He only got as far as Osnabrück, where he was bled a second and a third time, but died apparently of apoplexy during the following night, that of June 10th, 1723.

An equally ghastly legend deals with the last hours of the infamous Countess von Platen, whom all sides in the strife between husband and wife unite in reprobating. She lived to be old and blind. In her darkness she was haunted by the fancied presence of Philip von Königsmark with a blood-stain on his mouth. But of all the curious traditions which have gathered round the melancholy story of George I. and Sophia Dorothea of Zell, the most extravagant and self-contradictory is that which was gravely quoted in a recent article in the *Nineteenth Century*. It is said that the elder George caused the heart of Königsmark, with whose murder the Prince had nothing to do, to be taken from his body and burnt. The ashes were collected and put into a box, and the box was then inserted in a stool. This stool the inhuman husband habitually carried about with him and used as a footstool, so that he might have the satisfaction of realising that he thus trampled on the heart of Sophia Dorothea's lover! The story is fantastic enough to go unanswered, but it may be said in connection with it that no anecdote could be more foreign to the character of its hero—or villain. George I., like other members of his house, was, in his cold and coarse stolidity and doggedness, singularly free from vindictiveness. It was this, in common with a rough-and-ready sense of justice, which rendered the two earlier Georges, in spite of their glaring shortcomings, better sovereigns than their predecessors, the more brilliant—taking them as a whole, more personally attractive—Stewarts.

There is only one more word to say of Sophia Dorothea of Zell, and that word bears reference to a discovery supposed to have been made more than a century after her death. A packet of letters written under assumed names was found in Sweden, in the university library at Upsala. These letters, unlike the papers alleged to have been written by Sophia Dorothea in her imprisonment, are believed by many good judges to show both by external and internal evidence that they are genuine. They are love-letters written in two handwritings, and are full of mad passion and desperate schemes for clandestine meetings. The conviction is to a great extent warranted that they are the original letters written by Princess George and the Count von Königsmark. They are understood to have been secured and preserved by one of Königsmark's sisters, Amelia von Königsmark, who wrote of them: " Here are the letters, captured again at great peril, which cost a brother his life and a King's mother her freedom." Amelia von Königsmark married a General von Lowenhaupt, and her papers passed to her Swedish descendants. If these letters are genuine they are conclusive proofs of Sophia Dorothea's utter faithlessness.

III.

CAROLINE OF ANSPACH, WIFE OF GEORGE II., AND HER DAUGHTERS.

AUTHORITIES:

Lady Mary Wortley Montagu, Horace Walpole, Mrs. Delany, Dr. Doran, W. M. Thackeray, etc., etc.

CAROLINE OF ANSPACH, QUEEN OF GEORGE II. (AS PRINCESS OF WALES).

CHAPTER I.

THE ELECTORAL PRINCESS OF HANOVER AND PRINCESS OF WALES.

CAROLINE OF ANSPACH was the daughter of John Frederick, Marquis of Brandenburg-Anspach, and of Eleanor, his second wife, daughter of John George, Duke of Saxe-Eisenach. She was born in 1683, the same year in which her future husband, George II., was born. Her father died in her childhood, and her mother took for her second husband the Elector George of Saxony.

Happily for Caroline, she was not brought up in the riotous Saxon Court. She was sent to Berlin, to the Court of her guardian, the first King of Prussia. There she was under the care of the wise and accomplished Sophia Charlotte, the much-loved daughter of the Electress Sophia. From that time Caroline's education, hitherto neglected, was sedulously attended to. She made an ample return for the pains taken by her teachers. She was both intelligent and studious, with an excellent memory and a rare penetration, not only where books, but also where men and women were in question—an invaluable gift to a Princess. The result was that she was one of the cleverest, best-informed of contemporary Princesses, and she was as witty as she was learned. She had other qualities which she did not owe entirely to her instructors; these were her equable temper, her great power of self-control, her extraordinary tact. In addition, she was a beautiful young woman, with a quantity of fine, fair hair, a blonde complexion, and a stately bearing. In her early youth her admiration for the Queen of Prussia led to a remarkable likeness between the two in speech and movement.

Reasonable and dutiful as the girl Princess was, it did not follow that she had not sufficient spirit and determination to resist successfully the pressure put upon her by her Prussian friends to induce her to make an ambitious choice, from her many suitors, of the best-endowed with worldly goods, the Archduke of Austria, who became afterwards the Emperor Charles VI. But Caroline was a staunch Protestant, and refused absolutely to be converted to the Roman Catholic religion in order to fit her to receive a Roman Catholic bridegroom. It is possible that, unattractive physically and mentally—as one is tempted to imagine the Electoral Prince of Hanover (George II.) must have been to the brilliant young Princess—he had sufficient charm for her as the Queen of Prussia's nephew, the Electress Sophia's grandson, and the future King of England, to cancel his defects. Her love for him was unquestionable, and it never wavered, under the gravest provocation, any more than the Electress Sophia's regard failed for her Elector and Duke. On George's side the marriage is said to have been one of inclination, and in his way —not a very noble or honourable way—he showed the highest value for his wife to the end.

The marriage was celebrated at Hanover in 1705, when bride and bridegroom were twenty-two years of age. The second splendid wedding—that of George's sister, Sophia Dorothea, and the Prince Royal of Prussia —followed, when Addison, at Hanover, in the suite of Lord Halifax, had the first opportunity of seeing Caroline, whom, as his Queen, he celebrated in his verses with much eulogy.

Caroline spent nine years of her married life in

Hanover, where her elder children were born. It was the early summer of her life, and though it was a summer by no means without clouds and storms, it was, perhaps, to a woman of Caroline's serene and happy temperament, not deficient in the alternating sunshine which we are tempted to claim as our right in youth. Caroline, like the old Electress in her early days, took her husband as she found him, made an amount of allowance for his faults and foibles, which it is difficult, under different circumstances, with altered standards and ideas, to comprehend, expected little from him or any man, and got more than she expected, while she lavished on him the treasures of her faithful devotion and tender affection. He was a little, fair-haired, red-faced man, looking more insignificant than he was by reason of his blonde complexion and low stature. He was mean in mind and body; he had a narrow understanding and a hot, inconsiderate temper. There was a certain grotesqueness about him, bestowed by the vanity which led him to puff and strut and to ape the vices, no less than the virtues of abler men. His sullen, dogged, coarse-minded father, with whom he was on the worst of terms, was less ridiculous than the son. His redeeming qualities, of which Caroline made the most, were the little man's valour—which he amply vindicated at Oudenarde and Dettingen—a certain amount of stolid sense and prudence behind his folly, an equal allowance of rough-and-ready justice inherited from his father, and, what George senior was innocent of, some heart.

The Prince's quarrels with his father, which reached the height of the couple's not being on speaking terms for years, must have produced an atmosphere of jarring discord and strife, in which it is difficult for good feeling and good spirits to flourish. The air of the Court was still further disturbed by the waywardness and impertinence of the younger George's tone to the grandmother who had been a second mother to him. Deficient as George I. was in proper respect for his mother, he resented his son's attitude towards her. Caroline also must have been hurt by it, since a cordial affection subsisted between her and the old Electress. Besides, the young wife was far too shrewd not to be aware of the discredit which such conduct brought upon her husband, and of its utter lack of policy supposing the aged Sophia lived to occupy the throne of England. But all these family differences and alienations only served to throw the Prince to a greater extent on the society of his wife and to increase her influence over him—a consequence which a high-spirited, deeply-attached woman like the Princess could not regard altogether as a misfortune. She had no real fear of the rages in which he was wont to spurn his wig and coat from one corner of the room to the other. She only knew that she was first to him, and that to her he always turned for support and sympathy. For anything further, Caroline was philosophic, politic, patient, rather than sensitive. She was full of mental resources, and as food for her heart she had her husband, her children, her German and English friends. According to Toland, she was the most carelessly indifferent of the whole family to their splendid prospects in England. But the indifference might have been assumed in order to meet the conflicting humours of those principally concerned in the great future opening out before them; or Toland might have made his observation in an hour of apathetic languor, such as overtakes even the most energetic natures. Certainly the Princess showed no lack of appreciation, whether for herself or her husband, of what was involved in the sovereignty of England after she had her share in it.

The Court of Hanover, even with so gruff and glum a sultan as George I. at its head, had many good points to a German Princess of Caroline's faculties and tastes. It had still the lingering aroma of such borrowed splendour and mental superiority as the Elector and the Electress, in her husband's lifetime and in her prime, had been able to give it. Lady Mary Wortley Montagu visited it two years after the royal house had been transferred to England, and during one of the occasions when George I. revisited his native country. The far-travelled lady found it a very tolerable place of residence. The town was small, but the palace was capable of containing a large Court. There were no houses of great nobles in the neighbourhood; in fact, the wealth and magnificence of Germany were confined to the Courts and the great burgher towns. The King dined and supped in public, after the Versailles mode introduced at an earlier date; and while he was still only Elector the members of his family, including his mother and his daughter-in-law, made part of the show, and learned to regard it as a becoming and agreeable detail of their rank and state. The King's opera-house was second to none in Germany, and he had French comedians in his service, who played twice a week for the delectation of the upper classes. In winter the speed and costly beauty of the Court sledges gliding over the snow were marked features of the scene. In summer there were the fine gardens of Herrenhausen, the delight of the Electress Sophia, the last scene on which her aged eyes closed. Lady Mary admired them even when she had the disadvantage of seeing the lime-tree avenue in winter. She was particularly struck by the great size and profusion of the orange-trees, which bore fruit throughout the year by means of the perfection of stove-heat applied to them.

Many English Whigs repaired to Hanover and sought to warm themselves in the beams of the Brunswick sun some time before the death of Queen Anne. Among

them was a young couple, obscure enough though of
good family, belonging as they did to the Howard
house. These Howards were so poor that it was said
Mrs. Howard sold her beautiful hair on one occasion
in order to defray the expenses of a dinner which the
couple gave, as a matter of policy, to the Hanoverian
Prime Minister. The husband was dissipated and
worthless; the wife[1] was a woman of singularly
pleasing expression and manner, rather than of beauty
of feature. She was above the middle height, with
what was then called "an elegant figure"; she was
quiet and ladylike. The notice she received was chiefly
from the Princess; the Prince treated her with indifference. Another English visitor, who was then of little
account, but who was destined to play a prominent part
in George I.'s government, was the lawyer Craggs,
eventually Secretary of State.

In the summer and early autumn of 1714 the deaths of
the Electress Sophia among the shades of Herrenhausen
in the weeping Caroline's arms, and of Queen Anne in
England, made the Elector George King of Great
Britain and Ireland. The Act of Succession secured his
inheritance, and the plots of the Tory leaders Harley
and St. John in favour of the exiled Stewarts were crushed,
at what might have been the moment of fruition, by the
energetic action of the Dukes of Somerset and Argyle.
They were Whig ministers of the Privy Council, and
they brought to a summary conclusion the masked plots
of the Tory Cabinet by demanding the immediate proclamation of George I.

The King, with a large German and English suite,
prominent in which were his son and daughter-in-law
(both then in the thirty-first year of their age), landed
at Greenwich in September 1714.

The King was in his fifty-fifth year, and could not

[1] She was the great-granddaughter of John Hampden.

speak English. He had to transact his business with his ministers in the Latin language. He announced that he brought with him his son (who spoke English but with a strong foreign accent and idiom) in order that he might be trained in English politics and government. But no trace of such training survives in the fierce discord which presently broke out afresh between the two. It ended in George II., as Prince of Wales, representing the young England of the day and heading a Court in opposition to that of his father. Caroline had need of her tact, for though she came to England in the dignified position of Princess of Wales, that position had many humiliations for her. There was no place for her any more than for her husband in the Palace of St. James's.[1] The rooms there—whose occupant was supposed to be the first lady in England, resident in the palace for the purpose of presiding over the royal circle—were given to Mdlle. Schulenberg, one of the King's old friends, a tall, lean, dull woman of his own age, whom the wits nicknamed the "Maypole." The King created her Duchess of Kendal, and the rumour was freely circulated that he had married her privately. He visited her daily, and when with her pursued his favourite diversion of cutting out paper. She "entertained" for the King at those evening assemblies attended by many Germans and a few English, the deadly dulness of which Lady Mary Wortley Montagu has described. The Duchess of Kendal's rival in the King's favour was not the Princess, his daughter-in-law, but a very stout, comparatively lively German lady of forty years, Madame von Kielmansegge, who was created Countess of Darlington. Her huge size, combined with the nation's contempt for these satellites, caused her to

---

[1] The Prince and Princess of Wales repaired to St. James's on their arrival in England, but were forced to leave the palace on the first violent outburst of the smouldering quarrel between the father and son.

be termed the "Elephant." On one occasion the pair driving together in one of George's glass and gilt coaches were mobbed and hooted. "My goot people," called out the more spirited Countess, lowering a window and making a protest to her assailants, "we have come for your goots." "Yes, and for our chattels too," was the derisive shout. The King would sit in the box of either of these ladies at the theatre or opera; but he went in no greater state than was implied by a sedan chair carried across the park, and he was attended not by two lords-in-waiting but by two negroes, also part of his old German *entourage*. These had been slaves acquired from the Turks in the frontier wars. George was a thrifty and unostentatious sovereign; he was fond of saving, and as he never felt the crown of England secure on his head, he did not lose sight of the probability of a successful rise of the Tory party, which would send him back, with his gains, to the little German kingdom, which he loved so much better than his English inheritance.

Caroline had little to do with her father-in-law and his Court except when she had to appear there on public occasions and at State ceremonials, and then, by taking the initiative, she compelled him to acknowledge her and speak to her with the respect which was her due. He simply detested her as part of his son's belongings, and as that son's most ardent and loyal adherent. Besides, she had as witty a tongue as his mother had possessed; and, though Caroline was rather more careful in speaking her mind, she was not altogether silent. The King was in the habit of alluding to her as "*Cette diablesse, Madame la Princesse.*"

By a curious family arrangement, which has received no explanation, but which may have had its origin in the family quarrels already raging, and in a conviction that the hostility between the father and son might be renewed in another generation if the first-born son of

George II. and Caroline grew up amidst the factions and intrigues of a strange Court, little Prince Fritz did not come to England with the rest of the family. He was left behind at the age of seven, and stayed under the care of his governor in Hanover apart from his near relations, seeing only his grandfather the King during his visits to Germany, till the young Prince was in his twenty-first year. If there was any such idea as that of preventing courtiers' intrigues and the strain of a contact which was liable to jar, the plan for preventing further domestic misery was singularly unsuccessful.

Denied lodgings in St. James's, the Prince and Princess of Wales withdrew to Leicester House in Leicester Fields, then on the verge of the country. There they established themselves; but the rupture between them and the King did not reach its height till subsequent to the anxious days of the '15 when Mar raised the standard of rebellion in Scotland. In 1717 Caroline gave birth to a second son, at whose baptism the royal grandfather took such furious umbrage, on grounds long since forgotten, that it became for a time little better than war to the knife between the two households. None of the courtiers of George I. dared present themselves at Leicester House. None of the frequenters of Leicester House were received at St. James's. A far more savage blow was dealt by the King at the Prince and Princess. George I., with the approval of the Lord Chancellor, Lord Macclesfield, declared it was the royal prerogative that the King should superintend the education of the younger members of his house. He therefore caused the three girl Princesses, Anne, Emily (or Amily as the name was then pronounced), and Caroline, with their little brother, to be withdrawn from the care of their parents at Leicester House and committed to the guardians whom he appointed. The insult and the injury of this interference with their natural rights were keenly felt and bitterly resented by the ill-used Prince and Princess. Caroline especially is said to have been much attached to her children, to whom she delighted to act in the double capacity of teacher and playmate. Neither did she decline the performance of less agreeable duties on their behalf. Sarah, Duchess of Marlborough, once found the Princess whipping one of "the roaring royal children," when George II., who was present at the performance, remarked complacently, "You have no good manners in England. You are not properly brought up when you are young."

The wondering, weeping little girls made it up among them, and succeeded in getting leave to send to the bereaved pair a basket of cherries with the children's respectful duty and love, and over the simple offering the poor father and mother wept in their turn.

It was not till three years later, in 1720, on the birth of Caroline's next child (Princess Mary?) that the breach between the King and the Prince and Princess was partially healed by the instrumentality of the Prime Minister, Sir Robert Walpole, who was sagacious and pacific in temper, if time-serving in his practice and systematically low in his principles. The children were restored to their proper protectors, from whom they were not again removed.[1]

[1] According to Horace Walpole the three elder Princesses, Anne, Emily, and Caroline, remained under their grandfather's eyes till his death.

CHAPTER II.

AT LEICESTER HOUSE AND AT ST. JAMES'S.

AT Leicester House Caroline did much to popularise her husband and to gloss over his defects. The English nation, accustomed to the Stewart dynasty, the representatives of which had been as a rule distinguished by their gracious bearing and their mental graces and gifts, and by their prestige as the native sovereigns of a great country, were repelled and disgusted by the surly uncouthness of George I., and by the unattractiveness together with the strong foreign element of the Court at St. James's. Caroline was resolute in the determination that she and her husband should amend these faults, and they were partly successful in the attempt. At Leicester House the Princess held an informal drawing-room every morning, which formed a precedent for long lists of balls, masquerades, and water parties. One refining taste the first three Georges had in common, and that was a love for music, and for Handel's music. George I. resented Handel's quitting Hanover for England in the reign of Anne; but the King forgave the great composer his temporary desertion, and required from him " the water music " played in the King's barge on the Thames. For once the King and the Prince were agreed in their admiration of Handel's stately operas and oratorios. George III. used to tell how he was taken, when a boy, by his grandfather, George II., then an old man, to listen to Handel, and was thus inoculated with the family taste.

At Leicester House there were distinguished gatherings not of old Hanover, but of young England, in her choice spirits: Chesterfield, Stanhope, the brothers Hervey, Pope, Swift, at times were included in the circle, the presiding genius of which was a brilliantly clever woman, who laughed over *Gulliver*, and appreciated *Robinson Crusoe*, though she had to pursue her reading in private, since the Prince detested books.

In proportion as George I.'s Court was ridiculed for such unornamental, unbecoming fixtures as the "Maypole" and the "Elephant," the Princess of Wales—herself a dignified and charming woman—was highly approved of for surrounding herself with a group of English ladies, well-looking, well-informed, well-bred, according to the standard of the day, and with a bevy of as pretty and lively girls as England could produce for maids-of-honour.

Among the ladies was the bedchamber woman, Mrs. Howard, Caroline's old acquaintance in Hanover. Mrs. Howard was now living apart from her ne'er-do-well of a husband—in fact, was in such dread of him that the Princess's protection was regarded as necessary for her safety. In England George professed a gallant admiration for Mrs. Howard, visiting her rooms every afternoon and spending several hours with her, condescending to be soothed and entertained by her agreeable conversation. Even Caroline could not eradicate her husband's follies, but she could render them more respectable and less absurd. She could consign him to the company of her "good Howard," who took nearly as much care of him as Caroline herself did. Convinced as the Princess was of her superiority to all other women in her husband's eyes, and of her unbounded influence over him, she could suffer his idle homage to Mrs. Howard as the safest and least pernicious of such platonic gallantries. But politic Princess as Caroline was, she was a woman still, and not always a generous woman in her dealings with her woman of the bedchamber. She is said in later years to have relished her husband's rude disparagement of Mrs. Howard's lean arms and scraggy neck in comparison with the beautiful arms and neck of her royal mistress, to whose toilette the bedchamber woman was putting the finishing touches while George was lounging in the background. Caroline is also reported to have taken a malicious satisfaction in blandly requiring, as Queen, services which the lady at first indignantly refused to render, such as kneeling and thus presenting the silver basin and ewer with water that her mistress might wash her hands.

Mrs. Howard was agreeable and cool-headed, never losing her temper or making a scene. To men her society was gently soothing and mildly stimulating; she was emphatically "a man's woman." Pope and Gay celebrated her attractions long after she was laid in the dust.[1] Her laudatory biographers were won by the simple tastes, the unaffectedness and kindliness which her letters revealed; neither was she without cordial friends among women. But Caroline's special friend among her ladies was another woman of the bedchamber, Mrs. Clayton. She was of comparatively humble birth, though the wife of Sir Robert Clayton, Clerk to the Treasury, and afterwards created Lord Sundon. She was appointed to her post on the recommendation of the Duchess of Marlborough. Very conflicting opinions of Mrs. Clayton are expressed in the biographies and letters of the day. John Lord Hervey praised her as of good understanding and excellent heart. Horace Walpole, who had a bitter feud with Hervey, described her as "pompous and pretentious." His gossiping version of the origin of her intimacy with Caroline was, that Mrs. Clayton,

---

[1] They even praised her infirmity of deafness, which was slight to begin with.

apart from George II. and an old German nurse, was the only person acquainted with the existence of the internal complaint against which the Princess struggled secretly for many years.

In most respects Mrs. Clayton was very unlike Mrs. Howard, and between the two women of the bedchamber there was a chronic quarrel. Mrs. Clayton was ardent and impulsive and got into many difficulties through her hot temper. She had solid intellectual tastes in common with the Princess; doubtless this is all the reason required for their mutual regard. Lady Mary Wortley Montagu, with her sharp tongue and her sharp pen, refers to the pair of friends as "playing" at studying philosophy and metaphysics under the learned divine Dr. Samuel Clarke. He dedicated to Caroline the publication containing his discussions on natural philosophy and religion with the German philosopher Leibnitz. What associations Leibnitz's name must have recalled to Caroline of Hanover and Herrenhausen—the long lime-tree avenue, where the bees hummed in summer, the fragrant orange-trees, the philosopher's royal patroness, his "Serena," who was also the wise and kindly kinswoman of the Princess's early life!

The most renowned of Caroline's fair and gay maids-of-honour with whom and with their merry doings Leicester House, Richmond Lodge, and Kensington Palace were closely connected were Mary Bellenden and Mary or Molly Lepell. They were as vivacious as they were lovely; for in those days sprightliness was considered an excellent thing in woman, especially in her youth. On one occasion little Mr. Pope was taken possession of by the lively pair. They gave him a dinner after one of the royal hunting parties, and Molly Lepell spent several pleasant hours strolling with him in the moonlight according to the free-and-easy customs of the time. The two beauties sobered down as they grew older, and merged into exemplary wives and mothers. One of them, this Molly Lepell, left behind her a series of letters written in her declining years to a friendly clergyman, breathing much earnest religious feeling and devoutness of spirit. "Sweet Molly Lepell," as she was called in the *vers de société* of the period, married—the engagement having been conducted with all "the mystery and secrecy" which is said to attend even Court trifles—one of the most conspicuous figures of the reign, John Lord Hervey. The poetaster sang in his tuneful jingle how great was the sensation when "Hervey the clever" wedded in orthodox style " sweet Molly Lepell." Thackeray writes of Hervey's ghastly beauty, his "ghastly painted beauty," and of the impossibility of putting trust in him. Indeed, any truthful representation of his finely-chiselled supercilious face bears out to this day all that is known of a singularly heartless man of wit and fashion, till one is tempted to cry, " Poor Molly Lepell ! "

Caroline bestowed on Lord Hervey—or " Lord Fanny," the nickname which his effeminate airs brought on him—all the affection and confidence that with happier domestic relations she might have lavished on her elder son. In return he betrayed her confidence, exposed and made game of her foibles. Even her death-bed was not sacred to him. With regard to its " grotesque horror " and Hervey's share in recounting the scene, Thackeray made the emphatic comment: " The man who wrote the story had something diabolical about him."

Mary Bellenden[1] married Colonel John Campbell,

---

[1] A doggerel verse in her honour refers to the dismissal of the Prince and Princess of Wales from St. James's :—

> "But Bellenden we needs must praise
> Who, as down the stairs she jumps,
> Sings, ' Over the Hills and Far Away,'
> Despising doleful dumps."

and survived to an advanced age, when she was burned to death in an accidental fire at a county-house near London, where she happened to be staying.

The levity of a third maid-of-honour, Sophy Howe, ended in scandal and disgrace. There was much coarse licence of manners and morals in the England of the day. To mark the great changes in public opinion Thackeray has given various quotations from old news prints. Here are two: "Mary Lynn was burned to ashes at the stake for being concerned in the murder of her mistress." "At night (Twelfth Night) their Majesties played at hazard with the nobility, for the benefit of the groomporters, and 'twas said the King won six hundred guineas, the Queen three hundred and sixty, Princess Amelia twenty, Princess Caroline ten, the Duke of Grafton and the Earl of Portmore several thousands."

There was yet another maid-of-honour of Caroline's while she was still Princess of Wales, who was neither fair nor wise, who was only passing honest. This was Jenny Warburton, the daughter of a Cheshire squire. She had been one of the maids-of-honour to Queen Anne, and on Caroline's arrival in England Jenny Warburton was appointed to the same post in the Princess's household. Her extreme rusticity and ignorance, together with her personal plainness, caused her to be the butt of her better-endowed companions. Nevertheless, when John, Duke of Argyle, bravest of soldiers and most patriotic of statesmen, a handsome man and a brilliant talker, returned from the wars, he conceived a sincere friendship for Jenny, whose sterling simplicity and integrity rendered her fair and worthy in his eyes; so open and honourable was the friendship, that not even the most unscrupulous tongue put a bad construction on it, though the Duke had been entangled when a boy in a loveless marriage, and had been long separated from his wife. Suddenly the wife died, and the Court was occupied with keen conjectures of what the result would be where the two sworn friends were concerned. Certainly the Duke would marry again, making a great marriage, such as many a fine lady of his society would willingly figure in, and his friendship with poor Jenny would be dropped.

It is in connection with the supposition, that a little story, very creditable to the Princess's good nature and kindliness, has been preserved. When she heard of the death of the Duchess of Argyle Caroline said to Mrs. Howard, "How I pity that poor Warburton! Her agitation must be cruel; and she must dread appearing in public, where everybody will be whispering, and every eye watching her looks. Go and tell her I excuse her from attendance; she need not wait to-day, nor, indeed, till all the tattle has subsided."

Mrs. Howard found Jenny busily sewing, as if nothing was the matter, and had some difficulty in making her message understood.

"Not wait to-day! Why not? Why mustn't I wait? What's the matter? Is the Princess angry with me? Have I done anything?"

"Done! Bless us, no, my dear Mrs.[1] Warburton; it is her Royal Highness's kind consideration for you. She concludes you cannot like to wait. She is afraid of your being distressed."

"Dear! I always liked waiting, and I ain't in distress," replied the sensible, matter-of-fact Jenny.

But there was no need for undesired sympathy, since the great Duke immediately laid his strawberry-leaves at Jenny's feet. It was entirely as a concession to her sense of propriety that the ardent wooer was induced to

---

[1] Young and unmarried women in a respectable position were addressed as "Mrs.," not as "Miss," in the last century. Mrs. Hannah Moore was the last single woman who was so styled.

allow the marriage to be deferred till six months had elapsed. We have it on the testimony of a descendant of the couple that his faithful love for her never waned. On entering her room he would clasp her in his arms in the presence of their daughters, when she would appeal to them, "Do you see, you young folks? On such a day we shall have been married so many years. Will your husbands' love last as long, think ye?"

Unfortunately, Jenny had a voice both loud and shrill, which she transmitted to her daughters. The Duke used to say he knew if his ladies were at any party the moment he crossed the doorstep of the house where it was held. The family attribute procured for the members the nickname of "the bawling Campbells."

Caroline's intimacy with Mrs. Clayton was well known, and was much exaggerated in the popular mind. It was said that she ruled the Princess and Queen, as Mrs. Howard ruled George. In neither case was there more than a few grains of truth in the assertion. The Princess, not Henrietta Howard, ruled the Prince; as for Caroline herself she was cast in a stronger mould than to be readily ruled by anybody, least of all by one of her bedchamber women. But the impression was that Mrs. Clayton could command much preferment through her influence over the future Queen, and that the woman of the bedchamber accepted bribes given for the purpose of securing her advocacy on the side of the petitioner. Lady Mary Wortley Montagu, who was nothing if she was not brilliantly scurrilous, coolly observed, in relation to the jewels Mrs. Clayton wore, which were believed to have been given to her as an acknowledgment of her support in applications to her mistress, "You would not know where wine was sold if the seller did not hang out a bush"; in allusion to the old custom still practised in some foreign towns of distinguishing a vintner's by a green branch suspended over the door or window.

Lady Mary's verdict on Caroline was that in her youth " she was judged a German beauty," and that she had " the genius which qualified her for the government of a fool—a genius unknown to witty Lady Mary in her capacity as a wife. The foundation for the charges against Mrs. Clayton was probably the fact that the Princess granted her the privilege of introducing aspirants for the royal notice. In this light she probably presented Sir Isaac Newton and Halley to Caroline, as George in his aversion to intellectual pursuits was little likely to bestow any grace upon them. The Princess, on the contrary, was eager to mark her respect for their attainments. She would fain have secured Halley as governor or tutor for her second son William, Duke of Cumberland, still hardly beyond his infancy; but Halley declined the dubious honour.

It does not seem to have propitiated Lady Mary Wortley Montagu in Caroline's favour that the Princess lent her ready countenance to the scheme for mitigating the ravages of small-pox by the process of inoculation as it was practised in Turkey. Lady Mary had caused her infant son to be inoculated. The Princess followed suit with two of her elder daughters after the experiment had been tested on a group of condemned criminals, who had their lives granted to them in consideration of their services on this occasion. The eldest Princess, Anne, was exempted from the trial because she had already suffered from small-pox, by which her face was pitted; otherwise she was a buxom, rosy-cheeked girl.[1]

In 1727 George I. paid his parting visit to Hanover. He had a foreboding that it would be his last and that

---

[1] Caroline herself had small-pox soon after her marriage, but was only slightly marked.

he would not return to England. Accordingly, before he set sail, he took a friendly farewell of those members of his family whom he had persistently treated as enemies. Presently the news of his death reached London. The tidings were brought by Sir Robert Walpole in person to Richmond Lodge, where the Court was in its country quarters. The bluff, heavily-built Prime Minister rode post-haste at midday through the June heat and dust, and sought an immediate private interview with George. In vain the Princess and her ladies represented the impossibility of granting his request, since the Prince was at that moment enjoying his after-dinner nap. Sir Robert, knowing the importance of his errand, was not to be denied. He took it upon him to enter the royal bedroom, and knelt down stiffly in his jack-boots by the bed. The Prince started up, shouting furiously who dared to disturb him.

"I am Sir Robert Walpole," said the panting but undaunted intruder. "I have the honour to announce to your Majesty that your royal father George I. died at Osnabrück on Saturday last the 4th instant."

"Dat's one big lie!" was the first exclamation of the son and heir.

The coronation took place on the following October 11th. George and Caroline were then each forty-three years of age and had been resident in England for thirteen years. Mrs. Delany gives a pretty description of the coronation. The Queen was carried in a sedan chair through the park to Westminster Hall, by which she and the King went to and came from the Abbey. Both walked under canopies : the King was not well seen, the Queen was distinguished by everybody. She was never so "well liked" (so much admired), for already her personal appearance was spoilt by the *embonpoint* which had increased with years. Her dress was "extravagantly fine," but she walked gracefully and smiled on all as she passed by. Mrs. Delany might well comment on Caroline's fine clothes, for she is said to have worn "twenty-four hundred thousand pounds worth of diamonds on her petticoat, in addition to the diamonds and pearls on her head, neck, and bodice." Horace Walpole and Hervey do not hesitate to state that the diamonds were borrowed from the Jews, and Hervey adds that she got from her ladies the use of their necklaces for the coronation. Yet the Queen had many fine jewels of her own, though those of Queen Anne had been so made away with that a single pearl necklace was the sole relic. After the gorgeousness of the Queen the three elder Princesses—Anne was then twenty—who held up the tip of the mother's train were in comparatively modest array. "They were dressed in stiff-bodied gowns of silver tissue, embroidered or quite covered with silver trimming, with diadems on their heads, purple mantles edged with ermine, and vast long trains. They were very prettily dressed and looked very well." But Mrs. Delany's enthusiasm is for the bedchamber women, among whom was Mrs. Howard in scarlet and silver, her head with long locks, puffs, and silver ribbons, "so rich, so genteel, so perfectly well-dressed."

Almost as brave a show as that in the Abbey was the dining in public in the Hall, and there the zeal of the privileged spectators, who had been at their posts since four o'clock in the morning, was rewarded by the humane consideration of the diners in the light of "the eighteen hundred candles besides those which were on the table." The mindful feasters in the Hall filled baskets with cold meat, bread, sweetmeats, and wine, and sent them, "drawn up by a string," to solace the needs of their friends among the company in the galleries.

9

CHAPTER III.

THE QUEEN.

CAROLINE was destined to reign as Queen-Consort for ten years. During this time her influence over her King was paramount. It was first exerted, as Queen, in inducing the King to keep in office his father's Prime Minister, Sir Robert Walpole, whom George, when Prince of Wales, had heartily detested. She is said to have been perfectly aware of the abominable rudeness and coarseness—characteristic of the period—with which Walpole had spoken of her as "that fat beast the Prince's wife." On the other hand, she was sensible of the absolute necessity there was for retaining his services at the head of the Government, and she appreciated his shrewdness and good judgment as a statesman. His ignoble creed that "every man has his price" (by which his support may be bought) is well known. As an illustration of this cynical conviction, on George I.'s death Walpole made it be spread abroad that, if he continued in office, he would raise the Queen's allowance to a hundred thousand pounds per annum. But the inference adopted by Dr. Doran that Caroline was thus bribed to espouse Walpole's cause is gratuitous. Her devotion to her husband's interests is beyond question. She needed no bribe to uphold the claims of the only man who had afforded any promise of ruling England peacefully and successfully. She understood and felt to the full the value of money, but she was awake to higher obligations. She was far above the ordinary grasping harpy to whom money is everything.

The Queen sought to recommend herself, and by doing so to recommend her husband, to all around her. Her manner to English ladies who flocked to her Court and appeared at her drawing-rooms was frank and agreeable. Her personal attractions might be on the wane, but a great charm was lent to her address by her captivating voice, while her graceful hands were still "beautifully small" in their plumpness. Here is an instance of the Queen's graciousness and tact, given by a fine lady of the day, whose opinions are to be depended upon because they are remarkable, in general, for their fairness and forbearance: "On Saturday, the first day of March, it being Queen Caroline's birthday, I dressed myself in all my best array, borrowed my Lady Sunderland's jewels, and made a tearing show. I went with my Lady Carteret and her two daughters. There was a vast crowd, and my Lady Carteret got with some difficulty to the circle, and after she had made her curtsy made me stand before her. The Queen came up to her, and thanked her for bringing me forward, and told me she was obliged to me for my pretty clothes."[1]

Frederick, Prince of Wales, who had received various titles—those of "Duke of Gloucester," "Duke of Edinburgh," etc., etc.—while he was still in Hanover during the life of his grandfather, George I., was now summoned to England. His continued absence from his family, acting on an utterly undisciplined and peculiarly wayward nature, had entirely alienated him from them. Apparently, he did not entertain a particle of respect or regard for father or mother, brother or sister. For his mother, indeed, he had a particular aversion. He was looked upon by all his kindred with the utmost distrust and dislike, though it is admitted that the Queen tried

[1] At Caroline's last drawing-room on the King's reminding her that she had passed the old Duchess of Norfolk, the Queen turned back, though ready to sink with fatigue and pain, and spoke a few courteous words to the venerable Duchess.

at first to find excuses for her son; and to the last—whether from policy, whether from some lingering regret in the mother's heart where her first-born was concerned—sought to reconcile him to the King his father. But George I.'s feud with his son was as a trifle compared to the bitter strife which raged between George II. and Frederick, Prince of Wales. The animosity on both sides was expressed with the scurrilous violence of the times, in which Caroline was not behind her neighbours.[1] French, which she habitually spoke, though the most polite language in Europe, did little to soften the sound of her rancour. "My dear lord," said Caroline, speaking to Lord Hervey of her son, "I will give it you under my hand, if you have any fear of my relapsing, that my dear first-born is the greatest ass, and the greatest liar, and the greatest *canaille*, and the greatest beast in the whole world, and that I most heartily wish him out of it." The furious resentment in which everybody concerned indulged, and the exceeding plain language in which all expressed their wrath and disgust, is inconceivable unless to readers of the diaries and letters of the period. When the gentlest member of the royal household, Princess Caroline, spoke of her brother, the mere circumstance of her devotion to her mother caused her speech to be that of a reckless virago. And when Princess Emily made a few attempts to be on terms with him she was freely accused of double-dealing, of a desire to stand well alike with the present and with the future King.

In person the Prince was a tall, rather handsome young man, with long fair hair (his mother's hair), curiously curled above the forehead and at the sides of the face, then tied back in a bag-wig or a *queue*. In mind and character he was less illiterate than his father,

---

[1] Caroline's wit was often of a coarse description, but those were days when delicacy of sentiment and expression was rarely to be found.

though his tastes were not more refined, and he had drunk, gambled, and been a profligate from his early youth. But what turned Caroline utterly against him was not so much his vice, and his rudeness and lack of all natural affection towards herself, as his attitude towards his father, the object of her life-long solicitude and tender fidelity. "Prince Fritz" was disobedient, defiant, and insubordinate, till the very jealous bravado and senseless perversity of the young man lent to some of his unwarrantable proceedings a tinge of the morbid, unreasoning hate which is akin to madness.

In his extravagant conceit and treachery of disposition the Prince of Wales made bids for popularity in every quarter. He attended an evening party at the Countess of Huntingdon's in order to hear Whitfield preach when Methodism, in high places, was dividing public attention with the Mississippi and South Sea schemes. He praised the sermon, and rebuked the levity of some of the fine ladies present, to the great gratification of his good hostess. He was equally ready to show himself at St. Bartholomew's—or "Bartlemy's—Fair, and join in the gross revelry certain to degenerate into excess and riot. Like his father, Frederick made a parade of the tone of a man of gallantry and licence. He professed to cultivate the Muses, and wrote detestable verses in his own person. In the midst of this chameleon-like versatility there was one aspect of the Prince which never changed, and that was his envenomed hostility to every member of his family. He was as unscrupulous in his private talk of them as they were in their talk of him. When his mother lay dying, at the very time when he was making, before the public, solemnly sympathetic inquiries after her health, and petitions to be permitted to see her, he congratulated his cronies on their being likely to hear "good news" soon, the news being that of Caroline's death. There is no page of family history so hideous in some lights, so painful in all, as that which records the relations which existed between Frederick, Prince of Wales, and his nearest blood relations.

The Queen was not only present at the King's interviews with his minister, but while apparently passive she was really prompting or modifying his consent to the various measures which Sir Robert Walpole laid before him. During George's frequent absences in Germany Caroline was appointed Regent, to the hot indignation of her elder son, and, aided by the Cabinet Minister, she ruled the country constitutionally and with much discretion. Twenty-four months after his accession, George was absent for two whole years, and it was no easy matter for those left in power to preserve its balance and maintain the peace and honour of the country. It was during the interval between the rebellions of '15 and '45, and the entire kingdom was restless and unsettled. Much smuggling and many other disorders prevailed, and called for a strong hand to restrain them. The exciseduties were a vexed question, so were the opinions and prospects of those of the Established clergy who did not hold High Church views, and of the Nonconformists, who naturally looked to the House of Brunswick, as the champions of Protestantism, to support the Dissenters' claims. Thus the repeal of various Test Acts was urgently demanded, and the Queen, in her difficult position, was reduced to temporising. It was said of her, as it was said of the Electress Sophia by the opponents of what, for lack of a better name, may be styled the Low Church party, that the Queen was unorthodox in her favour for liberal Churchmen, and that this bent in her was due to the influence of Lady Sundon (Mrs. Clayton). Caroline resembled her husband's grandmother in having been always fond of theological discussion. She was much more likely to lead than to be led by her bedchamber woman in this respect. When the Queen's preferences are known to have included Dr. Samuel Clarke, Bishop Berkeley, and Bishop Butler, whose *Analogy of Religion, Natural and Revealed, to the Constitution and Course of Nature* she was accustomed to keep on her breakfast-table, it does not seem as if her lack of orthodoxy was of a very formidable description. It must, however, be said that the irreverence of the speech and manners of the day was on a par with their frequent brutality. In the accounts of the scenes which prove this fact the reader is forced to come to the conclusion that the claims of an earthly sovereign were allowed to figure in a controversy—the repulsive unseemliness of which did more than savour of profanity—with the prerogatives of the King of kings. In Anne's reign the indecorous practice had been established of the chaplain's reading prayers in the ante-room, while the Queen dressed in the room within. She was in the habit of causing the door of communication to be shut occasionally. On one occasion when this happened the chaplain stopped the service, and the Queen sent to ask the reason why, on which the high-spirited and indignant prelate replied that he declined to "whistle the word of God through a keyhole." Prayers were read in the same disorderly fashion to Caroline. The chaplain's reading-desk was placed under a huge picture of the heathen goddess Venus. The Queen's toilette went on in regular stages, the last including the presence of Lord Hervey, her Vice-Chamberlain, as well as of her ladies and women of the bedchamber in attendance, and Hervey was there to discuss with his mistress the morning's highly-spiced gossip.

Amidst this autocratic and disrespectful carelessness, the Queen, in her affability and candour, was open to both remonstrance and rebuke when there was any one bold enough, under the seal of his commission, to administer them to her. Dr. Whiston had the courage to tell her frankly of the scandal created by the royal conduct in the square pew in the little chapel in the palace at Kensington. The King demanded that the shortest [1] of "good sermons" should be preached; yet, in spite of their shortness and goodness, he either fell asleep, or conversed with the Queen in German so loudly as nearly to drown the voice of the preacher, who, on one occasion, was so hurt and distressed that in place of challenging the offenders, as his predecessors challenged the "lion's cub" Elizabeth, the unfortunate man burst into tears. Caroline acknowledged the reasonableness of the protest, but pled in self-defence that the King would speak to her and she had to answer him.

Whatever the fate of England might have been had Caroline lost the influence over her husband which she was persuaded was only to be secured by the appearance of unqualified deference to his wishes, she would have been infinitely more respected, and more worthy of respect, had she cherished and given voice to a mind of her own, on questions of right and wrong, in her intercourse with her husband. It would almost seem as if a blunted sense of decent propriety, when joining in religious worship, was hereditary, in addition to the fact that the growth of bad example had done its work, since we read that, in the next generation, Princess Emily received a public rebuke for carrying a little dog in her muff to church.

Gay had just brought out his popular *Beggar's Opera*, which, under its rollicking fun, contained a smart satire on the Government embodied in Sir Robert Walpole. For this indiscretion the poet (he is said to have been the first man to bring the news of Anne's death to Hanover,

---

[1] There is the excuse for George, that he—a stupid unintellectual old man—was required to listen to a sermon in what was practically a foreign language to him.

he had been certainly in such favour with Caroline that she had asked him to write a book of fables for the use of her little son William, and offered him a small place in the household) fell into disgrace at Court. As a consequence the performance of the play, which had " run " for many nights, was interdicted. Gay's part was immediately taken by " Kitty," Duchess of Queensberry, one of the most headstrong and whimsical of the fine ladies of the reign. She had such confidence in her own beauty that she went to the coronation of George II. and Caroline without either ribbon or feather. " This," writes well-mannered Mrs. Delany, in the dainty fault-finding which offers so marked a contrast to the robust vituperation of her contemporaries, " was not to her " (the Duchess's) "advantage." With a like conviction that her charms were beyond embellishment, the same wilful, egotistical " Kitty "—no longer young, but an aged woman—walked at the coronation of George III. in her " milk-white locks," unsheltered and unadorned. The Duchess was an ardent patroness of Gay. She chose to resent the disgrace into which he had fallen, and to go about making subscriptions for him—at one of the Queen's drawing-rooms of all places. When she was called to order for her conduct, she wrote so saucily impertinent a reply that she too was forbidden the Court; she indemnified herself by espousing Gay's cause more vehemently than ever. She repaired to Bath, like the rest of the world then, and got up private theatricals, which the Prince of Wales went to admire, in order to display, in the eyes of the world, his disagreement with his family.

In 1733 the first arrangements were made for the marriage of Princess Anne, Caroline's eldest daughter, who was in her twenty-fifth year, with the deformed Prince of Orange. The match was not greatly approved of by the King and Queen. Holland was not in the first rank among European countries, though its rulers had wedded with English Princesses more than once since the States became independent. The bridegroom's income was not much above ten or twelve thousand pounds a year, while his person was ill-suited to the buxom youth and comeliness of the bride. A far greater alliance—that with Louis XV. of France—had been talked of for her, but the proposal had been dropped on account of the Roman Catholic creed of the suitor. The decision with regard to the Prince of Orange was left to the person most concerned—the Princess, a young woman of much character and some estimable qualities, though she was of too haughty and imperious a disposition to be generally liked. She immediately pronounced for the Prince of Orange, declaring, in scorn of the ridicule of his deformity, that though he were a monkey she would marry him.

Nobody was more astonished, or well-nigh affronted, by her daughter's choice than was Queen Caroline. During the whole of the preparations, and even during the celebration of the marriage, she never ceased to dwell on the Prince's defects, and to bemoan with showers of tears the hard fate of the Princess. With outrageous exaggeration Caroline was in the habit of styling her future son-in-law "that animal, that monster"; yet surely dapper, red-faced, conceited, and irate George was neither an Adonis nor a Solomon that his partner in life should have commented, with overwhelming severity, on the shortcomings in person and manners of a man who is said to have had a fine and good face to counterbalance his crooked body. As for his share of the silence and phlegm which distinguished his race it was more than compensated by his quiet, magnanimous dignity under the unmerited rudeness and neglect with which he was treated on his arrival in England. He was so ill in health that many weeks had to elapse before he could resort to Bath to drink the famous waters for the purpose of hastening his convalescence. It was not till March, 1734, that the ceremony of marriage, of which so many gossiping details have been given, could take place. In the meantime William received no visit of formal politeness, no mark of friendly sympathy from Kensington or St. James's. The Prince and his retinue were treated with marked slights by all save London city and the people at large, to whom the stranger's conspicuous Protestantism recommended him. One is tempted to ask oneself whether there was not a seamy side of clownish selfishness and rudeness to the Sir Charles Grandison era of exquisite bowing and curtseying, just as, in the Middle Ages, the fantastic courage and generosity of chivalry had its reverse aspect of savage cruelty. The very bride, who had elected of her free will to accept the offer of William's hand, showed herself strangely indifferent to his feelings and sufferings. She did not display the slightest impatience to see him; she did not give utterance to the smallest regret that he should be seriously ill under trying circumstances. Like her family, she took little or no notice of him till the moment which was to make them husband and wife. However, her subsequent behaviour indicated that her apathy was due, partly to her position with its difficulties, partly to the pride which led her to guard jealously her own prerogatives, and would not allow her to concede anything till she had granted all.

The foremost in contempt for his brother-in-law, and in animosity to Princess Anne in the light of a bride, was, as might have been expected, her brother Frederick, Prince of Wales. He is represented as ludicrously angry because his sister was to be married while there was still no mention of his marriage. One of his modes of annoying his sister was to get up an opposition opera to that of Handel, her old master, for whom she had a high regard, so that for a time the great composer, whom the rest of the royal family delighted to honour, was thrown into the shade by an unworthy rival.

The Court life, in spite of courtiers' intrigues and fierce family squabbles, was formal and monotonous. The King, with his aspirations to be gay and gallant, was heavily dull and methodical in his habits and amusements. A round of residences at St. James's, Kensington, Richmond, and Hampton Court, formed the rule; a sojourn at Bath or Tunbridge Wells, then in their glory, was the exception. Caroline had a passion for landscape gardening, which she indulged with least hindrance during the King's absences in Hanover. Among her improvements were the removal of the labyrinths of ornamental hedges from Kensington Gardens [1] and the substitution of the Round Pond in their place; she also projected the formation of the Serpentine. Her taste in art was at least superior to that of George, and to her alert intelligence is due the discovery and preservation of one of the art treasures of the country. The reference is to a priceless set of chalk drawings by Holbein, able sketches of the notabilities of the Court of Henry VIII., with the names supplied by Sir John Cheke. The drawings, which are now in the possession of the Queen at Windsor, were found by Queen Caroline, long after they had been lost sight of, stowed away in the drawers of an old cabinet.

There was royal hunting for three days a week in Richmond Park and similar localities, when the Queen always hunted in a chaise, and appointed her vice-chamberlain Hervey, who cared no more for the sport than she did, to ride by her coach and entertain her with his lively conversation. It has been already mentioned

[1] There is still a pastry-cook's, in the main street of Kensington, where Caroline's recipe for German gingerbread is preserved. The Queen gave it to the pastry-cook's predecessor of her day, who had a shop on the same site.

that Lord Hervey, along with his heartless cynicism, was an effeminate fop, affording warrant for the nickname "Lord Fanny" which Pope first applied to him. He used rouge, was sickly—for which he was less to blame—and is said to have been subject to epileptic fits. He went constantly to London, on the plea of hearing what the world was saying and doing, and retailed what he had learnt to the Queen and the Princesses, with whom he walked "every other day." He was always at the Queen's breakfast-table. His society was so necessary and agreeable to Caroline that, when she was confined to her room with gout, she made the excuse of her mature years and high character in order to admit him to sit by her and enliven her with his sallies. He was so secure of his position, and so convinced of her regard, that in one of the *jeux d'esprit* which he was in the habit of perpetrating he not only described himself as waylaid by highwaymen on the country (!) road between London and the courtly little town of Kensington, but he went on to picture, in the freest manner, the news of his misadventure with the report of his death reaching the palace and the different amusing ways in which, according to their idiosyncrasies, the various members of the royal family and the Court circle would receive the information. In these details the author did not hesitate to comment slyly on the peculiarities of the individuals dealt with. This paper Hervey read aloud to the Queen, the Princesses, and the ladies-in-waiting, to the accompaniment of their appreciative laughter. In another paper, supposed to be his diary written after death, he painted his spirit as constantly occupied in serving his royal mistress. He was driving a bat out of her bedroom ; he was shading her from the sun ; he was taking the chill off the strawberry-water she was about to drink when she was hot ; he was sitting on the shaft of her Majesty's carriage, so as to brush away the dews and worms from her path; he was hovering over the chaplain in chapel, and tearing six leaves out of his sermon in order to shorten it, etc., etc. Caroline said, laughingly, she endured the impertinence of which the creature was guilty because she could not live without him. The return for all this indulgent affection was the cold-hearted analysis of her life and character, the elaborate narrative, as if given *con amore*, of every sorry circumstance, every grim and ghastly feature of her last days and hours. Why did Caroline, with her well-known penetration, lavish so much confidence and regard on so frivolous and false a servant? Even her son Frederick, of whom she was accustomed to think and speak as "a poor fool," formed a more correct estimate than his mother did of Hervey, whom Frederick detested with all his heart. The explanation is to be found in the matter-of-fact, philosophic, pessimistic side of the Queen's disposition. She had been early accustomed to put up with a great deal which was mentally and morally inferior. Hervey could not be called mentally inferior. He was a man "of parts" as people said in his day, of keen wit and lively talent, while she was a witty woman, with her perceptions of what was pure, honest, lovely, and of good report, long blunted, alas! by disuse and abuse. She was oppressed—as only such a woman could be oppressed—by the extremity of dulness and levity on the part of the King, in whose society she spent seven or eight hours each day, listening to him, humouring him, guiding him by apparently endorsing his views and opinions, with a constant restraint put on herself. During these long hours she is said by Hervey himself to have "looked, spoke, and breathed" but for her husband. It must have been an immense relief to her, faithfully as she loved and served George, to exchange his vapid boasting and tiresome garrulity, his causeless frets and unreasoning furies for the society of a companion as quick in perception and apt in tongue as herself, who could divert her thoughts and entertain her and her daughters by his racy version of what was passing in and out of London. She fancied here was a gossip with whom she could be at ease, whom she could trust, to whom she could speak her mind without fear of ulterior consequences. It should be remembered that Caroline's eldest son, who might have been her friend, had utterly failed her. Her communications with him were only less forced than those which he held with his father. Unless when it was necessary to notice the Prince in public, which the King was induced to do with difficulty, George passed Frederick by in dogged silence, as George's father had passed his son by in his youth, and habitually acted as if no Prince were visible.

Caroline's younger son, William, Duke of Cumberland, to whom she was sincerely attached, who returned her attachment, was not more than seventeen years of age at the date of his mother's death. His education and the offices, military and civil, to which he was early appointed, as if for the purpose of mortifying his elder brother, kept mother and son apart.

Queen Caroline, like the Electress Sophia, got into trouble by her tongue. Her speech was always pointed and vigorous. That her strong language was frequently an offence to proper feeling and good taste is attributable, in part, to the licence then permitted and encouraged in conversation. The fact that the Queen spoke mostly in French, as has been stated, ought also to be borne in mind, since that language lent a certain airy piquancy and drollery to her talk. It served to modify the pungent phrases and broad illustrations of her meaning, which her biographers have rendered in the plainest of plain-spoken English. Her " sprightliness," as it was called, tempted her to tease her listeners, and to "play off" or show up their peculiarities, though it was never done ill-naturedly. She was dining in company with Sir Paul Methuen at Lady Walpole's, and kept attacking him on his notorious love of romance-reading, pressing him with the question, " Well, Sir Paul, what romance are you reading now ? " At last he was provoked into answering, " I have got into a very foolish study, madam, that of the Kings and Queens of England " ; a smart repartee which she deserved and probably enjoyed.

At Richmond Caroline walked for more than an hour every morning with the King. The amount of exercise was often exceedingly difficult for her, on account of her great stoutness, her gout, and the fatal complaint which was gradually developing itself. But rather than disappoint the King, who would have been annoyed by any failure to attend him on her part, she would plunge her foot and leg up to the knee in cold water, and trust to the dangerous shock to the system, and the violent perspiration thus induced, to enable her to do what she conceived to be alike her privilege and her duty. The Queen's devotion to her husband has been freely ascribed to ambition and self-interest. Thackeray judges it more justly, though he does not profess to account for it : " One inscrutable attachment that inscrutable woman has. To that she is faithful through all trial, neglect, pain, and time. Save her husband, she really cares for no created being. She is good enough to her children, and even fond enough of them, but she would chop them all up into little pieces to please him. In her intercourse with all around her she was perfectly kind, gracious, and natural ; but friends may die, daughters may depart, she will be as perfectly kind and gracious to the next set. If the King wants her, she will smile upon him be she ever so sad, and walk with him be she ever so weary, and laugh at his brutal jokes be she in ever so much pain of body or heart. Caroline's devotion to her husband is a prodigy to read of. What charm had the little man? What was there in those wonderful letters of thirty pages long which he wrote to her when he was absent? . . . Why did Caroline, the most lovely and accomplished Princess of Germany, take a little red-faced, staring princeling for a husband and refuse an emperor? Why, to her last hour, did she love him so? . . . With the film of death over her eyes, writhing in intolerable pain, she yet had a livid smile and a gentle word for her master."

Card-parties for basset, quadrille, loo (spelt "lu"), etc, etc., etc., with occasional heavy gains and losses, were formed every evening in English as in other European palaces.

Before going to bed, the King and Queen spent an hour or two each night when they were in the country, and three nights a week when their Majesties were in town, with a respectable pair, who were under the royal protection and were members of the household. These were French Huguenots of high birth. The King created the brother Earl of Lifford; the sister, Lady Charlotte de Roncy, was governess to the younger Princesses Mary and Louisa. According to Lord Hervey, the two were more worthy than amusing; according to Horace Walpole, they were poor, and received more of the honour of the King and Queen's countenance than of substantial remuneration for genuine services. In the company of Lord Lifford and Lady Charlotte the King walked up and down and talked of armies and genealogies; the Queen knotted[1] and yawned, and occasionally " went from yawning to

---

[1] Knotting was a favourite occupation of ladies in the eighteenth century. Like tatting (which it resembled), netting, and knitting, it was better calculated to send the workers to sleep than to keep them awake. Knotting resulted in the production of a strong kind of lace or fringe.

nodding, and from nodding to snoring." When Lady Charlotte was summoned to help to make up a game at one of the royal card-tables, her mistakes are said to have been treated with scant ceremony. The Queen tweaked her by the turban, the Princess Royal rapped her on the knuckles. These details are supplied by Lord Hervey and Horace Walpole, " Lord Fanny " and " Horry," as kindred spirits termed them. In these gentlemen's readiness to believe the worst of all save of their special cronies, in their incapacity for ascribing to the people around them higher motives than those which sufficed for themselves, they are not witnesses who can be taken without a pinch of salt. Their pens, like the brilliant pen of Lady Mary Montagu, were dipped in gall. Unfortunately, the authors referred to are not only the most graphic writers, they are the chief contemporary authorities on the manners and customs of the Court and on the social life of the reign. Mrs. Delany, who is a mildly vivacious, quaintly pleasing substitute for the men, while she is much more truth-loving and amiable, was in Ireland and in the country for part of the time ; besides, she deals more with an occasional ceremonial, such as a coronation, with the fashions, and with delightful records of her personal friends and her personal pursuits, than with any form of history. Lady Louisa Stuart with her Scotch shrewdness and old-world liveliness supplements by her reminiscences her family narratives ; but she is necessarily brief. There is no lack of material in Lady Mary Coke's voluminous diary and letters, but they are the literary remains of a woman styled characteristically, from the dead whiteness of her skin and from her fierce eyes, " the White Cat." She was nearly as crazy as Kitty of Queensberry, while her extravagant egotism was still more dominant ; neither was she more generous and gentle than the two distinguished men—

one of whom, Horace Walpole, used to welcome her to Strawberry Hill.

Caroline has been laughed at for her mistaken patronage of Stephen Duck, a Wiltshire labourer, who wrote poetry of little merit. The Queen procured for him an appointment as Yeoman of the Guard, and named him Keeper of her Grotto—grottoes and wildernesses were among the "fads" of the time—in Richmond Park. She even caused him to enter the Church and made him Vicar of Kew, a promotion of which he was not worthy in any light. The burden so weighed upon him that the unhappy man drowned himself. In the sad story there is only one pleasing element, and that is Caroline's genuine desire to reward intellectual effort under difficulties.

The Queen was very fond of English comedy, had the famous Anne Oldfield to "read" at Windsor, and on the actress's death, writes Dr. Doran, "bought her collection of plays for a hundred and twenty guineas."

An event of moment in 1734 was the withdrawal of Lady Suffolk (Mrs. Howard) from her Court posts. She held, first, that of bedchamber woman, and second, on her husband's accession to the Earldom of Suffolk, that of Mistress of the Robes, which was her office for twenty years—years during which she had not been absent from Court for six weeks in succession. The etiquette of the royal service required a bedchamber woman to come into waiting before the Queen's prayers were made, which was before she dressed. The bedchamber woman gave the Queen's underlinen to a lady of the bedchamber, who had also to be present; the lady of the bedchamber put the "shift" on the Queen. In the same manner the bedchamber woman presented the fan to the lady of the bedchamber, who handed it to the Queen. The page of the back-stairs brought the basin and ewer, and placed them on a side table. The bedchamber woman knelt and offered them to the Queen, the lady of the bedchamber looking on ; the bedchamber woman poured the water from the ewer on the Queen's hands ; later, she pulled on the Queen's gloves, if she did not choose to do it herself. The page of the back-stairs put on the Queen's shoes. When the Queen dined in public her glass was handed to her by a woman of the bedchamber, who also brought the Queen's chocolate.

Lady Suffolk's infirmity of deafness had increased to an extent which wearied the King in his daily visits to her. She, whose conversation had formerly been so soothing, had learnt a habit of contradicting Majesty itself—a liberty in which Queen Caroline rarely indulged. Horace Walpole mentions that Lady Suffolk was a strict lover of truth, and was very apt to be circumstantial about trifles. These peculiarities may have had something to do with her contradiction of the King which was not agreeable to him. She persisted in her friendship with Gay, who was in perennial disgrace at Court, and with Pope, who had openly satirised the King and the royal family. Puffing, strutting little George protested ungallantly that he was weary of a deaf old woman, and ceased his daily visits to her. Lady Suffolk declared that the rooms assigned to her in Kensington Palace were three feet underground, and were injurious to her health. Another reason for the resignation of her office was that the worthless life of the husband from whom she had long lived apart was ended, and although she was upwards of fifty years of age she was about to marry, for the second time, the Honourable George Berkeley, a younger son of Earl Berkeley, Master of St. Catharine's in the Tower, and Member of Parliament for Dover. Her retirement from Court was more regretted by her mistress than by any other member of the royal family and household. In spite of the cordial regard entertained for Lady Suffolk by her intimate friends, her early contemporaries in office, and by the sardonic editor of her letters, together with the warm tribute paid to her memory by Thackeray, her departure from the circle was welcomed, rather than regretted, by all save the Queen, who was "both glad and sorry," with whom, and with whom only, Lady Suffolk had a long and friendly parting interview, in which Caroline even sought to induce her servant to reconsider her resignation. George had been bored by his old friend and *confidante*. The elder Princesses had resented her influence with their father, and were pleased to see her go; only Anne, in her blunt, disrespectful fashion, pitied her mother for having the King for ever on her hands. A quarter of a century afterwards Lady Suffolk happened to pay a visit to Kensington. There was a review of the household troops, of which she had not heard, and her coach got wedged in among other coaches, so that it could not move. As the old woman sat there, the King, whom she had not seen for many years, passed, and did not recognise her. Two days afterwards she heard of his death. She survived the Queen thirty years, and the King seven; she outlived her second, as she had outlived her first husband, and died, comparatively poor, in 1767, in the eightieth year of her age. Apart from her deafness, she was well-nigh as pleasing as ever to the last.

Lady Sundon (Mrs. Clayton) succeeded her former rival as Mistress of the Robes and remained with Caroline to the end. Lady Sundon's death, which occurred five years after that of the Queen, is said to have been caused by grief for the loss of her friend and mistress, or, as sceptical spirits understood it, by the mortification of the check to her ambition. She was said to suffer from attacks of madness after Caroline's death.

In the years 1735 and 1736 the King revisited Hanover, while the Queen again acted as Regent in her husband's absence. When in Germany, George experienced one of his violent attacks of gallantry and extravagant admiration for a German lady, Madame Walmoden. She was a descendant of the family of disreputable adventurers, of whom the Countess von Platen, George's mother Sophia Dorothea's deadly enemy, was the most conspicuous. George's letters—from forty to sixty pages long—in which he gave the minutest account of his proceedings abroad for his wife's benefit, were full of ecstatic praises of the lady. Caroline must have read them with a rueful smile at her King's ineradicable follies and absurdities. She replied to them with the time-serving dissimulation and subserviency which spoilt an otherwise fine character. She professed to sympathise with him fully in his enthusiasm for this new paragon. Madame Walmoden came to England at a later period and was created, by George, Countess of Yarmouth. Lady Louisa Stuart remembered her, and describes her as a dull, orderly, harmless woman, not possessed of any particular personal or mental attraction, and not disposed to meddle with anybody.

On the King's return to Kensington in October, 1735, Dr. Doran describes the Queen, with her ladies and gentlemen, hurrying to the gate to meet him as he alighted from his coach. She took his hand and kissed it in her office as Regent, then hastened to kiss him on the lips, with a very unceremonious, hearty, *brusque* kiss, as his loving wife. But George, who chanced to be in one of his cross, ungracious humours, led her upstairs "in a very formal, stately manner." If the King was in this frame of mind he spared nobody. Lord Hervey describes two similar scenes at this time. One was when Caroline and her daughters were drinking their morning chocolate in the gallery, with the Queen's second son William, Duke of Cumberland, standing by. " George snubbed the Queen... for being always stuffing;

the Princess Amelia for not hearing him; the Princess Caroline for being grown fat; the Duke of Cumberland for standing awkwardly; and then he carried the Queen out to walk and be re-snubbed in the garden."

On the other occasion, when there was an argument on the obligation of giving "vails" or gratuities to the servants in any house which the King or the Queen visited, the Vice-Chamberlain took it upon him to hint that such liberality was expected from the Queen. "Then let her stay at home as I do," said the King rudely. "You do not see me running into every puppy's house to see his new chairs and stools." Turning to the Queen he added, "Nor is it for you to be running your nose everywhere, and to be trotting about the town to every fellow who will give you some bread and butter, like an old girl who loves to go abroad, no matter where, or whether it be proper or no."

The Queen coloured, and knotted a great deal faster, during this speech, than she had done before, while the tears came into her eyes; but she said not one word. Lord Hervey still ventured to defend his royal mistress, the result being that George burst into a torrent of German which sounded like abuse. The Queen made no reply, but knotted on till she tangled her thread, then snuffed the candles which stood on the table before her, and put one of them out; "upon which the King, in English, began a new dissertation upon her Majesty, and took her awkwardness for his text."

The King had several pictures painted of the balls and entertainments which he had most enjoyed in his visit to Hanover. These pictures, containing portraits of his Majesty's guests, were hung up in the Queen's dressing-room. "Occasionally, of an evening, the King would take a candle from the Queen's table and go from picture to picture with Lord Hervey, telling its history, explaining the joyous incidents, naming the persons represented, and detailing all that had been said and done on the particular occasion before them. "During which lecture," says the Vice-Chamberlain himself, "Lord Hervey, while peeping over his Majesty's shoulder at those pictures, was shrugging up his own, and now and then stealing a look to make faces at the Queen, who, a little angry, a little peevish, a little tired at her husband's absurdity, and a little entertained with his lordship's grimaces, used to sit and knot in a corner of the room, sometimes yawning and sometimes smiling, and equally afraid of betraying those signs either of her lassitude or her mirth." Alas! for the coarse-minded insincerity, disloyalty, and mockery, in which, if we are to believe Hervey, Caroline played a part.

In spite of these domestic fracas, no one, either then or since, ever doubted George's warm attachment, after his uncouth fashion, to his Queen, and her unalterable supreme regard for her King.

In April, 1735, Frederick Prince of Wales, was married to Princess Augusta of Saxe-Gotha. It was more than time that he should be settled in life ; he was in his thirtieth year. Already a bold scheme, with which his family had nothing to do, had been planned to marry him to one of his father's subjects—a scheme which was baffled by Sir Robert Walpole. The schemer was Queen Anne's former favourite, the haughty termagant Sarah, Duchess of Marlborough, freely styled "Old Sarah" by her later contemporaries. She had secretly arranged an alliance between "Prince Fritz" and her favourite grand-daughter Lady Di. Spencer. The Duchess was to give the bride a portion of a hundred thousand pounds, a sum which would have been particularly acceptable to the needy bridegroom, over whose proposed income of fifty thousand pounds a year, paid in monthly instalments at the King's pleasure, George—or rather Frederick's friends—and the Parliament were wrangling. But it was the question of a separate establishment, which would give the undutiful, wayward son still greater opportunities for mischief, in heading cabals against the King's authority, that delayed any suggestion of a fitting allowance for the future King.

It is just possible also, if there is any truth in the assertion, of Caroline, as well as of George, having long cherished a hope that England and Hanover might be separated, the Queen had trusted Hanover might pass to the Prince of Wales, and England to the son of her love, William, Duke of Cumberland; or, *vice versa*, England to Frederick and Hanover to William. Such divisions of territory were not unknown to the House of Brunswick. But if Frederick married and had heirs, the subsequent distribution of the royal possessions would be rendered doubly difficult.

If Caroline ever entertained the idea attributed to her, she must have relinquished it before the date of Frederick's marriage, which she was certainly anxious to promote. The King first looked to Prussia, and to the daughter and son of his sister the second Sophia Dorothea, for marriage-contracts where two of his children were concerned. He had planned a double marriage—the Prince of Wales to the daughter, and one of his own daughters to the son (afterwards Frederick the Great) of the King of Prussia. But Prussia, influenced by Court intrigues, and by reasons best known to her brutal tyrant, broke off the treaty. George then selected for his daughter-in-law a Princess of Gotha, a blooming girl of seventeen, eager to avail herself of the promotion offered to her. She landed at Greenwich on St. George's Day, 1736. Her fresh, happy face made her awkward, ungainly figure be forgotten, and recommended her to the people, who crowded to see her as she sat in the balcony of the Queen's house overlooking the park. The people's hearty greetings were the only welcome she had, for the bridegroom came late, and he was unaccompanied by any member of the family, with whom he was at chronic strife.

The marriage took place in the Chapel Royal, St. James's, on May 8th, 1736, in spite of the old superstition against celebrating weddings in the month which had been dedicated to the Virgin. The King and Queen were pleased with the Princess on first acquaintance, but in the troubles which followed she always seemed to them a mere tool of her husband's. Caroline looked upon Augusta as a poor, dull, stupid girl, against whom the clever woman of mature years could not condescend to bear malice.

George went again to Germany in the course of the summer, leaving behind him orders that the Prince and Princess of Wales should occupy rooms in whatever palace the Queen-Regent chose to reside. Prince Fritz, with the petty but galling spirit of contradiction which uniformly possessed him, thought fit to evade the order by inventing a succession of excuses. He pleaded an illness of his wife's on one occasion as his reason for not attending his mother when she was removing to fresh quarters.

Caroline was sufficiently provoked to take a journey in person—urged, as she professed, by her anxiety to ascertain the state of her daughter-in-law's health—in order to discover whether the Princess had measles or not. But in a darkened room, with the compliant Princess laid up in bed, and instructed in the evasive answers to give to every searching question put to her, it was difficult to discover whether the patient had so much as a slight cold.

The Queen had enough weighty business on her hands to occupy her otherwise. First, there was rioting everywhere, so that the guards had to be doubled at the entrances to the palaces where she was in residence. These disorders culminated in the Porteous mob in the Scotch capital, when the execution of the smuggler Wilson was avenged by the murder of the captain of the city guard, who had directed his men to fire on the ringleaders of the excited crowd engaged in attempting to cut down Wilson's body. The breaking open of the Tolbooth where Captain Porteous lay, the manner in which he was seized, half dragged, half carried through the streets of Edinburgh, and hanged on the very spot where Wilson had suffered the extreme penalty of the law, was so daring a usurpation of justice, while the affair was conducted so deliberately and systematically that it was exceedingly like the beginning of a general insurrection.

Next, Caroline was vexed by the prolonged injudicious absence of her King, extending even beyond the anniversary of his birthday. She was piqued and mortified into abridging her usual letters to him, which were as prolix as his were to her. But entreated by Walpole, who believed that his position as Prime Minister dedepended on Caroline's influence over the King, she sought to make amends for her brief rebellion by inviting Madame Walmoden to England, even by offering to take her into the Queen's service; an invitation and offer which were not, however, acted upon at the time.

The last straw which threatened to break the poor burdened camel's back was the bad passage which George had, in crossing from Hanover to England, in the month of December. He was so tossed by the storm, delayed, and turned back, that the liveliest apprehensions for his safety were current in England. The Prince of Wales began openly to brag that when he appeared in public the mob shouted "Crown him! crown him!" in anticipation of his speedy succession to the throne, when his mother and sisters were likely to fare badly at his hands.

But the Queen kept up her spirit and courage, and read Rollin's *Ancient History* to pass away the time. She spent Christmas Day without breaking down. It was only when Sir Robert Walpole thought it right to tell her that the ships which had been the escort of the King's vessel had struggled back in a disabled condition to England, bringing news of the tremendous hurricane they had encountered, but unable to say a word with regard to what had become of the King's yacht, that she broke down at last and wept bitterly. Nevertheless she went to service in the Chapel Royal as she was accustomed to do, because her absence would have been like sealing the King's death-warrant in the eyes of the Court and the people; besides, what better place could be found for an afflicted wife, over whose head the dreaded sentence of bereavement seemed impending, than the House of Prayer? In the middle of the service a letter from the King was brought to the Queen. His vessel had been able to put back to the port from which it had sailed, and was waiting there for more favourable weather. In the month of January, 1737, George arrived in safety; he had the grace on this occasion to express his gratitude for the Queen's concern on his account, and his fervent regard for her.

When the Prince and Princess of Wales's first child was born the Prince gave another illustration of his hare-brained recklessness, and of the miserable terms on which the royal family were living together—still together though the King refused to speak to his son, and while the Prince led the Queen by the hand to dinner, with terrible enmity reigning in the hearts of mother and son. The King and Queen, the Prince and Princess of Wales, the Princesses Emily and Caroline, with their younger sisters, Mary and Louisa, were all at Hampton Court towards the end of the month of July. "On the evening of the 31st the King and Princess Amelia were playing 'commerce' below stairs; the Queen, in another apartment, was at 'quadrille'; and the Princess Caroline and Lord Hervey were soberly playing cribbage." The party separated at ten o'clock under the impression that the Prince and Princess of Wales were also retiring to rest in their suite of apartments. At two o'clock in the morning the Queen was aroused by the bedchamber woman, Mrs. Tichborne, with the startling intelligence that the Prince had taken away the Princess to St. James's in order that their child might be born there.

"My good Tichborne," cried the Queen, using a form of address which was common with her, "are you mad, or are you asleep?" When satisfied of the truth of the information thus conveyed to her, the Queen announced her determination to follow the runaway couple as soon as it was daylight. She entertained, or professed to entertain, a fear that her son and his submissive Princess would attempt to palm off a supposititious child on the King and the nation. Caroline declared she would be at the bottom of the business; accordingly she started in one of the royal carriages with her two elder daughters, and reached St. James's by eight o'clock in the morning. There the indignant Queen found that her daughter-in-law had given birth to a daughter an hour after her arrival from Hampton Court. The Prince met his mother with many fluent explanations and apologies, such as that the Princess wished the child to be born at St. James's; that she was under the impression she would get better medical aid in London, etc., etc., from which the Queen turned away in scorn, viewing the excuses as "a pack of lies." She was, however, satisfied that there was no imposition. When she heard the poor young mother, who was putting a brave face on the situation, declaring she was very well and had not suffered from the Prince's action, Caroline was softened, and spoke kindly and encouragingly to her. The Queen took the infant in her arms, and said, half in pity, half in sarcasm, " May the good God bless you, poor little creature! Here you are arrived in a most disagreeable world."

Within a fortnight the Queen and the Princesses paid another visit to the Prince and Princess of Wales. On this second visit the Prince did not address a word to his mother during the hour she remained in the palace, though he went through the form not only of conducting her to her coach, but of kneeling in the muddy street and kissing her hand in presence of the gaping crowd collected at the sight of the royal liveries. This was the last time that the unhappy mother and son met. The Queen was not present at the christening of her grand-daughter. The incessant quarrelling—thinly veiled—which went on between the King and Queen with their household on the one side, and the Prince and Princess of Wales with their household on the other, reached a climax. The Prince and Princess were requested to quit St. James's, as Caroline and George had been told to leave the same palace at an earlier date. The royal outcasts were bidden establish themselves elsewhere, and they settled for the time at Kew.

Caroline's health had long been manifestly failing, undermined as it was by the internal injury which she had sustained and had imprudently concealed to the last. The fatal termination of her complaint was also hastened by her compliance with the King's inconsiderate and exacting demands for her company at all times, so that she would walk with him when she was totally unfit for the exercise, and drag herself out of bed in order to undergo the fatigue of standing by his side in public assemblies, till outraged nature compelled her to withdraw. Sir Robert Walpole, with his keen, if sardonic, insight into characters and motives, was one of the first who suspected the truth. He founded his suspicions on Caroline's persistent and particular inquiries with regard to the course of Lady Walpole's illness, which had been a case of rupture. He guessed that Caroline's malady arose from a similar cause. In the month of August, 1737, the Queen was so ill that her death was reported in London. She rallied presently, but in the following November grew so much worse that her dangerous condition could no longer be hidden, to the grief and consternation of the King, her daughters, her second son, Sir Robert Walpole, and of every candid and intelligent person in the country who esteemed her virtues and was aware of the active part she had taken in the government.

Caroline's last and fatal seizure occurred on Wednesday, November 9th, but the indomitable woman struggled gallantly against mortal pain and weakness. To please her King, she made her final public appearance at one of the drawing-rooms, which he was in the habit of saying were destitute alike of grace, gaiety, and dignity without her presence; she was much worse for the effort. Her loving daughter Caroline watched over her the next night, while poor George—obtuse and selfish in his very affection—lay, in his morning-gown, outside the bed, rendering the tortured woman, tossing in her restlessness, unable to turn.

Then began the "grotesque horror" and "dreadful humour" of a death-bed scene, from which Thackeray shrinks, which John, Lord Hervey, the Queen's friend, dissects and exposes. First, there was the troop of doctors, striving in their perplexity to find remedies for the unknown ailment; and when one of them succeeded in arriving at the truth, and spoke of it in a low voice to the King, who had been in the secret from the beginning, the Queen, guessing what he was about, called him "a blockhead" for his pains. When forced to own the nature of her illness, however, she was patient, courageous, even cheerful, with her old ready wit. She was willing to submit to any treatment, be it ever so painful, even to undergo an operation, if the doctors thought it would do her good.

Next the Prince of Wales sent hypocritical inquiries, at which his father stormed, to which his mother, alas! had no further answer than that she begged he might be kept out of her sight. She had no faith in his pretended sympathy; she knew he would "blubber like a calf" at her condition, and laugh at her outright as soon as he was out of sight and hearing. Yet this was the woman of whom we are told, on George's authority, that she was the last to believe her son a fool and knave! The wholesome heart had indeed been turned to gall.

On Sunday, November 13th, the doctors believed the Queen's end to be near—an opinion which she heard with great calmness. She took a loving farewell of the children who were with her, being especially tender to the Duke of Cumberland—a lad approaching manhood —and to the Princess Caroline, the most upright, unselfish, and gentle of the family, to whose special care the Queen committed her younger daughters, Mary and Louisa, girls in their earlier teens. She spoke in their hearing—to no purpose, as it proved—of the womanish sensitiveness and silliness which had induced her to conceal a bodily hurt which, if attended to in time, might have been of little moment, instead of shortening her days as it was then doing.[1] She sought to console the sobbing King, telling him that what of happiness and greatness she had enjoyed in her life she owed to him,

[1] Louisa, when Queen of Denmark, sustained a similar injury, which she also concealed with like fatal consequences.

drawing a ring from her finger and putting it on his hand, and appointing him her heir. She counselled him to marry again—a recommendation to which he returned a vehement refusal, coupled with a characteristic and unseemly qualification, on which she made an equally characteristic and unseemly comment.

The Queen had a superstitious belief that she would live till the following Wednesday, because, as she said, all the great events of her life had happened to her on Wednesdays. She had been born on a Wednesday, married on a Wednesday, had given birth to her first child on a Wednesday, and been crowned on a Wednesday. Even this last violent illness had seized her on a Wednesday, and she believed she would die on a Wednesday. As it was, she only survived till the following Sunday, the 20th of the month. During that week of extreme distress the doctors had sometimes a faint hope that the Queen might yet recover. She did not share the hope; she might have pulled through at twenty-five, she said, not at fifty-five.

The King kissed the sleeping woman again and again, enlarging endlessly on her unrivalled excellences, and, when she was awake and conscious, scolded her for not lying still, and for staring into vacancy "like a calf with its throat cut."

Princess Emily, who among various good qualities was affected with a strong sense of the ridiculous, while she had also her full share of the propensity of the family and the generation to dispense with natural reverence and modest self-control, and to speak her mind without restraint, lost all patience with the noisy chief mourner. She feigned to be asleep, so weary was she of affecting to listen and respond to her father's excessive garrulous eulogiums on her dying mother; and when he was absent from the room, in the tension of her feelings, she forgot all filial regard and womanly compassion to rage at the stupid egotistical man, calling him " old fool, liar, coward, and driveller," of whose stories she was heartily sick.

The courtiers gossiped and speculated. Messengers from the Prince of Wales crept into the ante-room, in order to hear the doctor's last report and carry their master the assurance that the Queen was certainly sinking—an assurance which he received with undissembled satisfaction.

The public and the Prime Minister—not George or even his daughters apparently—were solicitous that the Queen should make a last formal recognition of the truth of the Christian religion, and should receive its consolations from the hands of an ordained priest. Accordingly, Potter, Archbishop of Canterbury, waited on her, and read the prayers for the sick by her bed morning and night. But those who made the matter one of personal interest, and who besieged the prelate every time he quitted the sick-room with the pressing question, "Has the Queen received?" could not learn that she had taken the Holy Communion. The reason usually assigned for this omission was that she was not at peace with her elder son. It is known, nevertheless, that she sent him her forgiveness and blessing, and that she earnestly recommended his younger brother the Duke of Cumberland, if he lived to see Frederick King of England, to submit and defer to him, and only to seek to surpass him in virtue. It is not impossible that Caroline's absolute devotion to King George was at the root of her refusal to have a personal interview with her son. She knew that his presence in the palace would be a torment to his father in his sorrow, and that, if the Prince were ever readmitted to the royal circle, there would be fresh difficulty and scandal in dislodging him for the second time. Hervey and Walpole agree in attributing these motives to the Queen.

On the final Sunday Queen Caroline asked one of her physicians, "How long can this last?"

"It will not be long," was the guarded reply, "before your Majesty will be relieved from this suffering."

"The sooner the better," said Caroline; and then she began to pray aloud; and her prayer was not a formal one, fixed in her memory by repeating it from the Book of Common Prayer, but a spontaneous and extemporary effusion, so eloquent, so appropriate and so touching, that all the listeners were struck with admiration at this last effort of a mind always remarkable for its vigour and ability. She herself manifested great anxiety to depart in a manner becoming to a Queen, and as her last moments approached her anxiety in this respect appeared to increase. She requested to be raised in bed, and asked all present to kneel and offer up a prayer on her behalf. While this was going on she grew gradually fainter, but, at her desire, water was sprinkled upon her, so that she might revive, listen to, and join in the petition which her family (all but her eldest son, who was not present)[1] put up to Heaven on her behalf. "Louder," she murmured more than once, as some one read or prayed; "louder, that I may hear." "Pray! pray!" was the Queen's cry, as others had it. Her request was complied with, and then one of her children repeated the Lord's Prayer. In this Caroline joined, repeating the words as distinctly as failing nature would allow her to do. The prayer was just concluded, when she looked fixedly at those who stood weeping around her, and uttered a long-drawn (German) *So!* (the familiar expression of assent in her mother-tongue). This was "her last word; but she was still able to wave her hand in farewell to her friends and to the world. She composed herself on her bed, breathed a sigh, and expired."

Thus died Caroline of Anspach, in her fifty-fifth year,

[1] Her eldest daughter Anne, Princess of Orange, was also absent.

on Sunday, November 20th, 1737. She was, without doubt, the ablest of our Queen-Consorts. Her coarseness and callousness belonged to her generation, her fine qualities were her own. She helped to steer England wisely and successfully through a transitional period of great peril. She was the most devoted of wives, and, apart from her relations with the wretched Frederick, Prince of Wales, a good and kind mother. She was a faithful friend and patroness of good men in the Church, and of men of letters, so far as was in her power. She deserved, in many lights, to be called, as she was, " the good Queen Caroline." Ambition, together with her temperament—half philosophic, half mocking—blinded her, and rendered her, as they rendered several of her predecessors, strangely indifferent to affectations and offences which would have half-maddened a more delicately sensitive and impulsively passionate woman. Ambition, too, taught her the time-serving dissimulation —foreign to her naturally frank, outspoken disposition —which caused Walpole, while always regarding her as his most valuable ally, to talk and write not only of her, but to her, with little respect and less reticence;[1] if, indeed, bluff, brutal Sir Robert was capable of much respect and propriety where either man or woman was concerned.

The death of Queen Caroline was widely and justly lamented by all save the Jacobite faction in the country. Eulogiums in prose and verse, some of them of the most extravagant character, were poured forth in her honour. Her loss was still more deeply and abidingly felt in the Court circle. George, with all his grievous vices and follies, never forgot her; he would look at her picture for an hour at a time, bedewing it with tears,

---

[1] Sir Robert was in the habit of complaining that the Queen "daubed," that is, over-did the graciously flattering manner under which she concealed some of her personal and party dislikes.

and asserting that he had never seen a woman fit to buckle his wife's shoes. He did what he could to retain in the royal service her much prized Vice-Chamberlain and gossip Lord Hervey. Political exigencies deprived Hervey of his post at last, and he did not survive the Queen more than six years. Princess Caroline, her mother's favourite daughter and namesake, ceased to appear in public, and led the life of a confirmed invalid and recluse from the date of Queen Caroline's death.

The Queen was buried with the splendour due to her rank, though with less picturesque pomp than distinguished the funerals of the earlier Queens of England. Her coffin was deposited in a vault beneath Henry VII.'s Chapel, Westminster Abbey. Instead of the King or either of his sons filling the office, Princess Emily, the eldest Princess in England, acted as chief mourner, according to old custom.

Handel's recently composed anthem, "*When the ear heard her, then it blessed her*," was first sung on this occasion.

In the preparations for the funeral of George II., who survived his wife twenty-three years, dying in 1760, one side of his coffin and one side of that of Queen Caroline were removed, according to the directions which the King had left behind him, in order that, as the coffins rested together in the royal vault, the dust of husband and wife might meet and mingle.

Caroline was the mother of nine children—four sons, two of whom died in infancy, and five daughters.

IV.

CHARLOTTE OF MECKLENBURG-STRELITZ, WIFE OF GEORGE III.

AUTHORITIES:

Horace Walpole, Dr. Watkins, Mrs. Delany, Fanny Burney, Dr. Doran, W. M. Thackeray, etc.

CHARLOTTE OF MECKLENBURG-STRELITZ, QUEEN OF GEORGE III.
(THE GIRL-QUEEN).

CHAPTER I.

A YOUNG QUEEN-CONSORT.

THERE was a young King in England in 1761. George III., who succeeded to his grandfather George II. a year before, was just twenty-three. He was then a handsome but rather delicate-looking lad, on whom the hopes of the nation were centred, for was he not the first English-born Prince of his line, and had he not from his youth upwards borne, in contrast to his predecessors, the highest character for manly modesty and virtue? His father was the unlucky and undeserving "Prince Fritz," whom nobody except his wife—not his father, still less his mother or his brother and sisters—held in the slightest regard; with reason, for a more contradictory, heartless, insubordinate Prince never existed. George III.'s mother was a Princess of the House of Coburg. She came to England a simple-minded, well-disposed girl enough, neither pretty nor witty. Though with her starched ways she was never popular in England, she was a dutiful wife to the most trying of husbands— one of whose few redeeming qualities, however, was a certain sense of her worth and of respect for her character. She was a good mother in a hard, intolerant way. Unfortunately, she was also a woman of no liberality of mind, no tact, no grace. She was accused of intermeddling with public affairs in an underhand, unwarrantable manner. Certainly so long as she lived, which was for eleven years after her son's accession to the throne, he was, in spite of the lesson she had given him to "be a King, George, be a King," and in spite of his firmness in all matters of conscience and his naturally obstinate temper, a good deal like clay in her hands and in those of Lord Bute, who by George's favour succeeded the elder Pitt as Prime Minister for a time. Bute was entirely in the Princess of Wales' counsels, and for that reason, among others, was detested by the nation at large.

The great question of the day was whom should the young King marry. His grandfather had desired an alliance with the royal family of Prussia, but that project, thwarted by the Princess of Wales and Lord Bute, fell to the ground.

There was many a noble English maiden who had aspirations to the crown matrimonial, and there was the fair Quaker Hannah Lightfoot, to whom, wild rumour would have it, the royal lad had made honourable proposals of marriage, nay, would have married had not George II.'s death intervened in time. Yet it was long centuries since a King of England had wedded with a subject—not since Edward IV. had married Elizabeth Woodville. But there seemed some danger of it in the present case because of George's innocent admiration for the beautiful Lady Sarah Lennox, daughter to the Duke of Richmond and cousin to Charles James Fox. Her kith and kin are said to have done their best to bring about the unequal match. There still exists round Holland House a remnant of the park in which Lady Sarah was wont to make hay when the young King rode past on his way from Kensington to St. James's. The whole scene was then sufficiently quiet for such a performance. Holland House was a country mansion, and Kensington, apart from its palace and its stately square—many of the picturesque old houses in which had served as residences for the foreign ambassadors in the reigns of William and Mary and Anne—was but a country village with a country road, having a bad reputation for foot-pads, between it and London.

The Princess of Wales and her adviser would on no account countenance a misalliance, and as George would not disobey his mother, and was too sensible, with all his simplicity, of what was due to his rank and office, not to appreciate the weight of the arguments against his stooping to place Lady Sarah by his side, she smiled her sweetest smile and tossed her fragrant hay in vain. It was well, for Lady Sarah's future life did not afford proof of a capacity to discharge with credit to herself and profit to others the duties of a Queen.

It was believed that the widowed Princess and Lord Bute dispatched a trusty messenger to visit the Protestant Courts of Europe and discover a suitable Princess to match with the royal George. He found one in a remote corner in the little duchy of Mecklenburg-Strelitz. It was a poor little kingdom, over which the young lady's brother presided with his widowed mother and a couple of sisters to bear him company. Charlotte Sophia—the younger of the sisters—had been brought up in wholesome economy and quietness, still with every attention to ducal dignity. For six days in the week she had been content to appear in a *robe-de-chambre*; on the seventh she had worn full dress in which she had attended church in state and afterwards driven out in a coach and six, escorted by guards. Notwithstanding this distinction she had not so much as dined at the ducal table; for she was only a girl of sixteen, very much occupied with her studies in which she had been carefully instructed. Indeed, she was an accomplished girl for her age and for the remote duchy to which she belonged. She could play on the spinet better than any lady in England, she could speak a little English,

French, and Italian, she could draw fairly and embroider with skill and taste. She was not pretty, though she had a fresh complexion in keeping with her chestnut brown hair, good eyes, and what was then called "a fine countenance"—that is, a face agreeably brightened by quick intelligence and cheerful good humour. Her mouth was large—so large that as she was, whether as a girl or a woman, thin, people said she was "all mouth," but her teeth were white and regular. In spite of her smallness and thinness her figure was good, and she held herself so well that the public who came in contact with her never failed to praise it in a variety of terms. She was "very genteel" in the original meaning of the much abused old French word *gentille* (*petite, svelte,* charming), or she was "elegance and dignity itself." "How she held her fan!" an enthusiastic painter recalled her attitude in one of her sittings for his picture. Her arms and hands were beautiful almost to the end of her life.

But it was not for mere accomplishments or for such a share of personal attractions as she possessed that Charlotte was chosen for her high destiny. The King of Prussia in one of his smaller warlike expeditions had devastated Mecklenburg-Strelitz, on which the girl Princess ventured to write a letter to him in which she dwelt on the scourge of war and the blessing of peace and pled that her country might be spared further suffering. Naturally the letter contained a few self-evident truths clothed in stereotyped language, such as might find its way into any school-room essay.

But the epistle, written as it was with perfect correctness and great neatness, was regarded in those days as a wonderful production for a girl of sixteen. It was so managed that it should fall into the hands of honest young George—the royal Cœlebs in search of a wife. He was filled with respect and admiration. He declared that the writer of that letter with its noble, just sentiments so eloquently expressed, was the wife for him, and acted accordingly.

Thackeray has a pretty story of the Princess strolling with her girl-companions in the ducal gardens and crying out as the chatter turned on marriage, "Who will take such a poor little Princess as me?"

"And at that very moment the postman's horn sounded, when Charlotte's chief girl friend said, much to the purpose, 'Princess, there is the sweetheart.'"

Sure enough that postman brought the formal proposals of the King of England.

Young as Charlotte was, it is hardly possible that she was so entirely ignorant of the coming event—of tremendous importance to her—as she is represented to have been, though it might very well be true that the Empress of Russia knew of the projected marriage before it had reached the ears of the bride presumptive. A widely received account has it that one morning, without previous intimation, Charlotte's brother, the Duke, entered, accompanied by the Duchess-mother, the ante-room free to the Princess and communicated to her what was in store for her. "In a few minutes the folding doors flew open to the saloon, which she saw splendidly illuminated, and there appeared a table, two cushions, and everything prepared for a wedding. Moreover, the proxy for King George was standing ready. Her brother then gave her his hand and, leading her in, said in French, 'Come, do not be a child. You are going to be Queen of England,' and a service was performed, after which all present embraced her, calling her 'the Queen.'"

Two English ladies, the Duchesses of Hamilton and Ancaster, were sent to Mecklenburg-Strelitz to represent the Princess's suite and to help to escort her to her future kingdom. They were what was called "fine women," the Duchess of Hamilton, though she had been twice married, being still strikingly handsome. "Are all English women as beautiful as you are?" asked Princess Charlotte naïvely and wistfully, though probably not without a perception of the acceptability of the graceful, gracious compliment.

Lord Hardwicke was the envoy who bore the King's credentials and was empowered to bring the Princess to England. A cloud came over the rejoicings and delayed the conclusion of the treaty, in consequence of the unexpected death of the Duchess-mother.

But a bridegroom so great as the King of England could not be kept waiting, and a fortune so august as that of his consort could not be received with a doleful face by a silent Court. There must be festivity following quickly on mourning, illuminations, balls, fireworks, and volleys of artillery in rapid succession. The little bride had to swallow down her tears for her mother and show herself properly grateful and glad because of the new honours heaped upon her and the new life stretching out before her. And this may be said for the coming Queen that *noblesse oblige* was a strong principle with her. From first to last she set an intrepid example of conquering herself and sacrificing her inclinations to do what was right and becoming in her station and what would satisfy the natural and lawful requirements of the nation. If she exacted much from others it was because she had been always prepared to grant them all they could claim, though she had to trample down her own heart in the process.

On August 17th, 1761, the girl-bride left Strelitz never to return; for then it was emphatically demanded of a bride in a high place that she must forget her people and her father's house. Her brother accompanied her to Stade, and she had with her a life-long friend who figured for many years at the English

Court as Madame Schwellenberg. George, like his successors, suffered his bride to come to him. Charles I. when Prince of Wales stole *incognito* to Spain to be introduced to the Infanta who was not to become his Queen. His father James when crowned King of Scotland dared the voyage to Denmark to bring Anne to Holyrood; but such gallantry was not to be found in modern Princes.

From Cuxhaven Charlotte embarked on the Royal Yacht convoyed by an English fleet under the naval hero, Lord Anson. She had a stormy passage of a week's duration. She bore the discomfort with courage, cheerfully declining to be ill for more than the first half hour. She played a great deal on the harpsichord which had been provided for her, and sang to her own accompaniment, doubtless anxiously practising the talent for which she was distinguished. She arrived on Sunday afternoon at Harwich. Not even as far as Harwich did the King go to welcome her. When the news reached London next morning there was great excitement about how and when the Queen was to arrive, but there was no effort on the part of George, willing bridegroom as he was, to anticipate the moment of the meeting. Neither did the bride show any indecorous haste to complete her journey. She did not land till Monday afternoon, when, after being received by the Mayor, she took coach. She only proceeded in a leisurely way as far as Colchester, where she was entertained at the house of a local magnate with tea and coffee, and received graciously the presentation of a specimen of a local production called "candied Eringo root." She then proceeded, on the August evening, as far as Witham, where she halted for supper and a bed at the mansion of Lord Abercorn. Her host happened to be in London, so that she arrived unexpectedly, but she was immediately received with all hospitality and honour. She supped in public with open doors where the people might gather to look at her, while Lord Hardwicke and Lord Anson stood one on either side of her chair. It was a severe ordeal for a youthful foreigner, but if ever a girl of sixteen could surmount it bravely, with dignity and grace, it was this little Charlotte of Mecklenburg-Strelitz. Whether she slept the sweet, sound sleep of youth after her fatigue and her first supper in public, or whether she lay awake in the summer dusk thinking how strange it was and looking forward with a beating heart to the next day's meeting with the handsome lad whose miniature she had eagerly studied, on whom so much of her future well-being and happiness depended, who can tell?

The next morning Charlotte journeyed to Romford where she was to stop at the house of a wine-merchant named Dalton and await the royal servants and carriages sent for her entrance into London. She had dressed carefully for the occasion according to what was considered "English taste" in "a fly cap with rich lace lappets" (think of the little girlish face in this matronly guise!), a stomacher ornamented with diamonds, and a gold brocade suit of clothes with a white ground. Apparently she changed her mind in the course of the day and put on garments which were less approved of. She is described by a critical observer as "hideously dressed in a blue satin quilted *Jesuit*" (Joseph or Spencer?) "which came up to her chin and down to her waist, her hair twisted up in knots called a *tête de mouton*, and the strangest little blue coif at the top." She wore jewels including ear-rings with many drops, the gift of the Empress of Russia.

One of Charlotte's ladies seems to have taken it upon her to hint that an improvement might be made on her toilette by curling her toupée; but the Princess at once showed that, juvenile as she was, she would not allow a liberty to be taken with her or submit to be dictated to by a member of her suite. She answered with spirit and good sense that she thought it (her toupée) looked as well as that of any of the ladies sent to fetch her: if the King bid her she would wear a periwig, otherwise she would remain as she was.

Charlotte and her suite, her German ladies and her English lords, occupied three carriages. She entered London by the wretched suburbs of Mile End and Whitechapel (so that it must have needed the rejoicing crowds assembled in the streets to gaze and shout a welcome, whose numbers and bearing surprised and amazed her, to turn aside her attention from the poverty-stricken aspect of this approach to the capital).

By a long *détour* the cavalcade reached Oxford Street and Hyde Park. As it entered on Constitution Hill, one of the ladies, probably with intention, made the disquieting remark, "We shall hardly have time to dress for the wedding."

"Wedding!" cried the young girl, who had not realised that her fate was to be sealed so soon.

"Yes, madam, it is to be at twelve o'clock" (that night).[1]

Courageous as Charlotte was the shock of the information after the long strain of excitement was too much for her, and she grew white and faint. Lady Effingham threw the contents of a bottle of lavender water on the Princess's face. Struggling back to consciousness Charlotte saw the Duchess of Hamilton smiling to reassure her, when she was herself again on the instant, and made the animated protest, "My dear Duchess, you may laugh; you have been married twice, but it is no joke to me."

[1] The old-established usage was for royal weddings and funerals to be celebrated at night.

In truth a royal marriage with all its authorised credentials must have seemed a simple matter to Elizabeth, double Duchess of Hamilton and Argyll. She was none other than one of the beautiful Irish adventuresses, the Gunnings. According to contemporary gossip, she had been induced by her friends (in order to acquire for the first time the coronet graced by the strawberry-leaves) to take the Duke of Hamilton at his word at the close of a debauch when the time and the place were alike so unpropitious that only a curtain ring could be found to serve as the token of the union of two hearts and lives.

These picturesque days had their dark shadows as well as their high lights.

At the garden gate of St. James's Palace the bride's lips trembled and she looked paler than ever, but her self-possession did not desert her. She alighted, assisted by her chamberlain, the Duke of Devonshire, and found herself face to face with the King, his mother the Princess of Wales, his brothers and sisters and the Court. She would have knelt on the crimson cushion put down for her, but the King took her kindly in his arms and "all but carried her upstairs." Sharp-eyed, sharp-tongued courtiers would have it that with his fancy filled with the images of the loveliest women of the time, when George's glance first rested on his little bride, with no more than an April charm, he winced and his face fell. If so, all that was best in his nature responded also to her youth, her sex, her absolute dependence on his generosity and tenderness. He was prepared from that moment to be a kind and faithful husband to her, as she was, in a manner in which wilful and light-minded Lady Sarah Lennox could never have been, to be a faithful and loving wife to him.

Charlotte was presented to the Princess of Wales, who welcomed her as the wife she had chosen for her son, and to those of his brothers and sisters who were of an age to appear in company; among them were Edward Duke of York, next brother to the King, and his elder sister the "Lady Augusta," as her father had chosen to call her. The King's uncle "Bluff Bill," the soldier Duke of Cumberland, was also present, a conspicuous figure in the scene. A drawing-room was held (drawing-rooms were evening functions then), when the various Court functionaries and the ten bridesmaids were presented to the bride. "There are so many of them, so many of them," she said dizzily in French. She might also have exclaimed anew on the personal beauty of Englishwomen, for among the "maids" were three famous beauties, Lady Sarah Lennox, of whom the Princess was the unconscious rival, Lady Caroline Russell, and Lady Elizabeth Keppel. The tenth was to afford one of the strong contrasts of the period. She was Lady Susan Strangways, a daughter of the Earl of Ilchester. She figures along with her cousin Lady Sarah Lennox and the boy Charles James Fox in Sir Joshua Reynold's renowned picture. Under the plea of giving "a sitting" for this picture she left her father's house in order to elope with a well-known actor whose fortunes she followed to America, where she died. Such a misalliance on the lady's side was unheard of in the great world of a century ago. Lady Susan was the original of Thackeray's "Lady Maria" in his novel *The Virginians*.

In the course of these drawing-room presentations Charlotte forgot to hold out her hand to be kissed, so that her new sister, the Lady Augusta, never loth to come forward, had to capture the dainty hand and hold it out to those who were to do its mistress homage.

At nine (not twelve) o'clock at night the crowning event of the agitating day took place. The marriage ceremony was performed in the Chapel Royal, St. James's. The bride was given away by the Duke of Cumberland. Her dress was white velvet, while her slight girlish figure was half shrouded by a violet velvet mantle lined with crimson. It was fastened on her shoulder by a bunch of large pearls, but the weight of the mantle dragged it half off her shoulders. When it is taken into consideration that the season was early September and the evening hot for the month, the costume must have been oppressive. But the wearied little heroine of the spectacle bore up gallantly under the infliction, till the guns from the Tower and the Park thundered out their salutation, prompting Charlotte to ask first herself and then her newly-wedded husband with ingenuous wonder was it all for her? Was she worthy of such honours?

There was still the great dinner or supper before and after which she exerted herself to converse with those nearest to her in the various tongues, with which she had a creditable speaking acquaintance. If she knew herself eclipsed in good looks she would show wherein she did excel. She fell back on her beloved spinet. She played with taste and feeling some of the lessons which such masters as Handel and Haydn wrote for their pupils, and she sang to her own accompaniment. Here she had young George at her feet. He dearly loved music, and he had learned from his grandfather George II. to appreciate Handel. She thus exhibited her different accomplishments modestly and with an innocent dauntless determination that she would do herself, her friends, and her training all justice. One is reminded of the Tudor bridegrooms and their brides and how even dignified Catherine of Arragon danced with one of her ladies before Prince Arthur in order to show that her education had not been neglected.

After dinner Charlotte appeared in the gallery and at various windows in order to be seen by the populace. The day after the marriage there was the wedding drawing-room, to which the ten bridesmaids came in their white lutestrings trimmed with silver. The Queen did not speak because in a sense she knew nobody and the company were only in the act of being presented to her. But the dulness and formality were brightened to her by the King's standing at her side and speaking much to her in the kindest manner. Even such a worldling and cynic as Horace Walpole augured well for the future happiness of the royal pair by their attitude towards each other in their early days of acquaintance and wedlock. There was a Court ball the same night. It was opened by the Lady Augusta, who danced with her brother Edward, Duke of York.

The King and Queen went in state, amidst throngs of applauding on-lookers, to Church, where George had forbidden the Court preacher to disgrace his sacred office and offend his sovereign's ears by personal, fulsome eulogy. They went also in state to witness a play at Drury Lane.

The coronation came next, for George had deferred it for himself till his Queen should be crowned along with him. . Then was the opportunity for masses of the people to see and greet her in the procession to Westminster Abbey. Unfortunately, they were not near enough to judge of the redeeming traits in her personal appearance, and for the play of countenance which made up for the absence of positive beauty. The public was disappointed, and did not hesitate to express its disappointment plainly. This was the only mortifying incident in the grand pageant—more splendid and more picturesque, in the retention of old usages, than those which had gone before it since the accession of the House of Hanover, or in subsequent coronations. The sermon was preached by Drummond, Bishop of Salisbury; the act of crowning the pair in their robes of state was performed by Secker, Archbishop of

Canterbury. George insisted, with manly reverence, on laying aside the crown when he took the Communion. Queen Charlotte was forced to retain her crown because it was so small it had to be steadied on her rolled-up hair and could not be withdrawn without the disarrangement of the entire *chevelure*. When the procession repaired to Westminster Hall for the banquet the King wore his crown, while he bore in his hands the orb and sceptre; the Queen, wearing her crown and carrying her sceptre and rod, followed him. The old custom was still observed of the courses of the banquet, which was served on gold plate, being ushered in by three peers—Earl Talbot, the Earl of Effingham, and the Duke of Bedford—on horseback prancing and curvetting up the hall as far as the daïs where the King and Queen sat. A comical incident marred the perfect gravity of the actors in this ceremony—the admired conclusion of which was the three noblemen causing their horses to walk backwards the length of the hall and so to pass out of the presence of royalty. Earl Talbot had carefully trained his horse in this the most difficult feat of the whole performance, and the animal had learned its lesson only too well. When the three gentlemen rode into the hall and proceeded to advance towards the high table, the conscientious brute insisted on turning its own back and its master's to the King and Queen and thus riding up to the daïs, so covering its unfortunate owner with discomfiture and awaking half-smothered laughter all over the august assemblage.

The ancient challenge by the King's hereditary champion was also delivered. He rode up the hall and flung down his gauntlet while he recited the claims of George III. to be King of Great Britain and Ireland and summoned any man who denied them to mortal combat. No partisan of the House of Stewart made his way to the front, caught up and carried off the gauntlet as Sir Walter Scott made Redgauntlet do in support of a Jacobite tradition. A third curious practice was maintained at the Coronation Ball on the night after the coronation, when the Duke of Ancaster, whose Duchess had escorted Charlotte from Germany and was installed as her Mistress of the Robes, presented himself in the complete dress which the King had worn the day before and had afterwards bestowed as a high compliment on the Duke.

When these inevitably grave ceremonies and gay rejoicings were ended the Court settled down into what was to be its every-day life. This was marked by a well-ordered simplicity and a virtuous, affectionate domesticity, rare in royal annals at any time, and especially rare a century ago. Dissipated men about town, women of fashion craving for excitement and finding it in a constant racket of routs, *ridottos*, auctions, etc., might complain of the dulness of the Court, but the nation at large, above all the better part of it, sick of the mingled coarseness, waste, and profligacy which had distinguished the last years of the Court of George II., welcomed gladly a new *régime*, a reverent, honest, sound and sweet reign which did much to reform social vices and abuses throughout the country. Whatever might have been the intellectual rather than the moral shortcomings of the young King and Queen this inestimable credit is due to them. They raised the standard of belief and behaviour throughout Great Britain. High and low, who had any worth themselves, were proud of their good young King and Queen and thought twice before indulging in senseless profusion, not to say in riot and debauchery, when they recalled that wisely temperate and modestly economical household in the highest place in the kingdom. If the quiet decorum and strict frugality were carried too far and provoked future rebounds into foolish and shameless excess, the error proceeded from defects in temperament and judgment which were perhaps inevitable. Neither King George nor Queen Charlotte had the smallest taste for display and extravagance, for late hours in the company of the great idle world which cared nothing for its sovereigns, and only desired to use them as tools to countenance its own frivolity and folly. The King and Queen could be splendid and sumptuous on occasions in dispensing or accepting hospitality, but they did not care for splendour or sumptuousness in themselves. A visit to the opera once a week, an occasional appearance at the theatre formed enough public gaiety for the couple. Their private relaxations were unceremonious visits to the City for the purpose of becoming acquainted with its industries and manufactures or of inspecting its lions; such was the witnessing the Lord Mayor's Show from the private house of Barclay, the great Quaker silk mercer, opposite Bow Church.

But the rural pleasures of Richmond and Kew far outweighed in the royal eyes the diversions offered by the town. At old Richmond Lodge, which was George and Charlotte's country house till the old palace at Kew, with the gardens adjoining those of Richmond Lodge, was left vacant by the death of the Princess of Wales, the Queen gave such simple little parties as a well-to-do citizen might have given, in which ten or twelve young couples were refreshed with tea and danced to their hearts' content for three or four hours. In the morning the King had his kingly business and his hunting, while the Queen had her reading, her music, her needlework, with her daily walk or drive. In the last reign nightly gambling had been the evening routine, in which not only the King but his daughters, the Princesses—notably Princess Emily—and the ladies and gentlemen of the suites won and lost large sums. This was replaced, under King George and Queen Charlotte, when the family were alone, by a game of chess, of which the King was fond, or a game of backgammon played by the King and one of his gentlemen, or a game of cribbage in which the Queen took part. If card-playing had a place it was in the shape of some innocent sociable game which did not drain the lightest purse. But mostly the evening was occupied with music, which the King loved, in which the Queen excelled, or the Queen worked at her embroidery and the King read aloud what were reckoned standard books.

With remarkable good sense for so young a girl the Queen devoted much of the first year of her married life to her education, not to gadding here and there pursuing pleasure in any form, or to the eager exhibition of all the fine dress and jewels to which the homely but well-bred little German Princess had succeeded, which she might now wear every day in the week. The resolution which she carried out was to accomplish a serious study of the English language under a competent tutor. A like course in French had been prescribed for poor Marie Antoinette; but the youthful Dauphiness, though she had the fairy gift of beauty, with an ineffable charm which Queen Charlotte lacked, was giddy where Charlotte was sedate, and idle where Charlotte was diligent. For practice in her attainments, Queen Charlotte had those evening readings of the King to which she listened dutifully and attentively for his sake as well as for her own, that his mind not less than hers should be cultivated as became his rank and dignity. When the two were in their happy country retirement the Queen not only rode and drove with the King in the hours when he was at liberty to enjoy her company, but a favourite resort in their afternoons for a period of years was a garden pavilion (these were the days of pavilions and summer-houses), where the

Queen's fingers were busy with her needlework and the King's readings were resumed with greater leisure. Unfortunately, George, who was dull as a boy, remained a stupid man; but that was neither his fault nor his Queen's—she made the best of him and of herself. The result where she was concerned was that, while she had not the brilliance any more than she had the coarseness and unscrupulousness (as far as a virtuous woman could be unscrupulous) of her predecessor on the throne, George's grandmother, Queen Caroline, and though Charlotte could hardly be called a woman of talent and was without a spark of genius, she was an intelligent, well-informed, and by dint of her energy and perseverance a fairly well-read English lady. She might prefer Beattie as a poet just as George preferred West as a painter to their more gifted compeers, but that was a defect in perception which no amount of culture could have prevented.

The young Queen in her seclusion was not insensible to the benefit to trade of such seasonable *fêtes* as she inaugurated at Buckingham House and attended in the houses of the nobility with becoming magnificence. Her presence along with that of the King at the weddings or the christenings of the golden youth of the kingdom; the royal progresses to this subject's country seat, to grace the great universities, to honour a favourite admiral on board his man-of-war, were all as they should have been, models of stately simplicity, of frank, well-nigh boyish cordiality on the honest King's part, and on the Queen's unaffected, gracious interest in all around her. As a bride Charlotte had no objection to deck herself with her ornaments; indeed, she had a woman's love of jewels, and she had not only the Queen-Consort's jewels for her lifetime, but George showed his affection for his young wife by magnificent presents of jewels to her in her own person.

Still she judged that jewels should be worn in season, not out of season. Walpole tells a story illustrative of the subjection in which the Princess of Wales, who was not a favourite either with the Court or the people, tried to hold her daughter-in-law. Charlotte and George were going to take the Communion, a solemn duty which was then discharged in semi-state. Charlotte's dead mother had made her promise not to wear jewels on so sacred an occasion, and she was prepared to keep her pledge. Her intention was discovered by the officious tattling Princess Augusta, who conveyed it to her mother. The Princess of Wales then, in spite of the Queen's promise and of her tears of remonstrance at being compelled to break it, so insisted, and so employed the authority which she had been accustomed to exercise over her son, that Charlotte had to kneel before the altar and confess her sins in glittering array. Long afterwards, when no doubt jewels, except for their marketable value, had palled upon the Queen, she told Fanny Burney that after the first few times of wearing the crown diamonds, when she had been entranced like a child with their splendour, they grew rapidly a care and burden to her; the trouble of having them selected and put upon her, the dread of losing them, the obligation to restore them with her own hands to the firm of bankers with whom they were habitually deposited, did more than qualify the passing intoxication of girlish pride and vanity.

The King and Queen rose at six o'clock and went to bed early to ensure health of body and mind. When in town the pair were carried in their sedan chairs every evening at eight from St. James's and Buckingham House to Carlton House to pay their respects to the Princess of Wales. There was a large household of young people under her roof—lads who were already, or were about to be Dukes of York, Cumberland, and

Gloucester; girls who were soon promoted to matronhood, as the Duchess of Brunswick and the Queen-Consort of Denmark.

The sickly little Princess Elizabeth, whose precocious ability and child-wisdom had impressed even a *moqueur* like Horace Walpole, was followed to the grave by Prince Frederick William, a promising boy of fifteen, and Princess Louisa, a bright amiable girl, who fell a victim to consumption in her twentieth year. None of the survivors, unless the young King, was distinguished by even ordinary discretion. Thick-headed and obstinate as George has been considered, he had the sense and stability in which his younger brothers failed. His elder sister, Augusta, who styled herself his "favourite sister," was a chatterbox, and was to merge into a vulgar gossip and mischief-maker. Caroline Matilda, a fair-haired, handsome girl, was indeed quick-witted and high-spirited, but she was rash, impulsive, and destitute of the self-restraint, reasonableness, and prudence which were Charlotte's safeguards. In looking back on the family one can understand why their clever aunt, Princess Emily, called her troop of nephews and nieces "the best-natured young asses in England."

For good nature in youth is frequently only another name for youth's light-heartedness and buoyancy. These are elements welcome to kindred youth; they must have lent somewhat of a gay and breezy atmosphere—in which there was room for skirmishes and jars without question, while it was still the natural environment of life in its early vigour—to Carlton House. It was the home of a staid and severe Princess, who had been a strict disciplinarian to her little boys and girls, but who was no more able to command her young men and women than similar mothers frequently find themselves.

Charlotte was not forgotten by her own family, neither did she forget them; though in those non-travelling days she could not hope to revisit Germany, nor could she trust that her sister or her girl-friends would brave the perils and discomforts of a journey of many weeks to visit her. She had to content herself with sending them letters and gifts, but she had the gratification of receiving each of her three brothers. She had the still further satisfaction of finding the appointment of Governor of Zell conferred by George on her second brother.

From the first Charlotte adopted the sagacious policy of non-interference in State affairs. It may be thought that a girl of sixteen had small temptation to such interference, but one must recall the kind of girl she was, serious, shrewd, capable of a keen interest in all which concerned the welfare of the King and country, in order to give her credit for her modesty and moderation in remembering her foreign origin and her proper sphere as a Queen-Consort. She refrained from every attempt to put her finger in the Government pie. She did not seek to wield any undue influence. She did not dictate or take the first place in any relation of life, a fatal fault not uncommon in Queen-Consorts, and not rare in women of all ranks who have decided views and resolute wills. Charlotte could hardly be called an ambitious woman. She usurped no province, was no interloper, no arrogant intruder into domains beyond her knowledge and scope. She had her reward in many years of domestic happiness, and in her early popularity with her husband's subjects of all grades of intelligence and all shades of political opinion. In this respect she stood in strong contrast to the Princess of Wales, who, rightly or wrongly, was accused of trying to rule the King, her son, in his public capacity. For this reason as well as for the absence in her of all winning grace and graciousness she was heartily detested by the nation. As for Queen Charlotte, she lived to realise in full the fickleness of the mob; but those dark days were still far ahead.

The Queen pursued the same upright friendly course in reference to her husband's family. She abstained from questioning their rights. She was on good terms, in the main, with her mother-in-law, to whom Charlotte always behaved with fitting respect. So long as George's sisters remained in England, and his maiden aunt, Princess Emily, survived, the Queen treated them with kindness and consideration. To have gone further, to have allowed them the privilege of more intimate friendship, would have been in all probability to undermine her position, and to render it difficult, if not intolerable, for her as Queen.

Augusta was a foolish Mrs. Malaprop, a creature without natural reverence or truthfulness, whose tongue was as disrespectful as it was glib. Dr. Doran, who was severe enough to Augusta's foibles in the end, seems to have adopted the spiteful gossip of the time on the King and Queen's behaviour to her at the date of her marriage with the brave, rough soldier, the Duke of Brunswick. Doran dwells on the shabbiness, the positive penuriousness of the marriage doings. Another authority, who must have had warrant for his statement, tells a different tale. He enlarges on the supper at Leicester House on the evening of the marriage day, at which the King and Queen, the Princess of Wales, and the younger members of her family, together with the bride and bridegroom, were present ; on the ball afterwards, which was opened by the Duke and Duchess of Brunswick ; on the special drawing-room given in the couple's honour, with the farewell concert, supper, and ball which followed. He mentions among the gifts to the fairly dowered Princess the King's diamond necklace, valued at £30,000, the Princess of Wales's diamond stomacher, and the Queen's exquisite gold watch set with jewels.

When the King was greatly displeased, with much

reason, by his brother's idleness and dissipation, and in the case of the Dukes of Gloucester and Cumberland by their misalliances with two widows—the Duke of Gloucester marrying the beautiful Lady Waldegrave, a kinswoman of Horace Walpole's; the Duke of Cumberland Mrs. Horton, one of a wild, racketing county family of the name of Luttrell—the royal sister-in-law of the culprits, however offended in her own sense of what was due to the King and to herself, did not seek to increase her husband's resentment. It resulted in the passing of the Royal Marriage Act, precluding the marriages of members of the royal family without the consent of the sovereign and the Houses of Parliament. Edward, Duke of York, who was nearest the King in age, was as unprofitable a representative of the race as were his younger brothers. He did not marry, though he kept the upper circles of society ringing with rumours of some more or less imprudent match on his part. However, he was not to blame for the persistent claim on his regard, and the mysterious hints of a secret marriage circulated by a third widow, one of the most incorrigibly wilful and perverse of the fine ladies of the day.

Lady Mary Coke, born Lady Mary Campbell ("the White Cat"), had more than the albino fairness of her skin, the light colour of her hair and eyebrows and the alternate sleepy blink and angry blaze of her eyes to ally her with the feline tribe. She was largely endowed with a certain tricksiness and mischievousness of conduct. To such an extent did she carry her unwarranted pretensions to the hand of the Duke of York, that though her assertions were unsupported by any attentions on his part, and were flatly contradicted by his family, she assumed the airs of an ardently wooed, privately wedded wife. She went abroad on an ostentatious visit to his aunt Mary, Princess of Hesse. When the news arrived of his death from fever at Monaco (he was the only one of the brothers who had developed a taste for travelling, and had repaired to Italy, possibly in flight from the craze of Lady Mary), she shut herself up as if in the extremity of grief, and reappeared in public presently in what was the nearest approach to widow's weeds, till the dead man's aunt, Princess Emily, took the audacious pretender to task for her mingled deceit and impertinence. The final froward act of this extraordinary being, after she had reached old age, was to refuse to change her dress, or to lie down in her last illness, so that she actually died with a steeple-crowned felt hat, adorned by a plume of feathers, on her head.

But the real tragedy among George III.'s brothers and sisters was the melancholy fate of his sister, Princess Caroline Matilda. With this Queen Charlotte had nothing to do either in advocating or in reprobating the disastrous marriage which led to the catastrophe. Indeed, no alliance could have appeared more suitable and promising beforehand. Princess Caroline Matilda was troth-plighted to Christian VII., the young King of Denmark, who was her cousin through his mother Princess Louisa, one of the younger daughters of George II. and Queen Caroline, a sister to Fritz, Prince of Wales, father of the present bride. She had shown no reluctance to the marriage with her kinsman, an idea with which she had been familiar for years, since at the time of the betrothal both bride and bridegroom were considerably under age. It was in the usual order of such alliances that the couple had not met, and were personally unacquainted with each other, and that even when the marriage took place at Carlton House, Edward, Duke of York, was proxy for the bridegroom. The only person who seems to have foreboded evil was the stiff and sombre Princess of Wales. Caroline's tears at parting from her mother and family were a simple tribute to the fact that she was not likely to see them again, that when a Princess married a foreign Prince she, of all women, was destined, in the quaint language of an old song, to "drink the brewst" she had brewed to the dregs, unsupported and unrelieved. Bitter indeed was the "brewst" which poor Caroline had to drink; but so little did she foresee it that she arrived in her adopted country in the fearless spirit which dictated the proud, cheerful message which she sent back by the captain of the frigate in which she had sailed to the King, her brother, that his sister had borne the discomforts of the voyage as an Englishwoman should. She might have been her predecessor Princess Louisa, whose memory the Danes long cherished, who, when she came to Denmark, consented to the return of all her English ladies and attendants, saying that she herself was thenceforth to be a Dane. But, as it happened, the circumstances and the sequel were wholly different. The King whom Caroline Matilda went bravely and light-heartedly to marry was so tiny in person as to be likened to a fairy Prince when he came to England a year or two after his marriage, unaccompanied by his wife, in the course of travel he was pursuing.

At the same time a resemblance was traced between him and his portly cousin, King George, and, what was felt to be a little ominous, between him and his wrongheaded uncle, Fritz, Prince of Wales. Still, though small and pale, King Christian was neither misshapen nor ugly in the sense in which his uncle by marriage, the Prince of Orange, who came to wed Princess Anne, eldest daughter of George II., had horrified his worthy mother-in-law on the occasion of his visit. King Christian was credited with a fair amount of brains, though the faithful chronicler goes on to state that he "strutted about like a cock-sparrow." In truth, he was weak, both in body and mind, and was completely in the power of the Queen-Dowager, Julia Maria, who rivalled in wickedness the most black-hearted stepmother of fiction. Her scheme was to get rid of the incapable King, either by his early death or by shutting him up as insane, and to place on the throne in his stead his younger brother, her own son, Prince Frederick. Caroline and the children she bore to King Christian were formidable obstacles in the Queen-Dowager's path, and she hated and plotted against them accordingly. Caroline behaved, in the miserable situation, as a very young, dauntless, passionate girl might have been expected to behave. Finding that her husband was an utterly untrustworthy stay, she went her own way in reckless defiance of the sharp eyes and cruel tongue of the Queen-Dowager and the malicious gossip of a divided Court. Not content with amusing herself by riding and hunting in a fashion not practised in Denmark, she played such pranks as disguising herself in a young man's suit of clothes and seeking foolish adventures under false colours. There was a picture of her, which may still be extant, in a page's dress, with her long fair curls (a reversion of her father's and her grandmother's beautiful hair) escaping from their confinement and betraying her sex, while she held the horse of Count Struensee, of all people. Alienated from her half-imbecile husband by the wiles and misrepresentations of Queen Julia Maria, Queen Caroline seemed to wake up to her danger; but alas! the steps she took only accelerated her ruin. King Christian had come across the clever young doctor Struensee and had taken a great fancy to him, ennobling him, and gradually entrusting a large share of the government to him in gratitude for the improvement in the King's health effected by his following Struensee's advice.

Caroline had recourse to Struensee to reconcile her to her husband and to counsel her in turn. There is no proof that Struensee abused the confidence of either husband or wife. Where his country was concerned, he strove to serve it as an enlightened reformer of many existing errors in the constitution. If personal ambition had something to do with his zeal it was the only fault that could be fairly and plainly laid to his charge.

For a time the King stood by his minister, and Caroline, eager in everything she did, courted his friendship, and entered warmly into his reforms. But a reformer is sure to create enemies, and there was one deadly enemy already in the field, who caught at the association of Struensee and Queen Caroline as a means of accomplishing their ruin and furthering her cherished project by one decisive blow. Julia Maria again secured the ear of the King and poisoned his weak mind beyond recovery. Struensee was arrested and executed on a charge of high treason. Caroline was also arrested in her palace on the accusation of complicity with Struensee and infidelity to her husband. She was hurried to Cronberg, where her life might have been taken also, had it not been for the spirited intervention of Sir Robert Keith, who was lying with his fleet in the Baltic. He obtained her liberation on condition that she should be taken to Zell, to remain a prisoner in the Castle of Zell. There, separated from her husband and her children, in disgrace and confinement, to the last solemnly asserting her innocence, she died after three years at the age of twenty-four. The Princess of Wales did not long survive her younger daughter's downfall; she died at Carlton House, dutifully waited upon by the King and Queen, and was buried in Westminster Abbey.

Quite early in Queen Charlotte's happy married life, a cloud no bigger than a man's hand, and yet sadly indicative of what might happen, appeared on the horizon, and though it passed away as quickly as it came, could never have been altogether absent from the Queen's mind in time to come, and must have left on it a shadow of doubt and dread haunting her even in her brightest moments.

When George was a mere lad, before his grandfather's death, it is said there had been occasional symptoms in the heir to the throne of threatening brain disease, hanging over his doomed head—such an honest, manly head in its very limitations and in its dogged blunders! He was not a strong lad, and the consumption which carried off his youngest brother and sister was feared for him. He escaped that danger, and by temperate dieting he was enabled to check the corpulence which was a tendency of his family. It culminated in "Bluff Bill," the "Butcher" of Culloden, William, Duke of Cumberland, George's uncle, who was enormously stout. But while the King and Queen's marriage was yet young, and every prospect was bright, George had one of his premonitory attacks, when it was necessary to seclude him from company and to avoid all excitement. The particulars were kept closely hidden from the public, but think of the shock to the young wife, the bolt from the blue which ever afterwards hung over her, even when the sky was most serene! And she had to mask her feelings, go in state to the royal chapel every day, and hold drawing-rooms in order not to alarm the country. Happily a few days' retirement dissipated the fever of body and mind, and for a long time the terrible malady was in abeyance. Charlotte celebrated her King's recovery by a birthday surprise for him in the shape of what was called the "transparency" of a temple, at the gate of which the King appeared, dispensing peace to all the world.

These transparencies were simple " make-believes," in great request at the time. They appear to have been composed of oiled silk cut and fastened together in the figures to be represented and illuminated from within. On one of the Queen's birthdays a famous exhibition of transparencies, in which the whole royal family were symbolised,[1] was part of an entertainment got up in Charlotte's honour by no less a person than Miss Chudleigh who, strange to say, was one of the good girl-Queen's maids-of-honour. Where will not folly and wickedness enter in? For Lady Mary Coke's performances were nothing to Miss Chudleigh's. She married privately a son of the Earl of Bristol, who was a sailor and for the most part of his time at sea. In his absence, his wife, still passing to the world as Miss Chudleigh, received an offer of marriage from the Duke of Kingston. Loth to lose the opportunity of becoming a Duchess, the lady drove down in her coach to the village church in which she had been married, asked for the register, and there in the light of day, before the astounded eyes of the clergyman, boldly tore out and demolished the page on which the marriage had been recorded. She was under the credulous conviction that by withdrawing this important piece of evidence she annulled the marriage; so she went back and without any further sign married the Duke of Kingston. But the sailor husband, who was by this time Earl of Bristol, returned and took his revenge by claiming his wife, and a trial for the crime of bigamy on the part of the Countess or Duchess ensued. She demanded the privilege of being tried before the House of Peers, as she herself was a peeress, whether as Countess of Bristol or Duchess of Kingston. Part of the sentence pronounced upon her—the part which was commuted—was that she should be branded on the hand by the common hangman in punishment of her misdeed. The lights and shadows of those bygone days were strong

---

[1] The emblems were somewhat far-fetched and consisted of birds of Paradise, orange-trees, etc.

indeed; the good were very good, the sinners sinned "as with a cart rope."

Great events were stirring and shaking the world at home and abroad: the rise of Methodism, when the Wesleys and Whitfield had the glory of re-christianising the dark places of England, and made converts among the noble women as St. Paul did of old—notable among them being Lady Huntingdon, Lady Chesterfield and in Scotland Lady Glenorchy; the American war ran its course, and to George's mortification he saw his greatest colony wrested from him; the "No Popery" riots convulsed London, which was for days at the mercy of the mob, while the King and Queen remained intrepidly at their posts, he at St. James', she at Buckingham House, or, as it was more commonly called, the Queen's House; Clive and Warren Hastings were annexing territories in India, Clive laying a portion of the spoils in a cluster of magnificent diamonds at the feet of the Queen, and still George continued sound in body and sane in mind.

CHAPTER II.

A ROYAL WIFE AND MOTHER.

QUEEN CHARLOTTE from the day when she arrived a girl-bride in England had a generous desire to be a Queen-mother to her husband's people.

It has been customary in later times to dwell on the homely but honourable thrift practised in the royal household as not only humdrum, but parsimonious, and to allege that Queen Charlotte, brought up at a small niggardly German Court, was the author of the parsimony; yet no more munificent Queen to the poor and destitute ever reigned in England, in spite of the fact that she had no privy purse and only received twenty thousand a year to keep up her house (Buckingham House) and discharge her personal debts. No doubt the economy enabled her to be munificent. One of the earliest institutions which she established and maintained during her whole long married life was a home for orphan girls of gentle birth—a little on the model of Madame Maintenon's school of St. Cyr. In the Queen's home the girls were instructed in the old womanly art of embroidery so as to earn a livelihood by it. The first specimens of their matured skill and taste were always offered to the Queen, who was pleased to accept them for bed and window curtains, and covers to chairs and settees in the palace, where they could be seen and recommended to the patronage of the royal tradesmen and to such mistresses of great households as loved to be in the royal fashion. For the support of this school Charlotte annually set apart five hundred pounds.[1]

Another benevolent establishment instituted by her was the great Lying-in Hospital (for the wives of respectable working men) which still bears her name. These were her public acts of beneficence; her private charities were as liberal as they were judicious.

To her own numerous children Charlotte was an assiduously careful and kind mother. If she was strict it was in what she believed was their best interest. She loved to have her family with her; she taught the eldest of them their first lessons, she overlooked their studies and shared their pleasures. While they were still young when they were sick she shut herself up with them and nursed them as far as was in her power; she braved public opinion and a mother's nervous fears in having the eldest children inoculated as a defence against smallpox.

A year after her marriage, when Charlotte was not more than seventeen, her Prince of Wales was born. Great was the delight of the King,[2] and the nation rejoiced with the pair. Cake and caudle were free to all who came to the palace (St. James's) to inquire for the Queen and the heir. The festivities threatened to become riotous.

But who can estimate the proud yet humble gladness of the mother of seventeen? She was devoted to the child—a singularly fine baby. It was her loving hand which placed in his lap the patent of his creation as Prince of Wales. His cradle was draped with crimson velvet and lined with white satin; the sheet was

---

[1] She supported entirely or partly a variety of schools; she took under her protection a number of widows in three classes, twelve in each class; to these she gave grants of money paid half yearly in advance, the lowest grant amounting to twenty pounds.

[2] He gave the messenger who brought him the tidings five hundred pounds.

covered with broad Brussels lace, turned over on a quilt of crimson velvet. A nurse sat in state with a crimson velvet cushion on her knee, on which the child was laid; a maid was on each side of the cradle to rock it when necessary. Thackeray refers to a charming picture of Charlotte, in which the beautiful infant lies asleep across one arm, while the other is free to raise a finger as if bespeaking silent respect for the baby Prince's slumbers. The Queen arranged, and she carried out the arrangement afterwards, to teach her boy—an apt pupil in childhood and youth—his letters and to hear him say his first prayers. Who would have dared to predict that he was to live to plant cruel thorns in his mother's breast?

A troop of boys and girls to the number of fourteen followed in the wake of George Augustus Frederick, Prince of Wales. They were brought up in the main wisely and simply. The King hearing from the Duke of Buccleuch that his nursery was flourishing on oatmeal porridge caused an order for oatmeal to be sent at stated intervals to Mr. Mutter of Middle Mills, Lasswade, that the royal children might breakfast on the same wholesome food; and great was the exultation north of the Tweed on this sign of the King's approval of the national dish.

When the Court was at Kew the Princes had a tiny farm which they were taught to cultivate. They sowed it and reaped it. They beat out the corn with their chubby hands; they ground it and baked it into bread which their parents and sisters helped them to eat.

One instance of a mother's fond folly can be brought against Queen Charlotte. She caused a miniature drawing-room to be held for the children of the nobility by the Prince of Wales, aged eight, and the Princess Royal, aged five. It was a pretty mockery of the real ceremony, and the small pair who presided in state and splendour for the occasion are said to have behaved with much dignity and decorum; but the affair was questionable as an interlude in their education. A more unmistakably false step was the separate household provided immediately afterwards for the Prince of Wales and the Duke of York, then styled Bishop of Osnabrück in consequence of his holding the lay bishopric of Osnabrück, which entitled him to draw the revenues without any obligation to assume the priestly office. The step was warranted by precedent, but it was unnatural and artificial, and it was grievously prejudicial in spite of the high characters of the Princes' governors and governess (Lady Charlotte Finch) and the watchful superintendence of the Queen.

The Prince of Wales was a lovely child, a handsome lad, a fine-looking young man. He was more highly gifted intellectually than either father or mother. Indeed, he gave promise of being an able scholar and accomplished gentleman, as his mother had set her heart on his being. But the promise remained unfulfilled. He was destitute of his father's good principles and his mother's conscientiousness; though he could learn quickly, serious application was detestable to him. He was entirely ignorant of the honest, honourable satisfaction of self-denial, of doing his duty in the teeth of opposing inclination. He frittered away his talents in the pursuit of trivialities and the coarsest pleasures. He grew always more effeminate, more insubordinate and overbearing in temper in proportion as he yielded to self-indulgence. The moment the restraints of his minority were withdrawn and he was his own master, his follies, excesses, and rapidly accumulating debts scandalised the King and the country. To be considered "the first gentleman in Europe" in superficial grace and manners, to be reckoned a man of supreme taste and fashion and copied by the other fine gentlemen of the day, were his chief ambitions. It was from no political consideration, but out of sheer desire to thwart and get the better of the father who sought in vain to show him his failure in all which could be claimed from him, that, surrounded as the Prince was by the gay and thoughtless, by unscrupulous sycophants, aspirants for the favour of the future King, he immediately headed the party opposed to that of the King in the House of Parliament and in the nation. The position of the father and son recalled the quarrels between George II. and Frederick, Prince of Wales, and between George II. and George I. when he was Prince of Wales, in the younger man's perverse disobedience and insolent defiance of authority. George Augustus Frederick was the despair of prime ministers, who from William Pitt to the Duke of Wellington were constantly counselling him and remonstrating with him, while they were compelled to endure his capricious arrogance and insincerity. Even his supporter and friend from political motives, Charles James Fox, and his witty playfellow, Richard Brinsley Sheridan, were bitterly ashamed of the Prince's falseness and complete disregard of his word.

Poor Queen Charlotte struggled hard not to realise that the idol of her young motherhood was of basest clay. She hoped against hope for him, excused him, strove to make his peace with the King and, almost to the last, forgave the stabs he inflicted on her dignity as a Queen, wife, and mother, and her tenderness as a woman. She would embroider with her royal hands a dainty vest to be worn on his birthday, and contrive family reunions, innocent dances, and diversions to make the Court livelier for him; only to have the vest received with perfect politeness and tossed aside after one trial, and the family gatherings rendered an affront and disappointment by his coolly and deliberately absenting himself from them.

The Duke of York was much less gifted than his brother. He was a big, burly, hectoring carpet soldier. He followed in his elder brother's footsteps except that his dissipation was of a grosser kind and his tastes lower. But he was bluffly good-natured and he had some fitful filial feeling and family affection.

The third son, the Duke of Clarence, the sailor Prince, had the merits of a sailor-like frankness and simplicity as a qualification to the circumstance that he lacked the good manners of his brothers. He had a rough and rowdy geniality about him when he dispensed lavishly the hospitalities of the Admiralty. He was better liked than his elder brothers, though he did not dream of mastering himself or attempting to walk in the paths of sobriety and moderation.

It was fixed he should come to Windsor for one of the Queen's birthday balls in order that he might dance the first minuet with his pretty lovable sister Princess Mary on her coming out. Unfortunately there was a dinner before the ball, and as no man could sit down before the Queen (unless when etiquette was relaxed in the rural life at Kew), only ladies were admitted to her Majesty's table. The Duke of Clarence, then Prince William, was consigned to the care of the equerries, at whose table he insisted on drinking bumper upon bumper of champagne till, after performing a variety of antics, it was clear that he could neither dance a minuet nor enter a ball-room. On another occasion when he was fit to be his sister's partner, Maria Josepha, daughter of Lord Sheffield and future wife of Lord Stanley of Alderney, was present. She recounts that every time Prince William turned his back to the King he put out his tongue, to the great alarm and distress of Princess Mary. Withal, in later years, when he fell into good hands which he had the grace to appreciate, he proved the genuine kindness of heart which underlay his errors and follies, those of the day still more than of the man. He ended his life very differently from the manner in which his elder brothers ended theirs.

The younger Princes, who grew up and were in succession the Dukes of Kent, Cumberland, Sussex, and Cambridge, did not, to their benefit, inherit the same amount of worldly influence and prosperity which had been the ruin of the firstborn in the family. In fact, during the period of the Regency their just claims were neglected and set aside, and they were condemned to something like obscurity and hardship in their station. With one exception, adversity helped to make better men of them. They were more or less unoffending citizens,[1] good husbands and fathers. The exception was Ernest, Duke of Cumberland, a man of singularly surly uncertain temper. He was, however, less of a carpet knight than the Duke of York. He saw active service, lost an eye and received a slight wound in the battles of the Peninsular War. He married so wilfully and unadvisedly, though his wife was a Princess, that no allowance was voted to him by Parliament, and his Duchess was not received at the Court of Queen Charlotte. He was comparatively little in England in his earlier years, and a story was long current against him to account for his absence. It was said that in a fit of passion he struck one of his servants a violent blow with a cane, which, happening to enter the unfortunate man's eye, caused his death. The story went on to say that on account of the rank of the culprit the affair was hushed up, but that the dread of being called

---

[1] The Duke of Sussex was accomplished for his generation, spoke well and figured as the president of various learned societies and the chairman at many banquets.

to account for the untoward accident kept the Prince out of England. He succeeded to his brother, King William IV., as King of Hanover, in which character he was, in spite of his despotism, borne with by his subjects, and even enjoyed a certain amount of popularity among them.

When William reigned at Windsor and a remark, attributed to the Duke of Cumberland, was repeated to him, he said wrathfully in the hearing of his Court, "The Duke of Cumberland knows nothing about it; but if the Duke of Cumberland can do mischief or say an ill-natured thing he will be sure to do it."

There were two baby Princes, Octavius and Alfred, who brought the royal ranks to a close and soon left their places vacant, dying in infancy.

In her six daughters Queen Charlotte was happy. They were good women, examples to their class and sex. They were the Queen's right hands in her acts of benevolence. For many a day she shared their pursuits, reading and working with them, and studying whatever they studied. In a woman with her strict sense of the obedience and submission due from children to parents and with her German notions of etiquette the association grew somewhat of a yoke which pressed and galled a little when the children themselves were no longer young, and yearned for independence of thought and action; but that was the other side of the shield which only became visible towards the close of the family life. The Princesses had every reason to respect the King and Queen; and while an element of pitying tenderness and anxious apprehension mingled betimes with their reverence for him, they clung in trouble to the strength of mind, authority and experience of the Queen. They were affectionate and attentive to her wishes and tastes. The daughters loved in brighter hours to surprise the mother on her own and on family birthdays with unexpected achievements in ability and industry in decorating Frogmore, which she had bought for her and their special delectation (during the King's life and her own), and as a residence for her unmarried daughters in the future. At Frogmore they could be a private family party holding their gatherings and celebrating their festivals in comparative retirement and peace. We hear most of the Princesses and their doings from Fanny Burney when she chronicled them in her diary during her stay at Court as one of the dressers to the Queen. Her favourite and special Princess was Princess Augusta, who was always affable and engaging to the little authoress whose literary career had been full of brilliance, while there was something of a cloud between Miss Burney and the Princess Royal, of whom we hear from other sources as an amiable and sensible woman. The origin of the cloud was to be found in the stout person and blunt German manners of Mrs. Schwellenberg, the chief dresser, whom the Queen had brought with her in the old days from Germany. Queen Charlotte remained faithfully attached to her old friend and countrywoman, and the Princes and Princesses had been taught to hold one whom they had known from infancy in kindly regard.

But Mrs. Schwellenberg's homely ways were by no means viewed with the same complacency by the King's equerries, over whose tea-table she was, oddly enough, chosen to preside. They were either stiffly distant to her, or they made game of her; but they could carry off the situation better than it could be endured by Fanny Burney, who shared the table. Accustomed to the most intellectual society in London, lionised and petted by its select circles, she could not bear to be condemned to the society of an illiterate old woman who did not hesitate to call her to order and find fault with her with what the younger woman held to be unexampled rudeness. The lively *protégée* of Dr. Johnson and Mrs. Thrale found these to be hard lines, and in spite of her own solid sense and worth showed little forbearance and magnanimity in the detestation which she entertained for Mrs. Schwellenberg; a detestation which the offended dogged elder woman naturally returned with interest.

In the chronic feud the Princess Royal adopted the side of Mrs. Schwellenberg with pardonable warmth, hence the " dryness " which existed between the Princess and the diarist. The Princess Royal married the Crown Prince of Würtemberg and was an excellent wife to him and a good step-mother to his children. The wittiest and most accomplished of the sisters was Princess Elizabeth. In her earlier years a marriage was projected between her and the exiled Duke of Orleans, afterwards King Louis Philippe of France. At his house at Twickenham he was in the neighbourhood of Kew and he was intimate with the Princess's brothers. It was supposed he was inclined to Protestantism. Eventually he gave up Elizabeth for Amelia, the richly endowed daughter of the King of Naples. Elizabeth, though a Princess, was jilted ! She became late in life the wife of the Landgrave of Hesse-Homburg, and like her elder sister was loved and respected in her new relations. The prettiest and sweetest of the Princesses was Princess Mary, who after long delay was wedded to her cousin and first love, William, Duke of Gloucester.

Princess Amelia, the youngest, was the pet and plaything of the others and the cherished darling of the King and Queen. She faded away ere her girlhood was well past, dying as King George's young brother and sister had died, of consumption. Her death was the last blow which overthrew the King's tottering reason. Thackeray in his *Four Georges* quotes some simple pathetic verses which Princess Amelia is said to have written on the contrast between her opening bloom and the swift blight which fell upon it.

Many customs of the time—some of them admirable, some quaintly picturesque, some singularly inconvenient and burdensome—have passed away. Among them was the procession to chapel for morning prayer at eight o'clock through the long corridors. The procession was headed by the King and Queen walking arm-in-arm. The Princesses followed in pairs, and after them the suite. The attendance was not obligatory on the members of the suite, but it was understood the Queen remarked and disapproved of absentees. On the afternoons of Sundays and royal birthdays when the Court was at Windsor and the weather was fine, the King and Queen with their family promenaded on the terrace, which was generally crowded with people of rank and fashion. They came down from London to look at the promenaders, by whom the spectators were graciously noticed as occasion served, the King and Queen stopping for the purpose, with their whole train arrested behind them. Admittance to the terrace was obtained by the public of suitable position who could command the necessary influence. One of the excursions craved by country cousins, come up to town to behold the wonders of the great Metropolis, was that to Windsor with the spectacle of the royal promenade, which enabled the admiring strangers to claim a knowledge by sight of their sovereign and his fine family. When we think of the grey tower of St. George's, the green slopes and glades of Windsor Park, and the splendid company walking on the noble terrace under the summer sunshine we are inclined to commend the taste of the country cousin of last century.

As years rolled on, when the King was blind and infirm, he could be seen walking on the terrace between two of his daughters, his devoted guardians.

The Queen's toilette, which, when she could have her will in a country Paradise, was simple enough in its details, had at other times to be conducted with much state and ceremony. In her dressing-closet she was attended by her dressers, who handed to each other in succession, and finally to Charlotte, the various articles of dress. At the later stages of the process, when she sat in her *peignoir* and had her hair dressed [1] she would receive visitors in the French fashion, or Fanny Burney would vindicate her appointment by reading aloud; but when the powdering crisis came Charlotte was enveloped from head to foot in another dressing-gown and left alone with the performer, who raised dense clouds of powder round himself and the lady whose head he was "drenching" in the approved style. When the Queen retired for the night the King handed her to her dressing-room, to which the grown-up Princesses followed her, kissing her hand as they wished her good-night. Then the requisite garments were handed to her as before, and the ceremony ended; but not without the Queen acknowledging by a punctilious curtsey every act of service rendered to her.

Queen Charlotte took snuff [2] and was a connoisseur with regard to the merits of the best rappee and an adept at having it properly mixed. The mal practice was well-nigh universal in contemporary European Courts. All that strikes us as offensive in the custom was condoned by the supposed elegance with which a fine lady tapped her gold, brilliant-set snuff-box and took a perfumed pinch between her delicate thumb and fore finger. If Queen Charlotte held her fan in one of those beautiful hands of hers, like a Queen, one may be sure that there was also royal dignity in her objectionable snuff-taking.

[1] This operation generally took two hours.
[2] The King's aunt Princess Emily was also a great snuff-taker.

Most biographers of Queen Charlotte quote from Mrs. Delany's letters a visit from the royal family to the Duchess of Portland at Bulstrode. It is a graphic picture of the large young family, headed by the King and Queen, of the lumbering elaboration of their transport and of the mingled state and simplicity which characterised the whole episode. "The King drove the Queen in an open chaise, with a pair of white horses" (to the late breakfast to which they had invited themselves and a large instalment of their offspring). "The Prince of Wales" (whose birthday, August 12th, it was) "and Prince Frederick" (Duke of York) "rode on horseback—all with proper attendants, but no guards—Princess Royal and Lady Weymouth in a post-chaise. Princess Augusta, Princess Elizabeth, Prince Adolphus—about seven years old" (afterwards Duke of Cambridge)—"and Lady Charlotte Finch" (the royal children's governess) "in a coach. Prince William" (afterwards Duke of Clarence and King William IV.), "Prince Edward" (afterwards Duke of Kent), "the Duke of Montagu, and the Bishop of Lichfield in a coach. Another coach full of attendant gentlemen, etc., etc."

Well might Mrs. Delany add that the cavalcade made a splendid figure "as on a brilliant day it drove through the park round the court and up to the house." Of the Queen, the amiable aristocratic letter-writer tells us: "She was in a hat, and in an Italian night-gown" (an anticipation of the modern tea-gown) "of purple lutestring trimmed with silver gauze. She is graceful and genteel.... The three Princesses were all in frocks. The King and all the men in uniform, blue and gold." Part of the entertainment was walking through the suite of eight rooms and examining the pictures and curiosities. The rallying point was the great drawing-room in which there were only two chairs placed in the centre for the King and Queen. "The King, whose conversation" (incessant) "and good humour took off all awe but what one must have for so respectable a character, immediately placed the Duchess of Portland in his chair. Breakfast was offered all prepared in a long gallery that runs the length of the great apartments. . . . The King and all his royal children and the rest of the train chose to go to the gallery where the well-furnished tables were set, one with tea, coffee, and chocolate, another with their proper accompaniment of eatables, rolls, cakes, and another table with fruits and ices. . . . No servants waited but those out of livery. When the Queen chose to have only a dish of tea and a plate of biscuits in the drawing-room, the Duchess brought them on a waiter and served her Majesty." Mrs. Delany stood at the back of the Queen's chair, which happened to be one of Mrs. Delany's working, "and gave the Queen an opportunity to say many obliging things." Her Majesty would not return her empty cup to the Duchess, but "got up and would carry it to the gallery herself. . . . The King desired me to show the Queen one of my books of plants.[1] She seated herself in the gallery, a table and a book laid before her, and I kept my distance till she called me to ask some questions about the mosaic paper-work. As I stood before her Majesty the King set a chair behind me. I turned with some confusion and hesitation on receiving so great an honour, when the Queen said, 'Mrs. Delany, sit down, sit down; it is not every lady who has a chair brought her by a King.' So I obeyed." When Mrs. Delany expressed to her Majesty the pleasure it had given her to pay her duty to the King and Queen and to so many of

---

[1] Mrs. Delany was an accomplished and exquisite worker from her own designs. She was also famous for her copies of plants which she outlined and cut out of paper tinted by herself, pasting the flowers on a black ground.

the royal family, "Oh! but," was the proud mother's answer, "you have not seen all my children yet"; and the King remarked : "You may put Mrs. Delany in the way of doing that by naming a day for her to drink tea at Windsor Castle." Accordingly the next day was fixed upon.

The royal visit to Bulstrode was the introduction of the charming old lady, Mrs. Delany, to the King and Queen. The acquaintance thus begun ripened into a close and sincere friendship highly creditable to the friends on both sides.

As " Mary Granville " Mrs. Delany had been forced in early girlhood into an unsuitable marriage with an old Cornish squire, a boorish sot named Pendarvis. He did not live long, but on his death left her with a bare allowance. The beautiful young widow, born in the reign of Queen Anne, was an acknowledged belle both at the Court of St. James's and in St. Stephen's Green, Dublin. In Ireland she married Dean Delany, a friend of Dean Swift's. A widow for the second time, old and in poor circumstances, she was obliged to her dear friend the Duchess of Portland for a home. When the Duchess's death deprived Mrs. Delany of that refuge the King and Queen assigned her a house in Windsor, close to the gate of the Castle, settled an annuity on her and doubled their kindness by treating her as a cherished personal friend. Hardly a day passed when the King or the Queen did not look in upon her for a dish of tea or a cheerful talk. The Princes and Princesses were constantly invading her little territory, and making much of her. To them she was the most delightful of grandames, full of old stories, endless in her indulgence of their youthful fancies and freaks—a refined, gifted Mrs. Schwellenberg.

An awful interruption came to these artless gaieties and genial charities. It was not the attempt to assassinate the King made by the mad woman, Margaret Nicholson, though that was bad enough. She got so near him that the knife which was intended to pierce his heart cut his waistcoat. He would suffer no one save himself to tell the Queen of the danger he had encountered with courage and composure. She was distressed and alarmed, but the knowledge that the attack had proceeded from a crazy woman, whose purpose had been frustrated, who would no longer be a source of apprehension, soon quieted her fears. But a darker shadow was about to fall on the pair. In the course of the year 1788 the King caught a chill and was seized with a feverish attack which speedily went to his brain. Always a great talker, in the habit of putting endless questions which he himself answered, he now spoke continuously and incoherently in a hoarse voice, the very kindness and good nature of which it was piteous to hear. He kept telling everybody that he was not ill, merely a little nervous, and that if he could get to sleep he would be perfectly well. The ghastly dread which must have hovered in the background of the Queen's happiest hours for more than twenty years was a ghastlier reality.

For a little time the Queen was suffered to remain by the King's side; and so wistfully did he cling to her that when she was still allowed to occupy a bedroom next the King's he would get up during the night, light a candle, and come into her room to convince himself that she was still near him. He needed no physician, he said pathetically, the Queen was the best physician he could have. "She is my best friend; where could I find a better?" When the doctors, urging the necessity of absolute quiet for their patient, induced him to remove to a distant room, the Queen was in despair. She had further cause for pain. She had now to experience the serpent tooth of the ingratitude of a much loved child. The Prince of Wales hurried with indecent haste to supersede his father and mother in their palaces. Assured by his friends that in case of the King's incapacity the eldest son was the natural Regent in the father's stead, he did not wait till Parliament conferred on him the office, he went down to Windsor, gave every direction in the Queen's as well as in the King's rooms, dismissed attendants and altered arrangements. When Charlotte was induced to remove to Kew in order to supply the attraction of his wife and daughters' being there waiting for him to tempt the King into going to the country, the Prince preceded his mother, had part of the palace shut up, and even caused to be chalked on the doors of the remaining rooms the names of the members of the family and suite whom he chose to locate in them.

He was accustomed to come over with his brother the Duke of York and to remain in the rooms adjoining the King's in order to be personal witnesses to his ravings. Then the sons reported to the Queen the doctors' opinion of the King's state. This the brothers did with such brutal plain speaking and indifference to the feelings of the miserable wife and mother—of her who had been so proud and happy in the attachment of her husband and of his fine children—as to shock the hearers. The poor Queen shut herself up, stricken and humiliated, with her sorrowing daughters and ladies. Fainting fit after fainting fit prostrated her strength, till fear for her life mingled with the grief for the King's loss of his reason.

In the meantime the Prince of Wales and the Duke of York, jubilant in the prospect of unrestricted power as Prince Regent and as Commander-in-Chief, repaired to town and plunged into every orgy which drink, gambling-tables, and attendance at the least reputable public and private places of amusement could accomplish. The country looked on scandalised and appalled. Were these the lawless hands into which the guidance of the afflicted King and the nation was to be committed?

But the Queen's high spirits did not fail altogether, particularly where her duty to her helpless husband and her younger children came into play. The great statesman William Pitt, at the head of the Tory Government, supported her and looked after her interests and those of the people in the dire strait. He swayed Parliament by securing large majorities for his measures. He compelled the Prince of Wales to the sullen acceptance of a conditional regency, among whose provisions were the stipulations that the King's person was to be entrusted to the Queen's care, and that her Majesty was to be also invested with the control of the royal household.

Almost as suddenly as the dark cloud had descended on Queen Charlotte's fortunes it rose again by God's mercy, and the whole complexion of the case was changed. In November the King had been pronounced still delirious; the fever had left him but the delirium did not subside. The change to Kew from which something had been hoped had brought no improvement. The doctors were baffled and at their wits' end. Happily some of them were not above calling in further counsel. They summoned from Lincolnshire (to the Queen's great comfort) a certain Dr. Willis, famous for his treatment of lunacy. He arrived bringing with him two grown-up sons accustomed to act with him in the management of his lunatic asylum. The three are described as sensible, humane, kindly gentlemen. From the time the King was committed to their charge every reasonable indulgence was granted to him and his health of body and mind improved rapidly.

On January 1st, 1789, he was heard praying aloud fervently for his recovery. On January 18th he remembered it was the Queen's birthday and asked to see her, which he had not been allowed to do for several months. The gardens were reserved for his use, and the Queen would watch him from her window. Not knowing the reservation, Fanny Burney ventured on a stroll, when a serio-comic incident occurred. To her horror, on coming round a corner, she saw the King at a little distance. Believing that he was forbidden all intercourse with the world, she turned and ran. But the King, who pined for the sight of his friends and acquaintances, had already seen her and came running after her, bidding her stop and calling her by name.[1] It was a command she could not obey. Presently the three Willises, who had been in the background, joined in the pursuit, when the extraordinary spectacle was presented of "Little Burney" running through the royal grounds with her revered King at her heels and his three doctors bringing up the rear. Happily, Dr. Willis was able to arrest the fugitive and to impress upon her that she would do the King harm if she contradicted him further. She did her best to behave as if nothing had happened, halted, and even turned and advanced respectfully towards his Majesty, acting on the supposition that she had only, during that instant, seen and heard him.

To Fanny Burney's confusion the worthy old King, in his delight at meeting one he knew and liked, with whom he could discuss Court news, opened his arms and folded her in an affectionate embrace, kissing her on each cheek. She accepted the salute, satisfied that it was given in the benevolence of his heart, and that it was such a one as he had been wont from the

[1] The relations of Fanny Burney with the King and Queen were intimate and friendly. They had great faith in her judgment and sent her to be one of the audience at the trial of Warren Hastings, that she might bring back to them a full report of the proceedings.

beginning of his reign to bestow with a mixture of fatherliness and gallant homage on all the young women who were presented to him. He talked eagerly in his accustomed monologue, speaking quickly, hoarsely, but only occasionally incoherently. He discussed his family affairs, those of Miss Burney, politics, and his beloved music. He commenced singing from Handel, but so hoarsely and out of tune as almost to scare his auditor. Still he would not consent to shorten the interview. He showed that he was aware of his condition and dropped hints that he was sensible it had been taken advantage of. He ended by threatening with a half-jesting energy that when "he was King again he would rule with a rod of iron."

Miss Burney's account of the interview filled the Queen with happy hopes, and by February 12th the reunited pair were walking together in Kew Gardens with thankful hearts.

A few days afterwards Lord-Chancellor Thurlow communicated to the House the welcome intelligence that the King's medical attendants had announced his recovery. The elder sons, who had striven hard to turn their father's illness to their own profit, affected not to believe in his restoration to reason. After it was placed beyond doubt they scarcely concealed their disappointment. When in the gladness of the nation a large ball was given by White's Club to celebrate the joyful event, the two Princes sold the cards sent for them and their friends, and absented themselves from the ball. At the solemn and affecting thanksgiving in St. Paul's, the King, seated by the Queen's side, humbly confessed his sins and gratefully acknowledged God's goodness. He was calm, but she could hardly restrain her emotion, while the Princesses wept in sympathy; but as for the Prince of Wales, the Duke of York, and their cousin the Duke of Gloucester, they outraged the vast congregation by the loud and irreverent conversation they maintained during the service. London was illuminated in honour of the day. The Queen and the Princesses witnessed the spectacle. It was thought too exciting for the King, who only saw it from a distance in the company of Princess Amelia, the prattling child to whom he was tenderly attached.

At the first drawing-room and on the Queen's first visit to the theatre after the King's recovery there were renewed gala displays. "The Queen sat on a chair of state under a canopy, surrounded by the great officers of her household. Her dress was magnificence itself. She was in a blaze of diamonds; around her neck was a double row of gold chain supporting a medallion. Across her shoulders was another chain of pearls in three rows; but the portrait of the King was suspended from five rows of diamonds fastened loose upon the dress behind and streaming over the person with the most gorgeous effect. The tippet was of fine lace fastened with the letter "G" in brilliants of immense value. In front of her Majesty's hair, in letters formed of diamonds, were the words 'God save the King,' easily legible. . . . The female nobility wore emblematical designs beautifully painted on the satin of their caps." One is tempted to think that because the King had regained his wits the Queen and the female nobility had lost theirs. On the King's birthday the Queen was in royal purple covered with rich Brussels lace and carried a superb bouquet of brilliants—a present sent to the King by the Nizam of the Deccan. "Queen Charlotte is as fond of diamonds as the Queen of France, and as fond of snuff as the King of Prussia," was the report of a foreigner. The first taste was a misfortune to both Queens. It led to the story of the diamond necklace and De Rohan, which helped to ruin Marie Antoinette. It brought upon Queen Charlotte the accusation of having accepted bribes from Lord Clive and Warren Hastings to cover their abuse of government in India. It gave point to the false charge of selfish rapacity brought against an upright and generous woman.

The foreign ambassadors vied with each other in the taste and luxury of their commemoration banquets. The Princess Royal gave a ball to the young nobility, the invitations being issued in her name, while the married people were asked in the Queen's name. The gentlemen were in Windsor uniform, the ladies in garter blue covered with white tiffany. Each wore a large plume of feathers, white, and sometimes tipped with orange, in her head-dress, and each displayed a bandeau bearing the inscription, " God save the King." The fashion of wearing feathers, though the Queen had at one time forbidden them to her maids-of-honour, was at its height. It had not waned since the Duchess of Devonshire had to stoop on entering a room when she sported a feather given to her by Lord Stormont, which was an ell and three inches in length. The fashion of wearing ostrich feathers still survives in the costume for Queen Victoria's drawing-rooms so far as even the youngest *débutante* is concerned.

The etiquette at these bygone balls was of the most stringent description, and the Prince of Wales, though he could trample upon more serious obligations, and could cast this one aside where it affected himself, when the fancy took him was a stern stickler for its maintenance by less exalted persons. The rule was that no person should stand up in a country dance who had not previously danced in a minuet. At one of these balls Colonel Lennox and Lady Catherine Barnard, who had not danced a minuet, thought fit to range themselves in a country dance. The Prince of Wales, who was dancing with the Princess Royal, was in high dudgeon at the liberty taken. When he and his partner reached the offending couple he refused to dance with them by at once walking with the Princess to the bottom of the set. The Duke of York coming next with Princess Augusta danced regardlessly right down the row. The Duke of Clarence with Princess Elizabeth condemned the couple by breaking off and going to the bottom like the Prince of Wales and the Princess Royal. The culprits, abashed or unabashed, danced down the set, till they came to the Prince of Wales and his eldest sister, when he immediately took her by the hand, led her out of the dance, and conducted her to the Queen with haughty words to the effect, " Madam, I will not see you or any of your family insulted." Then Charlotte wisely brought the ball to a close.

Fantastic as were many of the demonstrations of loyalty on the King's recovery, they were at least genuine tokens of the high regard in which he and the Queen were then held by all honest unprejudiced hearts. The unspeakable blessing of reason was spared to the good King for a further period of over twenty years —an interval during which his friends and subjects were delivered from the incubus of the threatened regency.

CHAPTER III.

AN AGING AND AGED QUEEN.

THE old routine of the Court was resumed, with perhaps longer and longer stays, on account of the benefit of the sea air to the King's health, at Weymouth, which he had selected as his seaside resort, and adhered to so faithfully that part of the town on its beautiful bay adopted the high-sounding name of " Melcombe Regis."

In the days when travelling was limited to excursions here and there in England, now to visit a subject of sufficient rank and substance, now to make acquaintance with one of the great University towns, now to inspect a portion of the navy, and again to go over a public work or centre of industry as in the early years of the King's reign, many such expeditions were undertaken both before and after the King's illness, and were highly popular throughout the country. The King, Queen, and several of the Princesses paid a couple of visits to Oxford with Nuneham and Blenheim as their headquarters. The King sat in the Sheldonian theatre in the Vice-Chancellor's chair, his head covered, and received an address from his "most loyal University." Afterwards the heads of the houses and principal professors were presented to him; when a quick, merry observer like Fanny Burney had an opportunity of remarking on their unfamiliarity with Court procedure—how they knelt on both knees instead of on one, pulled themselves up by the King's hand after kissing it, tottered and stumbled in walking backwards, etc., etc. The colleges were visited in solemn rotation and a collation was taken in one of them by the royal party, while the ladies and gentlemen in attendance formed a semicircle and looked on in hungry appreciation of the banquet they were not to taste. The lively chronicler records a feat performed by Lady Charlotte Bertie when the King stopped engrossed in conversation in the middle of one of the halls. It was necessary for Lady Charlotte to leave the room in order to follow the Queen, but she could not turn her back on the King. She had a sprained ankle; but those to the manner born can do wonders. "She faced the King and began to march backwards . . . she went perfectly upright, but without one stumble, without once looking behind to see what she might encounter; and with as graceful a motion as I ever saw anybody enter a room, she retreated, I am sure, full twenty yards." The woman of fashion in her own *rôle* defeated the men of learning.

The royal explorers, on another occasion, examined Mr. Whitbread's great porter brewery in Chiswell Street, the Queen and the Princesses entering the main vat, and they and the King being served at luncheon with old porter from a bottle of extraordinary size.

The King and his family had a desire to see Divine Service performed on board ship, and one Sunday at Weymouth they went on board the *Magnificent*, sitting together under the quarter-deck awning, on the starboard side, while those of the nobility in the neighbourhood who followed their Majesties' example were on the larboard side. The ship's officers were in the centre, behind them the ship's company and the marines in the form of a crescent, while the chaplain was at his post and preached a sermon to an attentive congregation met under unusual circumstances.

A more imposing incident was the visit of the King

Queen, and Princesses to the *Royal Charlotte* lying off Portsmouth, when the King carried a diamond-hilted sword which he presented to the Commander, Lord Howe. And a still more interesting event even than the Handel Festival in Westminster Abbey which had preceded it, was the naval thanksgiving in St. Paul's, when a procession headed by the Admirals Howe, St. Vincent, and Duncan, conveyed the enemies' colours which the sea-captains had won in their glorious victories to the steps of the altar, where they were received by the Bishop of London and ranged on each side. The King was in naval uniform, the Queen and the Princesses in mazarine blue.

When the Queen accompanied the King to military reviews or to camps, while he was in scarlet regimentals faced with blue, gold lace and epaulettes, she, to do honour to the army, wore in her turn a scarlet riding habit faced with blue richly embroidered, a black hat, feather, and large cockade.

Though the calamity of the King's madness was arrested for a number of years and Queen Charlotte was again royal mistress in her own domains, she had many heavy trials besieging her in the present and looming in still darker battalions in the future. Her two elder sons remained as unruly and as miserably unsatisfactory as before. The Whig party, which supported them effusively in order to oppose the King and the Tories, fell into the injustice of systematically and vehemently aspersing the Queen, who stood between two hostile factions and was attacked by both. She was supposed to confirm the King in his Toryism and so she was maligned by the Whigs. She was believed after all to favour the Prince of Wales and to side with him in his contest with his father, and so the extreme Tories and the mob, for once holding a cause in common, vilified her. Clever caricaturists, with Gilray and Peter Pindar at their head, began to mock at her continually.

Something was hoped where the Duke of York was concerned from his marriage with Princess Frederica of Prussia, the only child by his first marriage of the late King of Prussia. The match was very agreeable to the nation not only on account of the rank and dowry of the bride but also because of her Protestant nurture.

The Duke's income was raised to thirty-five thousand pounds a year and an annuity of thirty thousand a year was settled on the Duchess should she survive her husband. The ages of the couple were suitable: she was twenty-three and he was twenty-seven. She was a gentle little woman, handsome in her modest way, well educated, upright, and kind-hearted. She was a world too good for him, while she was innocently attached to him. If he had only seen it, his temporal salvation lay in her. He went to Berlin, where the couple were married. France was in a state of open revolution, which, as was evident, was infecting England. It was not without considerable danger in traversing the South of France that the Duke and Duchess at last reached London, where they were re-married by the Archbishop of Canterbury at the Queen's House (Buckingham Palace) in the presence of the King, Queen, and the rest of the royal family, on November 22nd, 1791.

When the King and Queen with the Princes and Princesses paid the young couple a formal visit, the entertainment on the occasion took the form for which the King and Queen had a predilection, of a tea-party, sufficiently stately in its simplicity. The King's tea was solemnly handed to him by the Prince of Wales, while the Duchess of York, receiving a cup from the Duke, presented it with much reverence to the Queen. Only the King's good-natured loquacity and the Queen's gracious fine manners were equal to such situations and could render them easy and cordial.

Unfortunately, in the Duke and Duchess of York's marriage the virtue was all on the Duchess's side. After six years of insulting neglect and shameless inconstancy the dutiful affection of the poor Princess was worn to the last thread. The Court of Prussia was not in those days an example of domestic loyalty and tenderness, but its Princes were less outrageous in their evil behaviour than this English Prince, who had brought his bride to a foreign country only to behave to her with insolent falseness. But she was too modest and too dignified to indulge in useless upbraidings. She kept her worries and her sorrows to herself. The pair separated by mutual and amicable consent. The Duchess, whose health was delicate, retired to the country house of Oatlands, where she led a quiet, blameless life, distinguished chiefly by its charities. On any special occasion she showed her respect for the King and Queen by coming out of her retirement to appear at the royal drawing-rooms, etc., etc.[1] In return she received every mark of respect from her husband's family and from the nation. Even the graceless Duke condescended to treat her with outward propriety in the circumstances. He paid flying visits to Oatlands at intervals in order to settle business matters and make polite inquiries after the Duchess's health and well-being. The Duke and Duchess of York had no children.

One of the younger Princes, Augustus, afterwards Duke of Sussex but then only Prince Augustus, a lad of twenty, who had at least been so far free from the

---

[1] When the Duke of York was under a cloud because of the reported sale of commissions in the army by the worthless Mrs. Marianne Clarke, the Duchess came up to town, stayed in the same house with him, and appeared in public in his company, in a generous effort to shield him from disgrace.

wild excesses of his three elder brothers, distressed the King and Queen by committing a breach of the recently enacted Royal Marriage Act. In Italy he met and fell in love with Lady Augusta Murray, daughter of the Earl of Dunmore. The Prince induced an English clergyman in Rome to marry the couple without seeking the consent of the Sovereign and the Parliament.

The lady's relations supported the pair, so that on their return to England they were publicly re-married in St. George's, Hanover Square, in open defiance of the statute which had been enacted to prevent a repetition of the misalliances of George III.'s younger brothers. The marriage was pronounced invalid by the Ecclesiastical Court in August, 1794, and Lady Augusta immediately withdrew from her husband, who had only attained his majority a few months before. Apparently he did not make any attempt to procure a reversal of the decree, or an exception in his favour to the Royal Marriage Act, neither was there any mention of a morganatic marriage,[1] to which possibly Lady Augusta would not have stooped. The separation was permanent. She was permitted to take by royal licence the matronly title of Lady D'Ameland. The two children—a son and daughter—bore the name of D'Este, and were acknowledged as connections of the royal family.

The following year, 1795, saw the ill-omened marriage of George Augustus Frederick, Prince of Wales, now a man of three-and-thirty years of age and old in dissipation. His continued misconduct could no longer be excused on the plea of youthful folly which he might renounce presently. His debts were enormous, and it

[1] A marriage between a Prince or Princess and a private lady or gentleman in which the couple are recognised as man and wife, but the lady or gentleman does not take the rank of her husband or his wife, and the children are not necessarily Princes and Princesses, and have no claim to a throne.

was understood that they would only be discharged by the King and the Government on his marrying and settling down to a more honourable course of conduct than he had hitherto pursued. He had obstinately declined to marry for a very good reason. It had long been an open secret that eleven years before, in 1784, he was married in her own drawing-room to the only woman for whom he ever showed a particle of real affection, the beautiful Mrs. Fitzherbert. The lady was of respectable but by no means very distinguished antecedents. Her father was a country gentleman of the name of Smith, and while still in the bloom of her youth she was for the second time a widow—her second husband having been a Colonel Fitzherbert. There had been nothing of Prince Augustus's boyish candour in his marriage with Lady Augusta Murray in the circumstances of the Prince of Wales's marriage with Mrs. Fitzherbert. It was conducted with extreme secrecy; the Prince denying the fact in the most absolute manner both in public and private. In fact, the marriage was doubly forbidden by the conditions of the Royal Marriage Act and by the light of a still older Act, that of the Hanoverian succession to the throne of England. Mrs. Fitzherbert was a Roman Catholic, and no Roman Catholic could be Queen-Consort of England.

There is a somewhat apocryphal story that the Prince of Wales confessed his marriage to the Queen, his mother, to whom, in spite of his conduct towards her on the occasion of George III.'s first attack of madness, he still came to ask her to intercede for him with his justly incensed father; not that the prodigal was repentant, but that he would fain have his mortgaged income increased and his pressing creditors staved off. If the Prince of Wales ever made such a confession to the Queen, she must have regarded his marriage as totally irregular and illegal; but she had certainly more pity than condemnation for the woman who had entered on the untenable contract. Charlotte held a rigid moral standard with regard to the character of her Court, even where the members of her family were concerned, but she always displayed forbearance and clemency to Mrs. Fitzherbert; she received her publicly at her drawing-rooms, and consented to be visited by her when the royal family were in semi-retirement at Brighton.

In 1794 the Prince of Wales's finances were in a desperate state and he suddenly announced his willingness to marry, the King only stipulating that the bride should be a Princess and a Protestant. The Queen was anxious that the choice should be a wise one, but eventually it fell on the King's niece, Princess Caroline of Brunswick, daughter of the old talkative mischief-maker, Princess Augusta, the King's sister who had married the soldier Duke of Brunswick and presided for thirty years in an undignified, indiscreet fashion over a small German Court whose morals and manners were the reverse of what was desirable. It is sufficient to say here that the poor Queen was aware, even before she saw Caroline, that the daughter-in-law proposed for her was utterly antipathetic to her. No two women could be more unlike; no two would so jar on each other. Caroline was the very reverse of what a wise mother might have sought for in the wife of her son. For such a son as the Prince of Wales the prospect of his wedded life with Caroline was dark indeed. The Queen saw her last hope for her firstborn, the darling of her young motherhood, extinguished, and she was powerless to prevent the catastrophe. Personally there was little to object to in Caroline. At twenty-six she had a pretty face, with delicate features, fair hair and complexion, and expressive eyes. Her figure, though already showing a tendency to stoutness, was not yet overgrown. But mentally she was "a bold, dashing, careless girl whose tongue was ever in advance of reflection" (in this respect going far beyond her mother's, who called the coarsest things by the coarsest names), "and was as complacently vain as she was reckless of the consequences of her words and actions."

The Earl of Malmesbury was sent to conduct Caroline of Brunswick to England, and the marriage was celebrated on April 8th, 1795, in the Chapel Royal, St. James's, in the presence of the King and Queen and the rest of the royal family. Queen Charlotte, whatever her feelings might have been, gave an entertainment at Frogmore in honour of the wedding, and "was civil if stiff," while the bride is said to have been "superbly dressed," and to have "looked as black as midnight."

Already the quarrels of the ill-suited couple had begun, and soon were notorious. The Queen's distaste to the Princess of Wales (the natures of the two women were absolutely irreconcilable) is said to have been confirmed and intensified by certain impertinently sarcastic remarks on the Queen contained in some letters of the Princess to her friends in Germany, which came to the Queen's knowledge.

The only child of the Prince and Princess of Wales, Princess Charlotte of Wales, was born in London in 1796, and shortly afterwards the father and mother separated. The Princess settled at Blackheath, where she was occasionally visited by her uncle the King, but not by the Queen. The baby Princess was left at Carlton House under a succession of governesses appointed by her father, and even when she was removed to Blackheath she had an establishment of her own, in a different house from her mother, whom she was only allowed to see once a week. This practical separation of the child from the mother, who was fond of her baby, was, to begin with, an act of heartless tyranny. Afterwards, when the child was older, and the foolish mother—living in a racket of company of all kinds—had so conducted herself as to cause many scandals, there was something to be said on both sides of the question.

Princess Charlotte of Wales was the only grandchild whom the old King and Queen lived to see, and in that light as well as from the circumstance that she stood, after her father, next in succession to the throne, the little creature was an object of much interest to them. The Queen had many plans for her grand-daughter's education. She wished to enlist in the service no less a person than Mrs. Hannah Moore.

A diversion in the trouble brooding over the divided house was effected by the marriage of Charlotte, the Princess Royal, to the Crown Prince of Würtemberg. But even this satisfaction was considerably alloyed. At this date it sounds strange, all things considered, to be told that the bridegroom had wedded for his first wife the elder sister of the little esteemed Princess of Wales. This Charlotte of Brunswick, first cousin to the English Charlotte, to whose hand the Prince now aspired, had undergone a miserable mysterious fate. The story went that the Prince, then in the service of Russia, had taken his wife and three children to St. Petersburg, where the Princess, under the influence of the Empress Catherine, was led into much that was evil. Her husband endeavoured to return to Germany with his wife and children; but the formidable Empress, while giving him leave to go with his children, declined to consent to the departure of her friend, his wife. After he was gone the Empress removed all her German attendants from the unhappy lady, and then, whether in one of the violent caprices to which the able but depraved woman was subject, whether in the wish to silence the Princess on incidents with which she was familiar in the Empress's life, the Princess of Würtemberg was sent to a castle at some distance from St. Petersburg and confined there. Two years afterwards Catherine caused letters to be conveyed to the Duke of Brunswick and the Prince of Würtemberg simply intimating the death of the Princess. Of the truth of the announcement the Duke of Brunswick and the Prince of Würtemberg convinced themselves, but the Duchess of Brunswick, whose opinion, after all, was not worth much, never believed the tale of her daughter's death. There were other people who held that she was still dragging out her existence in a Russian prison or in the wilds of Siberia. This was a ghastly tale with which a bridegroom went wooing to the near relative of his last wife. Rumour increased its ghastliness; never satiated with horrors, it added to them in this case by roundly asserting that the Prince was an accomplice in his wife's tragic end, that his treatment had led to it, and that he knew full well how she had fared if dead, and where she was if still alive. But Charlotte, Princess Royal, was too sensible and friendly to be scared by rumour, and she was fain to make up to an injured man, as she believed, for what he had suffered in the past. She was in her thirty-second year; she was old enough to judge for herself; she was not averse to the husband who had made proposals for her hand, or unwilling to resign her state as the lady of the second degree of importance in England to be the lady of the first rank in Würtemberg.

Naturally the King and Queen did not smile on so doubtful a match. They were both opposed to it at first, and the King did not yield till he was satisfied (with reason) of the baselessness of the charges against the Prince. Then the Queen too gave way and allowed herself to trust that her daughter knew what was for her welfare and happiness. When the marriage was finally agreed upon there was all the pleasant bustle and interest of the first daughter's marriage in a group of grown-up daughters, the first Princess in a cluster of Princesses. The Queen took a mother's proud and tender share in the preparations, embroidering with her own hand the white-and-gold wedding dress.

In 1798 the anxiety of the Irish rebellion following on the French revolution but ending in the quelling of the rebels was a heavy burden on the King's mind. Two years later there was still sufficient anarchical and revolutionary feeling in the country to cause the King to be fired at from the pit of Drury Lane Theatre, when the Queen and the Princesses were seating themselves in the royal box previous to witnessing a play. The King behaved with great courage and equanimity, remaining himself in the front of the box, but preventing his wife and daughters from coming forward till he was assured there would not be another shot. The whole family then sat down and stayed out the performance, thus quieting the audience in the midst of their own heart-throbbings. On another occasion when the King and Queen were driving in the City the carriage was surrounded by a riotous mob and a stone was thrown in through one of the windows which struck the Queen on the cheek. She who in the early years of her life as Queen-Consort had been followed with praise and admiration wherever she went, who had done nothing to deserve the withdrawal of the popular affection, but had been in all respects virtuous, discreet, and beneficent, saw herself superseded in the people's esteem by their sorry idol the Princess of Wales, and was not infrequently assailed with taunts reflecting on her son's treatment of his wife, and accusations of being at the bottom of the mischief.

The first book stereotyped in England was a religious

treatise translated from the German by the Queen for the use of her daughters, and suggested by her to Bishop Porteous as an antidote to the infidel publications which were being widely circulated throughout the country. She was greatly interested in the rise of Sunday-schools under Raikes, and had his worthy ally, Mrs. Freeman, presented to her.

When Lady Huntingdon ventured to remonstrate with Archbishop Cornwallis on the indecorum of the gay and giddy routs over which his wife presided at his palace, she had the cordial support of the King and Queen. The King even wrote to the Archbishop endorsing Lady Huntingdon's opinion.

In 1801 the King's health fluctuated alarmingly. The proposal of a Bill for Catholic emancipation preyed on his conscience, as the loss of the American colonies had filled him with mortification in the earlier years of his reign. He considered that his consent to the Bill would be a violation of his coronation oaths. The Prince of Wales openly rejoiced in the hope of a regency; but the Duke of York, though not unwilling to profit in his purse by his father's threatened incapacity, for the first time withdrew to some extent from his elder brother's influence and showed a little filial feeling.

The Queen was persuaded that it was the affairs of the Prince and Princess of Wales which were distressing the King. She dreaded further alienation between him and the Prince, while she thoroughly distrusted the appeals of the Princess, who in the midst of much company and outrageous folly was constantly crying out for justice and for the possession of her child.

The physicians, the Willises, were now in attendance on the King, who was suffering from a bad feverish attack, during which he was talking continually, now praying piteously for his recovery, now commanding the Queen not to reveal what he said to her private, now eagerly discussing the retirement from office of his minister Pitt. The Queen appealed through one of the Princesses to the Willises to calm the King, and though she would not see the Princess of Wales, she had the prattling four-year-old Princess Charlotte to pay frequent visits to Buckingham House and Windsor in order to gladden the old man with her pretty baby ways. He had proposed that the future Queen of England should reside under his care and the Queen's at Windsor, and should be educated there ; but he was thwarted by the wilful opposition—for opposition's sake—of the little Princess's father, the Prince of Wales.

The King rallied from this fresh threatening of his malady, but the Queen was kept in a constant strain of anxiety lest he should over-exert himself, lest his loquacity should suddenly pass into incoherent nonsense. He was unable to appear much in public, and she returned willingly to the quiet domesticity of the happy early days of her marriage. But her mind was never at rest : she would appear at a drawing-room which the King could not attend, and where the Prince of Wales was rude to her, pale and careworn, while the Princesses' eyes were red and swollen as if they had been weeping. But *noblesse oblige* ! They had to play their parts as if nothing were amiss.

It was observed that the Queen never took her eyes off the King while she went through the form of making one at an evening card-table. She did not possess the comfort of having the Doctors Willis to rely upon for judicious treatment and to consult confidentially. The King had conceived an unreasonable antipathy to his former physicians and was now under the care of Dr. Symonds, who appears to have lacked the necessary knowledge and experience, and was much less successful in his treatment of his royal patient.

Even Charlotte's strong nerves began to give way. The King, naturally kind and indulgent to his family, had in the waywardness of his disease grown rough and well-nigh violent. He declined doggedly to resume his former habits, his country walks, his attendance at chapel, his promenades on the terrace at Windsor, where his daughters were always in readiness to obviate the difficulties caused by his growing blindness. With regard to the last infirmity, he was more like his old self, he was patient and resigned, consenting to wear a flapping hat and a shade when the protection was judged necessary. Still, seeing the change in his temper, what wonder that the poor Queen grew reluctant to be alone with the King, and craved the presence of one or more of the Princesses in her interviews with him? Nay, in sudden panic would lock herself into the white room (her boudoir), where he was wont to be the most welcome of visitors.

The blow, however, was broken by the descent being very gradual. The King, who now dwelt habitually at Windsor, would be tolerably well for months. He would breakfast with the Queen and the Princesses, go to chapel as of old, would even ride out with the younger Princesses and his equerries. He dined by himself at two o'clock, but after the dinner of the Queen and the Princesses at four o'clock he would join them for a short time before he retired with his secretary to transact his share of the business of the nation. In the evening all the family, with the variety of company from the neighbourhood, met in the great drawing-room in social intercourse till ten o'clock.

In 1805 the Queen consented to receive Caroline, Princess of Wales, and young Princess Charlotte at Windsor. She behaved to her daughter-in-law with courtesy, though she could not affect to feel the King's hearty forgiving kindness.

In the Jubilee year of 1809 the King was evidently failing in health. He was unable even to attend the *fête* given on the occasion by the Queen at Frogmore. His horse was led when he rode out. He used a stick in making his way along the terrace. Handel's "Fatal Eclipse," of which he was fond, affected both King and Queen to tears. Once she surprised him repeating aloud Milton's lines :—

> "Oh dark, dark, dark, amid the blaze of noon,
> Irrecoverably dark, total eclipse
> Without all hope of day !
> Oh first-created beam, and Thou great Word,
> Let there be light, and light was over all :
> Why am I thus deprived Thy prime decree ?"

But the double climax which overthrew entirely the King's tottering reason was the defeat of the bungled Walcheren Expedition and the consequent odium incurred by the Duke of York (who was the King's favourite son, as the Prince of Wales had been the Queen's favourite among her seven stout sons), and the death from consumption at Weymouth in the springtime of her life of the darling of his old age, Princess Amelia. It is said the poor girl, knowing her end was near, had a ring made containing a lock of her hair, wore it for a little time, then gave it to her father, saying, "Take this and remember me." The King broke down, left the room, and was unable to see her again during the few days she survived.

Poor Queen ! her heart also must have been lacerated as she realised in 1810 that her darkest forebodings were accomplished, and that the King, upwards of three score and ten, was hopelessly, incurably insane !

The Conditional Regency, proposed twenty years before, was appointed with the Prince of Wales as Regent, while the Queen was entrusted with the person of the King—an office which left her still mistress of the palaces. The increased expense to her personally was provided for by an addition of ten thousand pounds to her annual income.

The Queen behaved with the dignity, patience, and good sense which might have been expected from her. In time she grew reverently resigned to the terrible calamity which had befallen her and the husband to whom she had been from her girlhood warmly and loyally attached. She ceased to entertain any delusive dream of his recovery. She did not wish the King to be buoyed up by false expectations, the disappointment of which only distressed and irritated him. Sometimes in her visits to him her feelings were sorely tried, as when she found him singing a hymn to his own accompaniment on the organ and afterwards kneeling down and praying for his family, the nation, and that God would restore to him the reason which he felt he had lost. Touched to the quick as she was, his simple, unfaltering faith and goodness must have been under Heaven her best consolation. That was a lucid interval differing from the frenzy which made him call for death and fancy himself dead, when he "asked for a suit of black that he might go into mourning for the old King."

Though the long disastrous wars with France had been brought to a close, their consequences, as it seemed, in ruined trade, much suffering and disaffection among the lower classes, were still strongly felt. The visit of the allied sovereigns in 1814 inaugurated a series of festivities in which Charlotte had to play her part whether her heart were heavy or light. She was now upwards of seventy, and is described as a little spare woman still remarkable for her gracious, graceful manners. Her health was giving way under an insidious disease. She was in a worse plight as the wife of a lunatic husband than as a widow. She was tortured by the ingratitude and misconduct of more than one of her children, by the disorder in their households and the evil example of their lives over which she had no control. Her early popularity with all classes was gone as far as the impulsive, unreasoning mob was concerned. She had been satirised and caricatured in higher circles. She was accused of parsimony and avarice, of using her influence with the King to stifle liberal measures, and of making a party with her eldest son the Prince Regent against his injured wife, Caroline of Brunswick. Caroline's name, in spite of her grievous offences against good sense and good taste, was fast becoming the rallying cry not only of the extreme Whigs and the Radicals, but of the great body of Nonconformists. As the Queen was carried in her chair from Buckingham House to St. James's to hold one of her last drawing-rooms she was surrounded and stopped for a moment by the scum of the streets. She was hissed and hooted at and demanded what she had done with the Princess Charlotte? For the populace's last craze was that the Queen was keeping the heiress to the throne out of sight, and had shut her up in durance vile. For aught the girl's champions knew, the cruel, relentless old woman might beat and starve her grand-daughter to death.

As an answer to the taunts and insults addressed to her the Queen drew down the glass in front of her chair and faced and addressed her assailants. "I am above seventy years of age," she said. "I have been more than half a century Queen of England, and I never was hissed by a mob before."

The boldest of her foes recoiled before the undaunted rebuke given by the queenly old woman. They fell back and let the chair pass. The Prince Regent, hearing of the disturbance, sent some of his aides-de-camp to escort his mother back to Buckingham House. She dismissed them. They remonstrated, urging that they had the Regent's order to accompany her home and that they were bound to obey him. "You have left Carlton House by his Royal Highness's orders," replied the Queen; "return there by mine, or I will leave my chair and go home on foot." She had her way, and her courage converted the base attack into something like respectful homage.

Various events, some vexatious, some cheerful, some deeply sad, crowded themselves into the last years of Charlotte's life. In 1815 there was the alarm of Napoleon's escape from Elba and the triumph of the final victory at Waterloo. In the same year the Queen was scandalised by the marriage made in defiance of all propriety and of her prohibition by her fifth son, Ernest, Duke of Cumberland. Unsatisfactory in all his relations and actions, his marriage was not an exception to the general tenor of his life. His bride was a Princess of Mecklenburg-Strelitz, a near relative of the Queen's—in fact, her niece, as Caroline of Brunswick was the King's niece; but nieces were not destined to be matrimonial successes in the royal family of England. The original disability of Caroline of Brunswick to occupy worthily the position she was destined to fill was nothing compared to that of Frederica of Mecklenburg-Strelitz. But closely related as the Queen was to her, Charlotte seems, in those days of rare communication and scanty intelligence, to have been unacquainted with the worst features of the case. She must have known that Frederica's first marriage with Prince Frederick of Prussia had been dissolved (a circumstance which on account of the presence in the country of a Prussian Princess, the highly respected Duchess of York, was in itself a difficulty), while Frederica's second husband, the Prince of Salms-Braunfels, had left her a widow. The Queen, however, did not consider the objection as insurmountable. When Adolphus, Duke of Cambridge, the Queen's youngest son, was disposed to make proposals for his cousin's hand, the Queen interposed no interdict. As it happened, the lady preferred Cambridge's morose elder brother either from a peculiarity of taste or because he stood nearer the English throne. Still, Queen Charlotte regarded the second projected match complacently. There is a letter of hers extant (and quoted by Dr. Watkins), which was written to her brother the Duke of Mecklenburg-Strelitz, discussing the coming marriage pleasantly and giving some good advice to the bride.[1] All at once it came to the Queen's knowledge that the marriage of her niece to Prince Frederick of Prussia had been no mere formal contract broken off for political reasons, it had been a marriage in which the wife's misconduct had caused her to be divorced by her husband. The particulars of the affair had been known to King George while he was sane, and he had kept them back from the Queen out of consideration for her family feelings; but he had expressed in the strongest terms his condemnation of the erring Princess. She would have been the last person whom he would have consented to admit into his family.

The Queen immediately withdrew her consent and urged upon the Prince Regent to add his veto to the unseemly connection; nevertheless the marriage was solemnised in Mecklenburg with unusual splendour for the little duchy, in spite of the Queen's opposition. Presently the couple arrived in London, accompanied by the Queen's brother, to make peace if possible with the Queen. But she was inflexible; she would never consent to accord her approval to a person of whom the King had entirely disapproved, and she would not agree to a step which he would have been the first to prohibit. She owed a duty to herself, to her good daughters, to her

---

[1] This letter contains also an intimation of the homely gifts of six pounds of tea and two cheeses which the Queen was sending to the Duke her brother.

husband's subjects. She had striven for more than half a century to preserve a pure Court, she declined to have it sullied by the admission within its precincts of a daughter-in-law whose reputation was worse than spotted.[1] The rebellious couple were re-married, according to custom, at Carlton House in the presence of the Regent; but neither the Queen nor the Princesses countenanced the ceremony, nor did the Queen ever see or acknowledge her niece and daughter-in-law. The Duchess of Cumberland was a pariah in the royal family and in the society from which she was virtually excluded. The result introduced further strife and division into an already divided house. The Queen's grey hairs were being brought down in sorrow to the grave.

On May 2nd, 1816, Princess Charlotte of Wales was married to Prince Leopold of Saxe-Coburg. "The old Queen played the part of mother to the bride on the occasion"; for Caroline, Princess of Wales, had been persuaded to go abroad, where she was spending her exile and illustrating her quasi-disgrace by the medley of unsuitable company, rowdy gaiety, and well-nigh crazy impropriety which she had begun to practise during her stay at Blackheath.

Queen Charlotte drove with the bride in semi-state on an afternoon of early summer across Hyde Park to the Prince Regent's residence, Carlton House, where the marriage was solemnised. This was a wedding which the Queen and everybody else approved. At the splendid drawing-room held afterwards in honour of the occasion the Queen's spirits were so unusually high that critics set them down as "affected." In like manner the pale bride's smile was declared to be "forced," and she was pictured as thinking indignantly

---

[1] There was another reason. Charlotte knew that it was believed she had been hard, from the first, on the King's niece, Caroline of Brunswick. She would not have it said in addition that she was more lenient to her own niece Frederica of Mecklenburg-Strelitz.

and sorrowfully of her banished mother, who had acted, as her daughter was well aware, more like an *enfant terrible* than a responsible human being. Be that as it may, the marriage was one of mutual affection and unclouded happiness during its brief duration. The Queen-grandmother might well be glad at the solution of a troublesome problem by the removal of the young Princess from the harsh thraldom in which her father had held her without the further exposure of domestic misery.

Within three months another marriage in which the Queen may be supposed to have taken a deeper interest was quietly accomplished at Buckingham House without form or parade. It was the welcome end of a pathetically protracted love story. More than twenty years before there had been certain innocent little love passages between pretty Princess Mary and her cousin, William, Duke of Gloucester, son of her father's brother and the Countess of Waldegrave, whom he had raised to the rank of a royal Duchess. The exigencies of the state soon put a barrier between Princess Mary and her lover. If little Princess Charlotte was to grow up heir to the throne, where, in the midst of European wars and rumours of war, was there to be found a fit husband for her? Surely she would be safer and the nation would be best pleased if she married the one English Prince who was not within the forbidden degrees of kindred. Even if a greater alliance could be found for her, it would be well while she remained unwedded that Gloucester should continue a bachelor as a respectable *pis aller* in case nothing better turned up. The years rolled on till Princess Mary's young bloom faded and her girlish spirits grew meek and subdued, while Duke William waxed stout and heavy in body and mind, till at last, after a Prince of Orange had been rejected, Prince

Leopold was found fit for the vacant post and proved signally acceptable to the bride and the nation; so on a July evening there was a quiet wedding at the Queen's House, and Princess Mary, a bride of forty instead of twenty, was promoted to the goal of her early aspirations as Duchess of Gloucester. What though the Duke was the "silly Billy" of the graceless clubs, and was more distinguished by stupidity than by brilliance, he was "a proper man" to her, her first love glorious in her faithful eyes. One is glad to know that here was an instance in which royal cousins married and did not disagree, and that the Duke of Gloucester—an honourable contrast to other Princes whom Princess Mary had known—was a true and affectionate husband to his Duchess throughout their married life.

In 1817, when the Queen was trying the Bath mineral waters as a check to her increasing illness, the news reached her of the death in childbed at Claremont of Princess Charlotte—"*dead mother and dead child.*" The hopes of the nation were quenched in addition to the pang of separation between husband and wife after one short year. The Queen was deeply grieved and shocked and the chances of any improvement in her health were seriously impaired by the melancholy tidings. Yet the prejudices against her had grown so envenomed and furious that a wild whisper actually went abroad that she had compassed the death of her grand-daughter out of hatred to Princess Charlotte's mother, and that an accoucheur and a nurse present at Claremont were the Queen's tools in perpetrating the crime by causing the death of the child and by administering poison to the Princess during the night following the birth of her son. It was further alleged that in remorse for their wickedness the doctor and nurse had afterwards committed suicide. Here the single grain of truth is to be found. The doctor, an eminent man of sensitive temperament, keenly pained and disappointed by the disaster which had not only deprived him of the honour of successfully performing his functions in the highest quarter, but had also cost two precious lives and plunged the country into mourning, himself succumbed to the blow, his reason was completely unhinged, and he took his life.

In dismay at what was the failure of an heir to the crown in Princess Charlotte's generation Parliament issued a recommendation to the Dukes of Clarence, Kent, and Cambridge[1] to marry, while proportionate additions to their incomes were voted to provide for the increased expenses of their households. Before any of these marriages were celebrated another of Queen Charlotte's daughter's was married in 1818. Princess Elizabeth, a distinguished looking—in spite of her great size—and a really highly endowed woman, at the mature age of forty-eight, married the Landgrave of Hesse-Homburg. In the society gossip of the day many absurd stories were told of the German bridegroom's uncouthness—how unaccustomed he was to the use of a bath, and that he walked stockingless in his long cavalry boots. Neither did the elderly bride escape reproaches for her marriage while the Queen was so ill that there was hardly a hope of her recovery. To account for the act on Princess Elizabeth's part it was said that there were differences of opinion and contests of will between her and the Queen. The real explanation seems to lie in the dread which not only the Queen but the Princesses entertained of their being left unmarried, scantily provided for in accordance with their rank, and in a measure dependent on the good offices

---

[1] The Duke of Sussex, to his credit, declined to marry (and so forfeited the increase of income voted to his brothers) while Lady D Ameland was alive. She had separated from him when their marriage was declared illegal, and he had consented to the separation, but he refused to treat the marriage as if it had never been.

of their brother the Regent. Princess Elizabeth, one of the eldest and the most high-spirited of the Princesses, doubtless felt the position most acutely and was most desirous of escaping from it. If any misunderstanding and alienation had arisen between the mother and daughter, it is known that it passed away with the marriage and that the two so long and loyally united parted good friends. Dr. Watkins mentions that the couple delayed setting out for Germany and lingered for a little time at Brighton to be at hand if any immediate change took place in the Queen's condition. But Charlotte, who, as a girl, left Mecklenburg-Strelitz before her own mother's grave was green because of the duties and obligations which awaited her in England, was the last person to permit a daughter to disregard similar obligations, or to accept from her and her husband a sacrifice which might cause them serious inconvenience and loss.

One more visit the old Queen paid to the City, when she made a request to the Lord Mayor that she might be received without ceremony. Her wish was complied with. Her carriage was surrounded, as her chair had been on a previous occasion, by a yelling mob. She was scoffed at and menaced. The old question containing a new and more horrible meaning was shouted—What had she done with Princess Charlotte? Men thrust their heads into the carriage and endeavoured to disarm her footmen. On her return to Buckingham House, while dining in company with the Duke of York, she was seized with the first of the spasms—an ominous symptom in her exquisitely painful disease, which was of a bilious nature.

Perhaps the last signal gratification Queen Charlotte received was derived from the suitable and promising marriages of her three sons—the Dukes of Clarence, Kent, and Cambridge—and their arrival in England with their respective brides, Adelaide of Saxe-Meiningen, Victoria of Saxe-Coburg and Leiningen, and Augusta of Hesse-Cassel. The couples had been married in Germany and were re-married in England. The first of the brothers to marry and come back with his wife was the youngest, Adolphus of Cambridge, forty-five years of age. His bride, Augusta of Hesse-Cassel, was more than twenty years his junior. They arrived in England at the close of May, 1818, and were re-married at Buckingham House in the presence of the Queen and her family on June 1st. Of the two remaining couples, the Duke of Clarence, a bridegroom of fifty-three,[1] did not go to Germany to fetch his wife. She came, a Princess of twenty-six years of age, accompanied by her mother, to London to meet her fate. The Duke of Kent, fifty-one, brought home his bride, whom he had married according to the Lutheran form at Coburg. She was the young widow of the Prince of Leiningen and the sister of Prince Leopold of Saxe-Coburg, the widowed husband of Princess Charlotte. The Princess of Leiningen was in her thirty-third year and was the mother of a son and daughter, the children of her first husband.

The Dukes of Clarence and Kent, with the two Princesses escorted by the Prince Regent, for once in his life considerate and gracious, came out on a July afternoon to the old palace of Kew, where the Queen had gone to stay, in order that the joint ceremonies of marriage and re-marriage might be performed in her presence if she were fit for the fatigue. She was not fit, but she received the couples in her sick-room, and her old keen, shrewd eyes must have been pleased to recognise for themselves, as they had already seen in the case of the third bride, the young Duchess of Cambridge, that the somewhat plain and homely

[1] All the Queen's sons were big, stout men.

Duchess of Clarence and the pretty, accomplished Duchess of Kent were alike in this, that they were modest and reasonable young women who would try their best to make good wives to the Princes.

Queen Charlotte, well as she had loved simple tea-parties, could not preside over this one on the palace lawn, which followed the great ceremony of the evening. But she could hear where she lay the volley of cheers, led by the Prince Regent, which followed the last of the two couples on their way back to town.

The Queen's health declined rapidly, dropsy and difficulty of breathing supervening on her other ailments. She had a passionate longing to be taken to Windsor to spend her last days under the same roof with the King; but the step had been delayed too long. In vain different easy carriages were constructed and small essays made at driving her out; the journey on which she had set her heart was of necessity abandoned. When the physicians regarded her case as hopeless and fast drawing to an end, a communication was made to her on the authority of the Prince Regent "that if her Majesty had any affairs to settle it would be advisable to do so while she had health and spirits to bear the fatigue." It is said that till the Queen got the grave hint she had still a faint faith in her ultimate recovery; but from that moment she turned her attention to setting her house in order and preparing for the great change which was near at hand. The most of her family—her four younger sons with their wives, the Duke of Sussex, and two of her daughters—were abroad. Those sons and daughters in this country gathered round her; Princess Augusta and the Duchess of Gloucester[1] watched and waited upon their mother devotedly, day

---

[1] The youngest surviving daughter, Princess Sophia, whether from physical weakness or mental depression, appears to have latterly lived her life apart. She is not even buried at Windsor, she lies at Kensal Green near her brother the Duke of Sussex.

and night. They had been accustomed to read to her and share her devotions for many a year. The gradual decay of the Queen's bodily powers, her suffering and approaching death, had not only touched the Duke of York, they had awakened some sparks of tenderness in the Prince Regent. Towards the close of his mother's life he behaved to her with deference and affection. He was a constant attendant on her death-bed. At the very last, when she roused herself from the unconsciousness stealing over her, it is said that with a faint smile she made a motion with her hand towards him. He had been her firstborn, her "might and the beginning of her strength." He had wandered far from the path she had destined for him, the path in which she herself had walked faithfully from youth to age ; he had failed her and tried her desperately, but in a mother's heart full forgiveness and love inexhaustible abide. It was on November 16th, 1818. She was in her seventy-fifth year and had been for fifty-seven years Queen-Consort of England. Mrs. Inchbald, then residing at Kensington, records how she had watched the royal carriages passing all day between St. James's, Carlton House, and Kew, where the old Queen lay dying. Her King, in confinement at Windsor, was ignorant of his loss.

The Queen's funeral took place at Windsor on December 2nd. It was conducted without any great display, but with the military pomp thought requisite for a royal funeral. By her will she only left four thousand pounds in money ; a sufficient answer to those who had accused her savagely of greed and rapacity, of robbing the country to fill her private purse.

A hundred and thirty-six thousand pounds' worth of personal property, including Frogmore, its plate, furniture, etc., was bequeathed to Princess Augusta, and the estate in New Windsor, with the house known as New Lodge, was left to Princess Sophia. The Queen owed nine thousand pounds, incurred by her allowing her charities to exceed the ready money at her disposal. The debt was to be paid out of her personal estate. The main provision for her daughters was her jewels.[1] These were to be sold, with the proceeds divided equally between four of the Princesses. The Princess excluded was not Elizabeth, Landgravine of Hesse-Homburg, but Charlotte, Princess Royal, Queen-Dowager of Würtemberg, and the reason given for the exclusion was that Queen Charlotte considered her eldest daughter already well provided for. To her the Queen left as a mark of her affection her set of fine garnets, which could be worn with a widow's mourning.

Unpropitious as the Würtemberg alliance had appeared at first sight, the marriage had turned out a happy one. When death dissolved it, the widow, known in her adopted country as the "Good Queen-Dowager," declined to lay aside her widow's mourning while life lasted.

Queen Charlotte's stores of priceless lace descended eventually to the Duchess of Gloucester, and from her, according to report, they passed to her god-daughter, Princess Mary of Cambridge, Duchess of Teck. The Queen's wardrobe was to be given to her chief dresser,[2] Madame Beckendorff.

There was no mention of the Queen's sons in her will. They had their incomes settled upon them by Government, together with their official incomes, and it was not in her power to do anything more for them.

---

[1] There were two exceptions in the disposal of her jewels. Those which the King had presented to her, to the value of £50,000, upon her marriage, were to go back to him if he recovered his reason. If not, they were to become part of the Crown jewels of Hanover. The jewels which Queen Charlotte brought with her from Mecklenburg-Strelitz were to be returned to the head of the reigning family there.

[2] The Queen's old friend, Mrs. Schwellenberg, who was in her service for fifty years, had died suddenly while playing at cards, in March, 1797.

The personal custody of the old King was transferred, on Queen Charlotte's death, to the Duke of York, on whom an additional ten thousand a year was settled—not that he might reside for the better part of the year at Windsor and bear the consequently increased expenditure, but that he might inquire periodically after the invalid's condition. At the same time the state which the Queen had seen maintained round this wreck of "the Royal George" was put an end to by the orders of the Prince Regent. The King's former household was to a large extent dismissed as a needless cost to the country. George III. survived his Queen two years; the Duke of Kent died a week before his father; the Duchess of York died eight months after the King, and the ill-fated Caroline of Brunswick ended her unhappy career in the following year.

Queen Charlotte was a woman, reverent, upright, and dutiful to the core. She had never blenched from her first honest cenception of a sovereign's obligations. Narrow in her notions she might be, and rigid in her standards, but England owes her to this day a great debt for her unshaken godliness and unfaltering virtue at a godless and dissolute period of the nation's history.

The Court of Caroline, wife of George II. (in spite of her many good qualities), which came before, and that of the regency which followed after Charlotte's Court, ought to serve as warnings of what English Courts could be. They should help us to judge what the influence of George III. and Queen Charlotte was, and how it "made for righteousness."

V.

CAROLINE OF BRUNSWICK, WIFE OF GEORGE IV.

AUTHORITIES:

Lord Malmesbury, Lady Charlotte Bury, *The Jerningham Letters*, Dr. Doran, Thackeray, etc.

CAROLINE OF BRUNSWICK, WIFE OF GEORGE IV. (ABOUT THE TIME OF HER TRIAL).

CHAPTER I.

A ROYAL BRIDE.

CAROLINE OF BRUNSWICK, wife of George IV., was born at Brunswick in May, 1768. She was the second daughter of the reigning Duke of Brunswick and Princess Augusta, or, as her father would have had her called, "the Lady Augusta," whose birth occurred under such peculiar circumstances in the reign of George II. and his Queen Caroline. We hear more of Augusta as the Princess Augusta, elder sister of George III., who sought to patronise young Queen Charlotte. Princess Augusta's voluble heedless tongue and meddling propensity got her into mischief from her girlhood and were in evidence throughout her long life. She had not learnt wisdom with years, and her innate coarseness of grain had increased with her surroundings, until an elderly English gentleman, accustomed to the free-and-easy speech of his generation, could have blushed at the language which the Duchess of Brunswick used before her grown-up daughter. Duchess Augusta never had possessed the romantic attributes of Caroline Matilda of Denmark in the midst of her imprudence and recklessness. Neither had it been Augusta's fate to meet the terrible retribution which befell her unfortunate younger sister. The Duchess had her trials, numerous and sore enough to have crushed a less "easy-going," thick-skinned woman, but they were of a more prosaic nature than those which are linked with the name of Caroline Matilda of Denmark.

The Duchess of Brunswick was good-natured and affectionate on the surface, but was destitute of truthfulness, high principle, and the very elements of common sense and right judgment. Her daughter Caroline resembled her mother in many respects, with a quicker wit, a still more unscrupulous tongue, a double allowance of self-will, and an utterly uncontrolled stock of sensibility and sentimentality—perilous endowments for a future Queen. She was one of a family of six: four sons, brave like their bluff, gruff father, and an elder daughter Charlotte, four years the senior of Caroline, whose disastrous fate coming to a climax after Caroline was old enough to understand its significance was without power to warn and subdue her.

The Court of Brunswick with such a woman as Augusta at its head was full of coarseness and licence, and had a reputation for scandal and impropriety beyond that of any other German Court of the day. In this Court Princess Caroline, irresponsible by nature, grew up. She had ruled her mother from her childhood. She stood in fear of her father, while she passionately admired and loved him. She was now applauded for her wit, now blamed for her folly, now carelessly indulged and now rudely checked by her father, who did not afford her the example of a virtuous life. She received a scanty education, which managed to include proficiency on the harpsichord while it left out all real culture and refinement. Even in her girlhood poor spoilt, undisciplined Caroline was guilty of spurts of froward defiance of law and authority for which she was punished in a primitive fashion, by confinement to her rooms or by refusal to let her appear in the ducal circle, without the slightest effect on her in the shape of amendment.

George III. had set his heart on his eldest son's marrying as the sole means left for steadying him.

The King had another inducement: the marriage of the heir to the throne was the only chance of the country's coming forward finally to pay his enormous debts.

Caroline was the King's niece, the daughter of the sister of whom, according to herself, George had been fond in the old days, whose faults he might not have had the shrewdness to detect. Caroline's father was a reasonably honest man as well as a gallant soldier, though he was far from a model in other respects. According to one report the Duke of York, George's favourite son, had visited Brunswick and reported favourably of the personal and mental attractions of the Princess.

Queen Charlotte, like most sensible women, knew better than to advocate the match for her firstborn, who, in spite of his heartless disrespect towards her when he was temporarily in possession of power, kept a place in a mother's long-suffering heart. She was aware of her son's distaste to the marriage; she remembered "the Lady Augusta" who was never tired of retailing mischievous or spiteful gossip where her loyal forbearing sister-in-law was concerned. It seems the Queen must have heard of the misbehaviour and miserable end of her namesake Charlotte of Brunswick, together with hints that Princess Caroline was likely to be as unmanageable and unsatisfactory. To crown her objections, Queen Charlotte had other views for her prodigal son. She had destined a beautiful and, as she believed, a well-brought-up Princess of her own house of Mecklenburg-Strelitz to be offered up for the reformation of the Prince of Wales. If this Princess was the "Frederica" who was admired by her cousin Adolphus, Duke of Cambridge, and married by his elder brother Ernest, Duke of Cumberland, it is possible that Charlotte might have witnessed the wreck of her scheme; but she could not foresee its destruction.

The King's wish and the plausible expediency of the union carried the day. The Earl of Malmesbury was despatched to Brunswick with the necessary credentials and to make formal proposals on behalf of the King and the Prince of Wales for the hand of Princess Caroline.

The envoy was received with all the flutter of excitement and of gratified vanity and ambition which might have been expected.

The Duchess, while senselessly abusing Queen Charlotte and England in the hearing of her daughter, was openly delighted with the splendour of the match. The Duke had more self-restraint, more foresight, and a greater sense of honour. These caused him to drop various hints of the unfitness of Caroline for the position offered to her and to enjoin on Lord Malmesbury the thankless task—far too long delayed—of warning her of the pitfalls in her path, and of strongly advising her to curb her inclinations and to bring under control her free-and-easy manners, which were far removed from the decorum of a Court.

The bride, to whom the bridegroom had not written a word of greeting, was more offended than hurt by the omission, and was not much daunted in her elation at the brilliance of her prospects. Caroline was twenty-six years of age and had refused various suitors, among them a Mecklenburg Prince, who had received the support of the Duke and Duchess of Brunswick, a Prince of Orange, etc., etc. She was nice-looking at that stage of her life, with delicate features, good complexion, and teeth only beginning to decay. Her figure was not graceful; she was short with a tendency to stoutness, her head was too large for the lack of length in her neck, while of her shoulders Lord Malmesbury, in describing her, quotes the expressive French phrase, " *des épaules impertinentes.*"

The bridegroom, who had been reckoned handsome as an Apollo in his youth, was still regarded, even after more than a decade of fierce dissipation had left sure traces upon him, " as a man of fine presence," whose air and deportment were those of "the first gentleman in Europe." He began, however, to display an inclination to the corpulence which prevailed in his family and was a great mortification to his vanity. He was in his thirty-fifth year, nearly seven years Caroline's senior, and, what was infinitely more fatal to any chance of happiness for the couple, he had been married privately ten years before to Mrs. Fitzherbert.[1] He was also a mere tool in the hands of a wicked woman, Lady Jersey, whom he was about to appoint to one of the principal posts in the unfortunate Princess's household.

Lord Malmesbury fulfilled his mission with dignity, tact, and kindness. He thought well on the whole of Princess Caroline. He certainly knew her to be too good for the Prince to whom she was to be given. Prompted by his desire to serve her, and by his duty to his King and country, Lord Malmesbury acted on the Duke of Brunswick's suggestion. He administered to the Princess much excellent advice on behaving with discretion, being agreeable to her husband and respectful to the King and Queen, on keeping her own place, avoiding all undue familiarity with the members of her suite, asking no questions, having no confidant, etc., etc. To all the wise exhortations Caroline listened with wonderful docility for her.

Just before the marriage by proxy which took place on December 8th, 1794, the miniature of the bridegroom arrived. What impression it produced on the

[1] Mrs. Fitzherbert lived to be upwards of eighty years of age. Apart from her so-called marriage with the Prince of Wales, she had an unblemished reputation. A considerable annuity was granted to her, she was even allowed to use the royal liveries. She was treated with much forbearance and was generally liked.

impulsive bride we are not told. A less gracious act than sending the miniature was his forbidding a German lady to accompany Caroline—as a reader nominally, though according to the Duke of Brunswick the office was not likely to be a sinecure. The reason the Duke gave for the cancelled appointment was that his daughter wrote badly and spelt badly.

The marriage contract was signed and sealed, the heavy burdensome festivities were nearly over, the day before the bride's departure had arrived, when an ill-omened incident occurred. The Duchess received a packet of letters. One was from her brother King George, strongly recommending that the Princess of Wales on coming to England should lead a quiet, retired life. Another was a malicious anonymous letter warning Caroline's family of the character of the bridegroom, and of the troubles which were in store for his wife.

It was consistent with the Duchess's character that she should at once communicate the contents of the letters to her daughter. It was equally consistent with Caroline's disposition that the letters excited in her more of roused inquisitiveness and cool speculation than of either alarm or indignation.

The travellers—including the Duchess, who accompanied her daughter part of the way—started on a December afternoon, the cannon on the ramparts of the city sending after them a parting salute. The journey was then an arduous undertaking in the depth of a severe winter, with war raging between England and France. Lord Malmesbury had time to notice one respect in which the characters of mother and daughter differed materially. The Duchess was careful to penuriousness where money was concerned, the Princess was liberal in a lavish, prodigal way; both were alike in their want of self-restraint, in laughing with hardly an attempt at concealment at anything which struck them as odd in the appearance and manners of the ladies and gentlemen presented to them at the different halting stations.

The party took a well-earned rest at Hanover, which they reached nearly a month after starting on their journey from Brunswick, and where they remained three weeks.

Of Hanover as of England Caroline would be the future Queen. While the Hanoverians entertained her with all honour, she was bound to make the best impression she could upon them, were it only in preparation for the more severe ordeal of her presentation to the English people. She seems to have acted with more propriety than could have been hoped for at this early stage of her introduction to Court ceremonial. Indeed, her volatile mind had been latterly full of the idea of reforming her husband (the man she had never seen), of making up to him and to the nation for his alienation from the King and Queen. She would stand between the divided factions, linking them together, herself a model of all that a Princess and a wife should be. She would earn the gratitude of the country by her good offices.

Lord Malmesbury, while gravely applauding her excellent intentions, must have had a depressing consciousness of the egregious vanity and presumption of the notion on the part of the young woman whom he had still to instruct in the A B C of self-respect and good feeling; for she would rattle on in conversation, in any company she happened to be in, on the most foolish incidents of her past life, and on the grandeur of her future, whose difficulties she was prepared to defy and surmount in the most marvellous manner; and she would laugh without scruple at the absurdities of her silly mother.

Lord Malmesbury had a still more delicate task to accomplish. He was scandalised at the coarseness of the Princess's under-clothing and the slovenliness of her toilettes. He had to impress on a German lady at the Hanoverian Court that something very different was called for. He had even himself to hint broadly to her Royal Highness that the quick dressing on which she prided herself was worse than undesirable, when it left such results of dirt and disorder as were patent to his enlightened eyes.

Poor benighted Caroline! to have what she had regarded as a cardinal virtue, the mark of a superior mind, thus classed as an offence, and to be humiliated by the information of how she, who had done what she liked and had received her meed of admiration from a Court circle no more dainty than herself, would be viewed by her fastidious, abandoned husband!

At Hanover the Princess parted from her mother, with profuse tears on the Duchess's part and some show of becoming regard on the daughter's. On March 26th, almost three months from the date of their leaving Brunswick, Lord Malmesbury embarked with his troublesome charge on board the fifty-gun frigate *Jupiter*, which at once discharged a broadside to welcome the Princess of Wales. A midshipman named Doyle was the proud lad who was permitted to hand her a rope to help her in ascending from the cutter to the ship. The Princess won golden opinions among the sailors for her affability and cheerfulness, and for her fearlessness of any such casualty as being captured by the French.

On April 3rd the *Jupiter* anchored at the Nore, and on the following day—Easter Sunday—surely a day of good omen, the Princess proceeded in a barge to Greenwich, her progress watched by shouting thousands. But at Greenwich her reception was very much like that accorded to her grandmother, Augusta of Saxe-Coburg, when she came to England to marry Fritz,

Prince of Wales. There was nobody to greet the stranger, and though she arrived at noon she had to wait an hour for the royal carriages. When they did come they brought no princely bridegroom. George Augustus Frederick did not choose to come in person to welcome his cousin and bride, but he sent in his place the ladies of her suite; conspicuous among them the detestable Countess of Jersey (Childe the banker's great heiress). She immediately began to take insolent liberties with the foreigner, laughing at her dress and attempting to put herself on an equality with her by seeking to drive in the same coach, even to sit by the Princess's side, on her entrance into the capital. It was all the worthy Malmesbury could do to rebuff the brazen-faced usurper. How fruitless his efforts had been may be guessed from the fact that short as was the time the Princess and Lady Jersey were left together, yet Caroline, though forewarned, and though acquainted with the character of her lady-in-waiting,[1] was so infatuated as to attempt to pit her shallow wits against the craft of the other. The consequence was that the Princess fell immediately into Lady Jersey's snare by taking refuge in mad bravado, in the course of which she gave the eager listener the gratuitous assurance that her heart was not hers to give, it was already bestowed on an enamoured and inconsolable German.

A tradition lingers of Lady Jersey in connection with Caroline's English, which she spoke badly and wrote and spelt execrably. It is said that Lady Jersey suggested to the Princess words Caroline did not understand, words which used in conversation before the Prince would inevitably repel and disgust him.

[1] Caroline eventually appealed to the King on the insult inflicted upon her by having Lady Jersey in the suite, and the lady was made to resign her office.

The Princess was taken first to the Duke of Cumberland's rooms in Cleveland Row, St. James's. There at last the Prince joined her. The account of the pitiable interview is preserved in Lord Malmesbury's diary.

He introduced Princess Caroline. She attempted to kneel as she had been told. The Prince raised her, went through the form of embracing her, said "barely one word, turned round, retired to a distant part of the room, and called, ' Harris, I am not well ; pray get me a glass of brandy.' 'Sir, had you not better have a glass of water ? ' was the amendment of the disinterested envoy. Upon which he, much out of humour, said with an oath, 'No, I will go directly to the Queen,' and away he went."

And what of the Princess? The poor girl was amazed and well-nigh scared. The first sight of the man whom she had meant to reform was not encouraging. " Is the Prince always like that ? " she asked her friend in French. " I find him stout and not by any means so handsome as in his portrait."

If she had known it and he had known it, the word " stout " would have cut into the Prince's sensibility far more than many a harsher word. He lived in horror of his increasing stoutness. Leigh Hunt's " fat Adonis of fifty," Beau Brummel's " fat friend," maliciously applied to the Prince in years to come, stung the over-grown, used-up exquisite in the most sensitive quarter.

The Sunday drawing-room was over, but the Princess was present at the dinner afterwards. It is not wonderful, perhaps, that her father's strict injunctions and all Malmesbury's elaborate instructions were cast to the winds. Caroline thought fit to appear to the new relations who had received her coolly in her very worst colours. She was noisy, flippant, and underbred, making allusions which no modest woman ought to have made, and using the coarse expressions of which Lord Malmesbury had tried hard to break her. If Europe had been sought from end to end no Princess, innocent of absolute wrong-doing, could have been found more repugnant to Queen Charlotte in her dignity, good sense, and in that scrupulous regard for the conventionalities of life which was born and bred in her very goodness, than was the forward, indelicate, vulgar hoyden [1] who was about to become the wife of the Queen's son.

If the first meeting of the troth-plighted, ill-suited couple was pitiable, the circumstances of their marriage were positively ghastly. The ceremony, which was performed by the Archbishop of Canterbury, took place on April 8th, 1795. All the royal family dined together at the Queen's House and dressed at St. James's Palace, assembling at the Queen's rooms there before walking in procession to the Chapel Royal. The only cordiality shown on the occasion was by the King, who kissed his niece affectionately and shook by both hands the graceless son, who had fortified himself with a stock of Dutch courage for the trial he was to undergo. If magnificent dress could have concealed the tragedy which was being enacted, the dress was not wanting. Hoops swayed, lace fluttered, ostrich plumes waved. Caroline was in white satin embroidered with pearls, she wore a mantle of crimson velvet lined with ermine and had a small crown on her fair hair. At that date, so adorned, she was a comely bride but for the flurry of ostentatious indifference amounting to defiance which was in her bearing.

The bridegroom was in a Court costume—a blue velvet coat, knee-breeches, buckles, and pointed shoes—while he held in his hand a three-cornered hat with

[1] Yet Caroline was not without brains and kindness of heart, and everybody agreed that she could be dignified when she liked.

a rich diamond buckle and loop. He had still the remains of a goodly physique, but according to Lord Holland the Prince was so intoxicated that he could not have kept his feet had he not been supported by two of the royal Dukes, his brothers; as it was, in the middle of a prayer he staggered up from his knees, and the ceremony would have been interrupted had not the King crossed quickly to his son, whispered to him, and induced him to kneel down again.

There was a supper afterwards at Buckingham House previous to the unhappy couple's departing at midnight for his residence, Carlton House. According to rumour they were heard wrangling the whole way. The quarrelling did not cease next day, when he found fault with her shoes and she flung down in a heap before him the letters of congratulation she had received from the heads of different European Courts, saying these were to show that she was not an impostor.

The income voted to the Prince was £12,000 a year apart from the revenue of the duchy of Cornwall; that to the Princess was £50,000 annually, with £45,000 in addition to provide her with jewels and to defray the expense of refurnishing Carlton House. The Prince's income did not satisfy him because a yearly deduction was to be made from it for the payment of his debts in the course of nine years. He complained bitterly of this arrangement as a breach of the pledge in reliance on which he had been induced to marry Princess Caroline of Brunswick.

CHAPTER II.

A CONTENTIOUS COUPLE.

THE estrangement of the couple was complete from the first, and neither made the slightest attempt to bridge over the gulf; though they went through the form of the usual appearance together at the theatre and went in company to an entertainment given in their honour by the Queen at Frogmore.

Queen Charlotte tried to do her duty, but according to Lord Malmesbury she was stiff in her civility, while the unruly daughter-in-law, superbly dressed, looked "black as thunder." The Princess had some excuse for her wrath. Ordinarily she was like her mother, good-natured with the easy good nature of a person of no principle, no earnestness or real depth of feeling. But a packet of letters written to her family and friends, in which she had descanted freely on her position, and had made sundry smart criticisms of the Queen's person, etc., etc., had miscarried, been opened, and the contents had, as Caroline suspected, come to Queen Charlotte's knowledge.

For about a year, till a little after the birth of Princess Charlotte of Wales, Caroline remained at Carlton House, but practically she and the Prince of Wales "lived in different houses and were never alone together." At the end of the year a formal permanent separation was agreed upon, and the Princess, accompanied by a small suite of ladies, removed with alacrity first to the village of Charlton and afterwards to Blackheath, in connection with which she held an appointment—that of Ranger of Greenwich Park. Her income was much what it had been previously. The one point on which George IV. showed some consideration for his wife was in not robbing her of the means of living according to her station. He expressed himself more than once as desirous that the Princess should be free from pecuniary difficulties.[1]

The King, her uncle, countenanced Caroline by occasionally paying her a visit, a kindly attention the Prince of Wales bitterly resented. The Queen never came: she disapproved as strongly of the separation as she had disapproved of the ill-starred marriage. The greatest injustice done to Caroline then was the withdrawal from her of her child. She was extravagantly fond of all babies, and she was naturally fond of her own. The child was consigned to the care of her father, who had little affection for his daughter. He showed how little by the repeated capricious changes he made in her household throughout her youth, without paying the slightest heed to her feelings in the matter. The poor girl had no sooner grown attached to her governesses than she found them removed and herself committed afresh to the care of strangers, from no apparent motive, unless that she was not to be suffered to know and be happy with her guardians.

However, there were limits to the Prince's harshness to his wife, or, what is more probable, he entertained a certain fear of public opinion. He sent the child, in the charge of Lady Elgin, to stay in a house of her own at Blackheath, and once a week the little Princess was permitted to go to her mother.

Caroline began her life at Blackheath with unusual credit to herself. She seemed to aim at living quietly,

[1] She never was exempt from them.

was content with her income, took pleasure in her garden, inquired into the wants of the neighbouring poor and sought to relieve them. She was generous to excess, though mostly injudicious in her generosity. She put out several poor children to nurse[1] and taught others, personally instructing them in English reading, writing, etc., etc. Her qualifications as a teacher were on a par with her attributes as a husband-reformer.

The Princess was not without society. From sympathy or from curiosity many distinguished and many more simply agreeable men and women sought her company. She was undeniably hospitable, she gave pleasant dinners and suppers, in which the chief fault was that everybody was too much at his or her ease and unbounded hilarity was the order of the day, until no room was left for a wise and respectful recollection of the Princess's rank, not to say of her peculiar position. Blind-man's buff was one of the games played at these unceremonious parties, which were often prolonged to midnight.

The Princess's spirits when high (they were either high or low) got the better of her. She delighted in astonishing and scandalising people—a weak and dangerous form of vanity. When the poet Campbell was presented to her she insisted on dancing a reel with him. In writing of her afterwards he described her as "a fine body." A story is told of her that an artist appointed to paint her picture and shown into her morning-room for the purpose found her sitting on the floor, without shoes or stockings, eating a potato. He would have retreated in dismay until she had assumed a more suitable dress and attitude, but she refused to let him go, treating his scruples with gay ridicule and bidding him

[1] Caroline told Lady Charlotte Bury that she had nine children, and in answer to Lady Charlotte's incredulous amazement explained that the eight boys and one girl referred to were adopted children whom she supported.

paint her as she was. A Princess so unsophisticated, or rather so regardless of the laws which govern society, is in a perilous way. What made it worse for Caroline, Princess of Wales, was that she had ceased to be in her first youth. A girl's impulsive thoughtlessness and giddiness could no longer be pled in extenuation of a woman's madcap pranks.

At last a very demon of mischief took possession of Caroline. Instead of avoiding the appearance of evil she sedulously cultivated it. She took what was little short of an insane satisfaction in outraging the prejudices of her neighbours, in mystifying and misleading them, so that they might believe her guilty of shameful vice —of which, in spite of her glaring follies, the general evidence shows she was incapable. It is hardly necessary to say that no woman with any strong sense of duty and any delicate purity of mind could have fallen over such an ugly precipice.

In a miserable hour for Caroline she made the acquaintance of an officer named Sir John Douglas and his wife Lady Douglas. The couple had lately returned from Egypt and were settled for a time at Blackheath. Caroline introduced herself to them in the erratic, inconsiderate manner she was fond of adopting. She had heard they had a beautiful child whom she wished to see. In order to gratify the whim, she set out, on a winter morning, to cross the heath, which happened to be covered with snow, in a lilac satin pelisse, primrose-coloured half-boots, and a small lilac travelling cap trimmed with sable. Unannounced and uninvited she let it be seen that she intended to make a call on the Douglases. She was politely received by the pair, who could hardly decline the honour of her acquaintance, which, thus unceremoniously begun, rapidly ripened into a violent friendship between the two women and into the appointment of Lady Douglas as one of her

Royal Highness's suite. The ladies were in some respects kindred spirits. Lady Douglas, a matron of doubtful reputation, was much the craftier and more evilly disposed of the two; Sir John, as far as can be discovered, was a mere tool of his wife's.

A coolness arose on the Princess's side towards her quondam friend, and she broke off the connection, refusing to give any explanation of the breach. It is said to have arisen from her having acted, rather late in the day, with a little more prudence than she was wont to display in taking to heart a friend's revelation of some of Lady Douglas's antecedents, with the advice to Caroline to be on her guard where Lady Douglas was concerned.

Lady Douglas was furious at the stop put to the friendship, and so pestered the Princess for an explanation that she had recourse for counsel and assistance to her brother-in-law the Duke of Kent. He succeeded with some difficulty in inducing Sir John Douglas, in whose eyes the matter was complicated by an anonymous letter and an offensive drawing which he ascribed, without proof, to the Princess of Wales, to submit to the Princess's decision.

But the malice of a slighted, vindictive woman who sticks at nothing to accomplish her revenge is not easily defeated. It was contrived that her story should reach the ears of the Duke of Sussex, who believed himself called upon to lay it before the Prince of Wales, and he was only too willing, in his unmanly hatred of his wife and his persecution of her when he dared, to receive every bad report against her. Had the King been in his usual health, he might have afforded his niece more effectual protection; but he was then hovering on the brink of madness, and nobody dared to appeal to him on a subject certain to distress him. As for the Queen, good woman as she was, she showed herself fatally biassed against her daughter-in-law. She had washed her hands of her from the first. Caroline's every word and act ran counter to Charlotte's keen sense of what was right, and she was now beyond the age when people's opinions and convictions are easily modified. Her position with regard to Caroline was very much that of the Electress Sophia towards the wife of George I., but, to begin with at least, the Electress was less rigidly hostile to the younger Sophia. The elder woman did her best to restrain and quiet the younger until the faithless wife broke all bounds. A woman with far rougher surroundings, in less happy circumstances than Charlotte, wedded to her loyal, dutiful George, the Electress was in some respects, because of her individual traits, perhaps, a larger minded, less intolerant woman than was the Queen. But there are other items to be taken into consideration. Both women had sons whom the mothers, as mothers will, regarded in the light of the victims of their erring wives. Charlotte especially, who had been so fondly attached to the Prince of Wales—of whose beauty, grace, and wit as a lad she had been extremely proud—clung to the one excuse for the Prince's debauchery, heartlessness, and falseness, that if he had married a better woman he might have been a better man; she might, in a homely English phrase, have "kept him straight," as, indeed, poor Caroline had proposed to herself to do. It would have been a wise woman who would have brought George Augustus Frederick to a sense of the obligations of a fairly honest, temperate, reverent man.

Queen Charlotte, besides getting and taking the greatest credit for the virtuous character of her Court, had also unmarried daughters, excellent young women, whom she had reared with the greatest care. She had their honour and interests to guard, and it was not to be supposed that their minds and morals would be improved by coming into contact with such a daughter of Heth as the Princess of Wales was proving herself.

The Prince of Wales called upon Lady Douglas to substantiate the accusations she was spreading abroad. The result was a deposition by Lady Douglas in which she made the basest and most odious charges against the Princess, taking advantage of their former intimacy to allege familiarity with the details and to bring forward many small incidents which had really occurred in order to corroborate the hideous story. The names of various gentlemen, including the gallant naval officer Sir Sydney Smith, and the eminent portrait-painter Sir Thomas Lawrence, together with others of less note, were coupled with that of the Princess. The main point on which the slander turned was that the Princess had adopted a baby (as she had busied herself with various babies before). The infant, a boy of poor parents named Austin, had been brought into her house and was kept constantly with her. This child, Lady Douglas declared, was Caroline's child by her own cool, careless admission.

The matter could not rest there. A commission was appointed and witnesses, chiefly the Princess's servants, were examined against and for her. These servants had not been appointed by Caroline, they were nominated to their posts by the Prince of Wales and his agents, and they regarded him—their future King—as their master, from whom their promotion was to come. Nevertheless, though some of them professed to confirm and even to render worse Lady Douglas's gross assertions, there were others who emphatically denied them. The different gentlemen concerned contradicted positively and indignantly on oath their share in Lady Douglas's accusation. It was demonstrated beyond question that the child Austin (whom his adopted mother called "Willikin," continuing defiantly to keep him in her house and to pet and play with him immoderately) was as had been said the son of poor parents—in fact, was none other than one of those nurslings whom Caroline had taken out of charity and to whom she had played the part of Lady Bountiful. She had a greater liking for him than for the others, and the fancy had seized her to have him constantly with her.

For some time the Princess was kept largely in the dark about the steps taken against her, and for nine weeks she remained in suspense as to the decision of the King, before whom and his ministers the unpleasant affair had at last to be laid. Naturally, but illogically, Caroline, like many other foolish women who have done everything in their power to provoke groundless aspersions of their characters, was highly indignant at the turn events had taken, and from that date posed as a cruelly wronged woman, with a shrill cry for justice, and a wild clamour against her enemies added to the other elements of flighty insubordination which were always to be found in her nature.

Fortunately for the Princess she consented at this season to be controlled by friends wiser than herself. One of them, the Cabinet Minister Perceval, wrote respectful but urgent appeals to the King to remove the stigma which had been cast upon her. Perceval let it be understood that if the appeals were passed by the version of the infamous charge held by Caroline and her supporters should be laid before the public. The threat was effectual, both the original commission and the King's ministers pronounced the Princess innocent of crime ; though by the mouth of the King, who announced to his daughter-in-law that she was exculpated, they considered, with reason, her conduct as unbecoming in a woman of her rank and position, and enjoined on her to behave with greater circumspection in the future—an injunction which Caroline, tingling with resentment at the light in which her conduct had been viewed, treated with scornful indifference.

If Caroline of Brunswick had been capable of serious thought there were other events then happening in her family which were calculated to sober and steady her. Her father, the old man whom she loved, fell fighting, bravely but in vain, with his Brunswickers against Napoleon at the battle of Jena. Her mother, an aging woman, was forced to return as a fugitive to that England she had assailed with abuse, which she had left as a bride forty years before. Unhappily, the old Duchess was not the style of woman to be of much benefit to her daughter. Neither adversity, nor the kindness which King George and Queen Charlotte showed her in her tribulation, had taught her wisdom any more than time had inculcated discretion. She still "babbled every thought which came into her head." She found her dinner-table, to which she had invited Lady Jerningham[1] among other guests, a proper place for the discussion of the state of the Duchess's soul, about which she delivered sundry pious commonplace reflections.

The Duchess lived partly in a house in Spring Gardens, shabby enough in relation to her rank, partly at Blackheath, where, though she occupied a separate house, she was near her daughter. In the course of years of separation an oddly shown affection had developed between them. It was greatest on the mother's side, while it had some place in the daughter's heart, though Caroline, Princess of Wales, was still less disposed than Caroline, Princess of Brunswick, had been, to brook contradiction or to give honour where honour to age and maternity was due.

The old Duchess replied with much spirit to the

[1] *The Jerningham Letters.*

insulting observation made by the Prince of Wales when he offered to come and pay his respects to his aunt, provided, he stipulated, that he was ensured from meeting the Princess of Wales.

The mother replied that she should be happy to see her nephew, but that as her daughter came to see her at all hours she could not engage that his Royal Highness might not encounter his wife.

After all, not only the King and Queen visited the pathetic wreck of "the Lady Augusta," the Prince of Wales condescended to call in Spring Gardens at the risk of encountering Caroline there. The Duchess received at last an invitation to Carlton House. Here was a temptation difficult for her to resist; she would see again her old home where she had spent her childhood and youth, she would be able to criticise the changes and improvements made on it—first for the reception of Caroline, whose stay in it had been brief, and second to illustrate the splendid tastes of its master. Besides, the simple, garrulous old woman was easily propitiated, and she was fond of such society as she would obtain, mostly made up of stranded old people like herself who remembered the boyhood of her brother George III., the heartless vagaries of their father, Prince Fritz, and the Court of George II. in its licence and coarseness. (Caroline nicknamed her mother's circle "Dullification" and openly yawned when she was detained in it.) The Duchess went so far as to hesitate whether to accept or reject her son-in-law's invitation, but her better and more motherly feelings conquered; for had she consented to appear at Carlton House she would have been considered as ranging herself on the side of the Prince of Wales and condemning her daughter.

Little Princess Charlotte had now a grandmother as well as a mother to fondle her when she was suffered to see them. (Caroline, in her Philistine spelling, termed her child a "dear Angle.") Princess Charlotte was treated more rationally and with more discipline by her relatives at Windsor, with whom at the same time she was a favourite. She was a pretty fair-haired child, the chief defect of her face being the lightness of her eyebrows and eyelashes. As she grew older she showed slight traces of an attack of smallpox. She was naturally lively, and her childish sallies amused her grandfather, whose sight was waning more and more, while over him hung the melancholy of his realisation of the mental cloud which was descending upon him.

As a seal to the justification of Caroline she was again free to attend the Queen's drawing-rooms; she went to two in 1807. Dr. Doran quotes the account given of her by Sir Jonah Barrington, who chanced to be present. It tallies to a remarkable extent with the mercurial temper of the Princess. She advanced down the room leaning on the arm of her brother-in-law the Duke of Cumberland, who was sure to espouse the cause of any man or woman of whom the rest of his family disapproved. She was in deep mourning because of the recent death of her father, and some emotion overcame her so that she "tottered" as she approached the Queen. Sir Jonah thought she feared a repulse; but his unprejudiced testimony was that her Majesty was "kind," while other onlookers commented on "the cold civility" which was all that was accorded to the culprit. Caroline's spirits, however, rose in a rebound at the concession. She talked much and loudly as was her wont, and "was bold." She did not hesitate to gather around her a cluster of sympathising members of the nobility, and with a total absence of tact she consented to have many presentations made to her, as if she were anticipating the day when she should be Queen and was holding a Court of her own.

At the second drawing-room that painfully dramatic incident of the last meeting and parting of the Prince and Princess of Wales took place. They came face to face in the centre of the crowded room among the throng of gay company when every eye was upon the two. Caroline had left off her mourning for her father: she was dressed in much splendour, even gaiety. Her love of striking effects came out in the border of her silver tissue train and of the petticoat to her silver and lilac bodice. The border was embroidered to represent vine-leaves and grapes by means of emerald, topaz, and amethyst stones, with which the dress was literally sown. Silver laurel looped up the drapery and edged the pocket-hole. Her head-dress was the usual ostrich feathers and diamonds.

The Prince was, of course, in a Court suit, with its lace ruffles, star and ribbon, knee breeches, silk stockings, and buckled shoes.

The magnificent miserable couple bowed, stood opposite each other for a moment, "exchanged a few words which no one heard, and then passed on, he stately as an iceberg and as cold, she with a smile, half mirthful, half melancholy, as though she rejoiced that she was there in spite of him, and yet regretted that her visit was not made under happier auspices."

Alas! poor Caroline, no man on earth would have made her a wise or a refined woman, but with a husband kind and humane she might have been respectable and happy.

Princess Charlotte of Wales, a girl of eleven, in a Brussels lace frock with a pink and silver sash, was present on this memorable occasion. What could she have thought, precocious as she was with a sad precocity, of this meeting and greeting between her father and mother?

The next trouble was the Princess of Wales's debts.

In spite of her large income and her simple enough personal habits, she was so incapable of managing money and so much at the mercy of her servants that she owed as much as fifty thousand pounds. The difficulty was surmounted by the execution of a regular deed of separation between the Prince and Princess of Wales, in consideration of which and of his ceasing to be liable for her further expenses he consented to pay her standing debts. Her income was settled at £22,000 a year and was put under the care of a treasurer, who was in a manner responsible for its proper disposal. The Princess in contending for her rights had asked for rooms in one of the royal palaces, and apartments were granted to her in Kensington Palace.

In 1820 George III. became hopelessly insane, and the Prince of Wales was appointed Prince Regent. Until then Caroline had kept up around her something like a Court, and her balls and dinners were freely attended by the Dukes and Duchesses of Portland and Beaufort and other prominent members of the nobility; but from the time that George was Regent the great world came no more, or only very sparingly, to the dingy red brick palace associated closely with the memories of Dutch William and his Mary, of Anne, of George II., his Queen Caroline, and their numerous family. Still Caroline, Princess of Wales, maintained her shadow of a Court, in opposition to that of the Prince Regent, neither of the Courts being by any means models of what they ought to have been. The Princess was as careless as ever of courtly etiquette. On her birthday, when she might expect a crowd of such visitors as were left to her, Lady Charlotte Bury found her in a pink flannel dressing-gown, encouraging her young daughter to disparage laughingly, with her "loud musical laugh," a valuable jewelled aigrette

which the Queen, seeking to keep the peace, had sent
as a birthday gift to her daughter-in-law. She was not
more discreet in other respects. She affected frankness
and sincerity to the extent of assuming an indecent
heartlessness which was foreign to her character. She
declared that she was only afraid Princess Amelia would
die because then she could not go out and amuse herself. She was fond of the play, but would sometimes
attend it more for the gratification of others than for her
own pleasure. On the birthday of the boy "Willikin,"
whom she kept with her in a very doggedness of fidelity,
she insisted, though ill and suffering, on taking him to
the theatre. She heard that the Prince Regent was
dangerously ill, and she wrote to one of her cronies that
she could not "flatter herself that the period to all her
troubles" was yet come. She was in the frequent
habit after dinner, when she was not restrained by the
presence of strangers, of moulding little wax figures,
which she supplied with horns, and into which she
stuck three pins taken from her dress, previous to
roasting them before a fire. She did it half in bravado,
half with the superstition that by destroying this curious
series of effigies of her husband she would in turn
destroy him. She would have no servants wait at
dinner, and had dumb waiters instead. With regard
to the dinners themselves, at which Princess Charlotte
was allowed to present herself every Saturday, "the
food was bad and the wine worse." She was never
happy unless when talking of her grievances, and then
she would constantly repeat the strong expression, of
which she was fond, " to tell you God's truth."

Her sole attempts at intellectual pursuits were reading
aloud and keeping a kind of diary, in which she made
in her bad English daringly sarcastic sketches of the
people she had known in England. She had her noisy
free-and-easy dinner parties and concerts on Sundays in

defiance of English habits.[1] She would go out sometimes in the evening and in dinner dress accompanied only by one of her ladies, to whose dismay Caroline would pass out of Kensington Gardens and stroll beyond Bayswater into the adjacent fields at the risk of being accosted and insulted. She would seat herself beside strangers on the garden benches, talk to them and entertain herself by leading them to speak of the Princess of Wales and to give their opinon of her disposition and of the treatment she had received. Caroline's brother, the Duke of Brunswick, was a refugee in England. His two boys, Duke William and Duke Charles, also came over and were lodged at the top of a house in Vauxhall. Caroline went to visit her nephews occasionally. In driving out one of her queer unconventional proceedings was not to send out directions to the coachman or even to deliver the directions to him personally, she preferred simply to point to him, at short intervals, where she wished him to go.

She was by no means so fond of these youthful Dukes —her kindred in adversity—as she was of the promiscuous collection of babies she adopted and reared. She never saw her nephews without apostrophising their ugliness.

The Princess of Wales removed in 1814 from her apartments in Kensington Palace to a house in Connaught Place, where she was still more her own mistress. The best of her supporters began to shrink from her friendship; she sank lower and lower in the company she kept, especially in relation to a cottage in the neighbourhood, to which she went *incognito*, where she saw people quite out of her sphere. There is no name for these expeditions except the slang term "larks." Caroline was partial to "larks" and to the incongruous company, the members of which felt no scruple in making her an

---

[1] The King and Queen had also given dinners on Sundays, but their dinners were of a different order.

object of ridicule and laughing to her face at her broken English and odd ways. She enjoyed every form of mystification and was fond of the silly tricks and vulgar practical jokes which would have been distasteful to any person of intelligence and honour and were far beneath her dignity.

Yet Caroline could act the Princess when she chose and so could her young daughter, who with many fine qualities was not without alarming indications of having inherited her mother's impulsive rashness and obstinacy, just as she had inherited her fair complexion and her full, somewhat voluptuous figure, early tending to *embonpoint*. Perhaps a perception of this likeness was one reason for the Prince of Wales's coldness and harshness to his daughter. The apprehension of what might be the result of frequent unrestrained intercourse with her mother, in intensifying the traits which mother and child had in common, might be in part the reason why Caroline and her daughter were so systematically and persistently separated, and why every vexatious obstacle which could be interposed was put between them. It is more rational to suppose that these considerations had some weight with the Prince Regent than to imagine, as the Princess of Wales and her more violent partisans took pleasure in believing, that he was solely actuated by a vindictive desire to thwart and affront his wife.

The poor young girl, Princess Charlotte, stood up with pathetic loyalty for the mother whose natural affection for her child won a return in kind, but who was incapable of inspiring respect. Charlotte had arrived at the age of being formally presented to the Queen her grandmother, and it was arranged that the girl's aunt, the Duchess of York, should make the presentation. Against this arrangement with its marked slight to the Princess of Wales young Charlotte struggled with all her might. She declared that she would be presented by her mother or not at all. But as the Prince of Wales, now invested with the additional power of Prince Regent, had intimated to the Queen that he objected to the appearance of the Princess of Wales at any function in which he might take part, her attendance at the drawing-rooms was thenceforth perforce dispensed with. The substitution of the Duchess of York for the Princess of Wales in the performance of a duty which was specially a mother's contained the additional sting that even before her marriage Caroline appears to have cherished an unexplained dislike to the good little Duchess. After her marriage it is easy to understand how a hot-headed, feather-brained woman would entertain an aversion for the far wiser, better woman who was always held up to her as an example, with whose conduct her own was perpetually compared unfavourably. The sequel of the contest was that the young Princess was forced to yield.

Under the exasperation of the circumstances Caroline allowed her defenders to publish a letter in her name which the Prince had refused to open. It contained a protest against the unmerited injuries and indignities she was suffering, chief among them being her practical separation from her daughter. The result of this letter and of the altercations to which it gave rise in the Privy Council and in Parliament was that the mother and daughter were forbidden to have any intercourse for the time—a prohibition which did not prevent the Princess of Wales from causing her coachman, on one occasion at least, to drive after the carriage of Princess Charlotte, who was then living at Warwick House under the guardianship of the Duchess of Leeds. When the open carriages were drawn up side by side Caroline and the young Princess leant over and kissed each other affectionately, and conversed for a few moments, to the edification of a cheering crowd which speedily collected.

The Duchess of Brunswick, after her many vicissitudes, died in her house in Spring Gardens somewhat unexpectedly towards the close of March, 1813. She had been ill for a little time and her daughter had been with her the previous evening. The Duchess had been of little service to Caroline whether as child or woman, but she was an old familiar figure never wanting in a certain fondness for her children—among them her wayward daughter and her brave son the exiled Duke, who was destined in the course of the next two years to fall in the preliminary skirmish at Quatre Bras. The Duchess of Brunswick was buried without any display in Westminster Abbey. She had been six years resident in her native England, to which she had returned under such disastrous circumstances.

The great event of 1814 was the visit of the Allied Sovereigns to London; but though they were old war comrades of her father's and he had been slain in their cause Caroline had little to do with the festivities with which all London was ablaze. She was not permitted to attend the drawing-rooms, and the greatest notice the visitors took of her was when one of them sent his chamberlain to make formal inquiries for her in his master's name. She was deeply wounded, for she had sat, day after day, in feverish expectation of the arrival of the Emperor of Russia, or the King of Prussia, or at the very least of her nephew, her unhappy sister's son, Prince Paul of Würtemberg, whom Lady Charlotte Bury described as "a squinting bird, dancing and scolding the ladies"; but not one paid her the small mark of respect which the briefest visit would have implied. It is well understood that this utter neglect was in compliance with the urgent solicitation of the Prince Regent. The time was not well chosen for such harsh treatment. The Princess had been acting with unusual submission to authority, and when there was a proposal in Parliament to restore her income to the original £50,000 per annum, she voluntarily gave up £15,000 of the sum. It was these careless examples of free-handed generosity in which justice was not always a conspicuous element which endeared her to the unthinking, easily dazzled populace.

Caroline did see, as she had a great desire to do, the Emperor Alexander of Russia at the Opera House. It was a strange scene, for in the royal box between him and the King of Prussia sat the Prince Regent. When the air, which was being sung as the Princess entered, was finished, the great audience in the pit turned to her with hearty applause. She refused to acknowledge the compliment, saying with a flash of the scathing wit, which was one of her attractions and at the same time one of her snares, " Punch's wife is nobody when Punch is present." After the Prince Regent and the Allies were gone the mass of the audience called for the Princess of Wales, when she came forward, " made three curtsies," and then withdrew modestly enough. In the street her coach was surrounded by a vociferous mob, saluting her, asking to shake hands with her, and offering if she liked to burn down Carlton House, opposite which the carriage was passing. The character of the Prince Regent was well known to the masses, and was detested by them with an exaggeration of detestation. The tide of popular sympathy turning to the Princess was equally exaggerated and unreasoning, and had already a strongly political colouring.

The Princess was pleased and touched by the clamorous demonstrations. She was at her best when she answered : " No, my good people, be quiet. Let me pass, and go home to your beds."

When the Prince went in dignified procession with

his distinguished guests to a banquet in the City, he was followed from Temple Bar to the Mansion House by hoots and hisses and jeering cries, "Where's your wife?"

In the meantime, Caroline, who was now in her forty-fifth year, had been attending a masquerade, to which she went at twelve o'clock at night with her amazed ladies by a back-staircase and a back-door, at which they met the gentlemen of the suite who escorted them on foot through the streets to the Albany, where the intending masquers changed their dresses. One is reminded of poor Marie Antoinette in the thoughtless frolics in which she indulged in company with her brother-in-law, the Comte d'Artois, when both were in the grace and the gracelessness of their first youth, and of all the woful consequences which resulted from the idle pranks of a boy and girl. But this was no girl, this over-grown, giggling, senseless woman with a daughter on the threshold of womanhood—nay, Princess Charlotte of Wales's marriage was already on the *tapis*; and here again her loyalty to her foolish mother stepped in and broke off the contract.

The Prince of Orange was the suitor, who was acceptable to the Prince Regent and the country. The Prince Regent indeed wished to be quit of his daughter in an honourable way, to get her settled out of the country where her disturbing presence would no longer interfere with his comfort and complicate his relations with her mother.

The Prince of Orange did not attract the Princess particularly, but she was not so happily situated as to be obdurate to friendly representations. The barrier arose when she clearly understood not only that she, the heiress to the crown of England, would be expected to live in Holland, but that her mother would not be a welcome guest there. It is said that matters had gone so far that the Prince of Orange submitted to the Princess a programme of the celebration of the marriage together with a list of the guests he wished to be invited on the occasion, and that when she saw that her mother's name was absent she promptly returned the list with the name of the bridegroom struck out.

The next proceeding on the part of the Prince Regent was to order that his daughter should remove at once to Cranbourne Lodge near Windsor and thenceforth reside there with a fresh household of ladies appointed by him. This new instance of tyranny, with the apparent purpose of separating her more entirely from her mother, drove the high-spirited girl to violent revolt. The plan which occurred to her was first to ask a short respite that she might take leave of her dismissed ladies and prepare for the journey, and then when the Prince was gone to Carlton House to steal out in the dusk of the summer evening (it was in the month of July and the weather was fine) and make her way to her mother. Princess Charlotte had never been out alone before, she had hardly put her dainty foot on the common pavement. Her mother's escapades had all been executed apart from her daughter.

It is like a fairy-tale to realise a young Princess threading the throng of ordinary wayfarers, clerks, porters, message-boys, and working-women, returning from their day's tasks, etc., etc. But Charlotte did not lose her head, she knew what she wanted. She walked straight to the coach-stand at the bottom of the Haymarket, hired a hackney coach, and bade the driver take her to Connaught Place. He had no idea of the rank of the young lady who had hired him until the page who opened the door of the house in Connaught Place and answered her question addressed her as "Your Royal Highness," and until she gave him three sovereigns for his fare.

Caroline was at Blackheath, and there her daughter sent a messenger begging her mother to return without delay. Reckless as the Princess of Wales was on her own account, she was terrified by the crisis in her daughter's affairs, and exercised on Princess Charlotte's behalf a foresight and prudence the mother had never exhibited on her own. Caroline was utterly opposed to Princess Charlotte's defiance of the Prince Regent's authority, and the first thing she did before returning home was to drive to both Houses of Parliament in a vain pursuit of her own principal supporters, Mr. Whitbread and Earl Grey. The next aid she sought was that of her eloquent counsel, Mr. Brougham—him she summoned imperatively.

No effort was to be left untried to soothe and calm the excited run-away. Even her girl-friend, Miss Mercer Elphinstone, was brought post haste to use her influence with Princess Charlotte.

That was a wonderful summer night in Connaught Place. Little did the other inhabitants of the square dream of the magnates who, to avoid publicity and the gossip of servants which would attend on the spectacle of their private coaches and liveries, drove up in a succession of hackney coaches[1] to overcome and turn from her determination one solitary, sobbing girl. There was the Lord Chancellor Eldon, sent by the Prince Regent. There was the Duke of York, who had been dining with the Prince when he heard, in the course of the dinner, of his daughter's attempt at escape, upon which the Duke deserted both host and dinner and came to the rescue. There was the Duke of Sussex. There was the Archbishop of Canterbury, who remained in his hackney coach, sitting well back, till he should be

---

[1] The neighbours would only see in them evidence of one of the Princess of Wales's "jumble" parties gathered together at a later hour than usual.

summoned to add his spiritual weight to the mundane arguments of the others.

For a considerable length of time Princess Charlotte, in a fever of indignation and wounded feeling, would not submit. She would not return to the guardians appointed by her father, who had shown little regard for her, she would live with her mother—whether that mother would or not. The young Princess would work for her bread (little she knew of working for her bread!) and subsist on five shillings a week, sooner than continue to endure what she had borne.

Brougham, her mother's able advocate, had to tell the girl that by the law of the land she was, while still under age, subject to the control of her father— not to say of the Prince Regent, who represented the high mightiness of the King. As for the Lord Chancellor Eldon, he roundly asserted that he would not go back without Princess Charlotte. (It was many a long day since the briefless barrister, Jack Scott, who had lived to become Lord Chancellor Eldon, had himself set parental authority at nought, when he eloped with pretty Bessie Surtees, the future Lady Eldon.)

At last, worn out and broken down, possibly mortified by her mother's secession from her side of the question, Princess Charlotte gave way and returned to Warwick House in the middle of the night. She was "seen home," in the royal carriage in which her former governess had been sent to fetch her, by her uncle the Duke of York, bluff and good-natured whatever his lack of probity.

CHAPTER III.

A WANDERING PRINCESS AND REPUDIATED WIFE.

It was, without doubt, this painful scene which confirmed Caroline in the intention she announced shortly afterwards of going abroad for a time. Her enemies were only too glad to get rid of her. Her friends were of two minds. Some of them thought it was the best thing she could do for her dignity and peace; others, with a truer knowledge of the woman, had a foreboding, which was fully warranted, that the greater liberty she would thus acquire might be her destruction. She offered to resign the Rangership of Greenwich Park and her house at Blackheath[1] in favour of her daughter. The last half of her proposal was met by the harsh reply from the Prince Regent that his daughter "could never be permitted by him to reside in a house which had been the dwelling-place of the Princess of Wales."

Early in August, 1814, nineteen years after she had come as a bride to England, Caroline left the country, apparently not without some serious thoughts and pensive regrets. She sailed with her suite from the vicinity of Worthing, followed to the beach by a silent crowd, in which the ladies waved their handkerchiefs and the gentlemen uncovered in token of sympathy. She was forty-five years of age. Her travelling-dress was a quiet enough version of the fashions of the day. She wore a dark cloth pelisse with large gold clasps, and a

---

[1] Lady Charlotte Bury describes it as "full of trickery and trumpery."

cap of velvet and green satin (of the Prussian Hussar costume) with a green feather.

The Princess's sobriety did not last long. On the Prince Regent's birthday the ship fired a salute by her orders, and at dinner she proposed her husband's health in a speech full of mocking pleasantry.

The foreign Courts which the Princess of Wales visited received her, at first, very courteously, while she was cordially welcomed by her own people in Brunswick, to which she went back for a short sojourn. But soon her wonted indiscreet and unbecoming behaviour awoke disappointment and ultimately contempt. In Switzerland she encountered and became intimate with two other Princesses separated from their husbands—Marie Louise of Austria, the wife of Napoleon, and Juliana of Saxe-Coburg, the divorced wife of the Grand Duke Constantine of Russia. Princess Juliana had a special attraction for Caroline because she was the sister of Prince Leopold of Saxe-Coburg, whose marriage with Princess Charlotte was being arranged. Her mother had no acknowledged voice in the arrangement in which she had so great an interest, but she liked the match and the handsome bridegroom largely gifted with the tact in which his future mother-in-law was lamentably deficient. She showed the fact in the very intimacy she immediately struck up with the black sheep of the house of Coburg.

The great historic and political changes which were transforming Europe were lost on Caroline, engrossed with her own attitude of protest and defiance to fate and her husband. Napoleon returned from Elba, Waterloo was fought and won, and she paid little heed to the fall of an Emperor or to the defeat of " *La Grande Armée.*"

In Italy the Princess of Wales, who appeared at masquerades, now as an elderly Venus, now as the Muse of

History, was the noisiest and danced the longest of the pleasure-makers. Her English suite, the members of which were unable to keep their mistress from grievously compromising herself, declined to be compromised in her company, and resigned their offices one by one. She engaged an Italian courier named Bergami, a big fine-looking man who had lost caste in the world. He was really descended from an old family, was entitled to be called "Il Signor Baron," and was respectably connected, though he could find no higher office to fill than that of a courier. For this man, who had previously borne a good character, Caroline conceived one of her ardent friendships; she had him constantly with her, promoting him to the rank of chamberlain, receiving him at her table, creating him a Knight of Malta (which she had not the slightest right to do), inaugurating an order of knighthood on her own account, naming it the order of St. Caroline,[1] and investing Bergami with the dignity of Grand Master. She wound up her absurdity with the old folly of adopting a little child of Bergami's and carrying it about with her everywhere. She did this in spite of the fact that she knew and said she knew spies were set upon her, and that there was actually a commission instituted to procure proofs of her misconduct. She gloried in deceiving the members; she did her best to make them think her guilty, not of egregious error alone, but of brazen-faced crime.

Before the Princess set out on what she regarded as an extended Eastern tour (it was certainly extensive for her day), which was conducted on the most careless, senseless principles, her whole English suite had withdrawn and she was surrounded entirely by Italians.

---

[1] The insignia of this order was a cross and heart tied together with a true lover's knot. The motto was that of the Garter, "*Honi soit qui mal y pense.*"

Thus unchecked she pursued her wild career on sea or on land, in storm-tossed old ships, in rickety open boats, on mules and donkeys; she was absolutely fearless, and her health, which a sedentary life did not suit, stood any amount of hardship in travelling. She went to Tunis and cultivated the Bey, procuring from him the release of a batch of Christian captives. She went to Athens and Constantinople. She went as far as Jericho and Jerusalem. Her progress, Dr. Doran says with truth, was no longer that of a wandering Princess, it was the rollicking, helter-skelter journeying of one of a troop of strolling players.

She bought a villa on Lake Como and settled down after a fashion, giving *fêtes champêtres* to her neighbours; but the management of the establishment was conducted on the most unceremonious lines—the Princess and a sister of Bergami's, an Italian Countess, occasionally acting as cook in order to show their skill in the science of gastronomy.

Caroline had ceased to receive the smallest attention from foreign Courts. Her reputation for impropriety had spread far and wide among the English abroad. The untimely death of poor Princess Charlotte with her child had failed to subdue her mother. It had filled Caroline with genuine sorrow, though the letters she wrote expressing that sorrow were as grotesque as everything else about her. "I have her not lossit," the bereaved mother explained to Lady Charlotte Bury. But the very sorrow from which she fled goaded her on to further extravagances of behaviour.

The event which really arrested the Princess was one long expected, that came to pass at last—the death of her uncle George III., the old King, blind and mad for ten years. George, Prince Regent, was about to be crowned King, and Caroline would return after her six years' absence to be crowned Queen, to have a Court of her own, to be prayed for by name in the liturgy, and to enjoy all the advantages in honour and revenue which a Queen can claim.

Her proposal to repair to England was met on the part of the Government by a counter proposal, unwise and damaging to their side of the question. The Princess's income of fifty thousand pounds a year would be secured to her provided she would remain away from England and expect no support from the English ambassadors at foreign Courts. In short, if she was innocent she was to be bribed to keep out of sight; if she was guilty she was to be equally bribed to renounce her claim to royal rights.

Caroline, who might have entertained, indeed, had entertained such overtures from the Prince Regent, regarded them with scorn when they came from the King; she dismissed her Italian suite in spite of the protests of Bergami, and, accompanied only by Alderman Wood, her enthusiastic friend who had come to fetch her, and by Lady Anne Hamilton, she embarked in an ordinary sailing packet, arriving at Dover and driving to London, which she reached on June 7th, 1820. Her request for a house in England had been ignored; she had no home provided for her and was glad to accept the hospitality of Alderman Wood. He conducted her, followed by a huge applauding crowd, to his house in South Audley Street, where she had to appear on the balcony several times a day in order to show herself to her riotous friends. She was a melancholy sight in those days—an unwieldy woman whose once pretty face was swollen, lined, and weather-beaten.[1]

Caroline's party could be ranged in three divisions:

[1] Lady Brownlow, who saw Queen Caroline often in the Park, thus describes her: "She had exchanged her fair hair for a black wig with a mass of long curls hanging on each side of her face, her eyebrows were painted black, her cheeks plastered with rouge, and the expression of her face most disagreeably bold and stern."

the mob which is not particular about the quality of its idol for the hour, while it greatly prefers when it can rave over the wrong inflicted, and treat as a victim its hero or heroine ; the Whig opposition to the Tory Government, which, whether its members believed Caroline innocent or guilty, caught at the watch-word " injured Queen " as a convenient rallying cry and made use of her cause as a vulnerable spot from which to assail their opponents ; the third section consisted of the large body of Nonconformists and Methodists who stood stoutly by Caroline. At a casual glance it is surprising to find the Bohemian Caroline with a host of Puritans condoning her faults, exalting what virtues could be found in her, and pleading passionately for her as a grossly ill-used woman. The lack of all kindliness and forbearance in her opponents, the crying injustice of the verdicts which society and the King pronounced on her, while the notorious offender sat in his high place unchallenged, and the foolish woman to whom he had shown little mercy was trampled in the mire, roused the more manly righteous spirits to fierce wrath.

A house was taken for Caroline in Portland Place from which she went shortly afterwards to Hammersmith to tenant Brandenburg House—the house once occupied by the Margravine of Anspach. She drove about freely ; to Blackheath, to visit her friends in the City, etc., etc. Once, in the neighbourhood of Kensington, her carriage encountered that of her cousin and sister-in-law, Princess Sophia, the two passing without exchanging a greeting.

Luckily for Caroline her case was conducted from the first by able and eloquent men, who, while keeping within the bounds which separate loyalty from treason, spoke and wrote in her name as, it is hardly necessary to say, she never could have done for herself. In one of their protests mention was made of the most cruel stab which her enemies could give her in the omission of her name, the name of the mother, from the styles and titles of descent of Princess Charlotte engraved on her coffin. Brougham, in referring to the insult of the further omission of Caroline's name from the liturgy, said that she was certainly present in the clause which has to do with "the desolate and oppressed."

The fear felt by Caroline and her friends after they knew that the evidence of the commission which had sat at Milan with the intention of obtaining proof of her guilt would be brought forward, was that her case would be privately disposed of before a Government commission, when her condemnation was a foregone conclusion. She demanded an open trial by the law of the land, and eventually it was granted to her. She was cited to appear before the House of Lords, Lord Liverpool having succeeded in introducing his Bill of "Pains and Penalties," which was tantamount to requiring a sentence of degradation and divorce to be pronounced on the Princess of Wales. Witnesses for the prosecution were brought over from Italy, and her counsel Denman and Brougham, who earned name and fame by their splendid services, won permission to cross-examine the prosecution's witnesses, to produce their own, and to speak in Caroline's defence. She announced her intention of being present in the House of Lords on each day of the trial, and to enable her to do so she came from Hammersmith and accepted the loan of a house in St. James's Square.

Queen Charlotte had died two years before. She had borne her share of the unpopularity caused by the grievous dissensions in the royal family and by the frantic zeal with which the masses had espoused the cause of the Princess of Wales; but at least the old Queen was spared the shame of this criminal investigation.

Just before the trial began Caroline's old rival, the

Duchess of York, whose life had been as honourable as Caroline's was humiliating, peacefully breathed her last at her house of Oatlands.

The trial began on August 17th, and was continued till the beginning of September, to be renewed in October. On the first day Caroline went early. She was dressed quietly and in good taste, in black satin with a white veil over a lace cap. Her former chamberlain, Sir W. Gell, and Mr. Keppel Craven, who had also been in her suite, had returned to their posts. Her sole gentlewoman was Lady Anne Hamilton. Alderman Wood was in attendance. Caroline was led into the House by Sir Thomas Tyrwhitt and one of her counsel, Mr. Brougham; she was conducted to the chair of state placed for her, the peers rising to receive her.

The evidence was the old story of incredible folly [1] accompanied by a total absence of refinement and delicacy. But although the witnesses—nearly all of the lowest classes—put the grossest construction on Caroline's actions, every inference was founded on conjecture. There was not a definite proof of guilt brought home to her. Indeed, her incorrigible indiscretions had been committed quite openly, without the smallest attempt at disguise. They courted rather than avoided publicity, and that alone was a strong indication of her comparative innocence. To have believed otherwise would have been to reckon her and her Italian chamberlain Bergami, who had borne a good character up to the time of entering her service, the most depraved wretches in existence.

The witnesses of good position who came forward

[1] On one occasion the Princess is said to have presented herself at a review in Germany with a half-pumpkin on her head. When the Grand Duke, who was presiding, and whom she was scandalising, ventured to remonstrate and to suggest a more decorous head-dress, she answered that the weather was hot and that nothing kept her head so cool and comfortable as a pumpkin.

for Caroline did much to explain away or to invalidate the base suspicions of the witnesses on the other side. The comparative licence and gallantry of foreign manners, which allowed a man in Bergami's position to kiss his mistress's hand, etc., etc., was made plain to a strictly English tribunal, the members of which even in 1820 had little familiarity with the habits of other nations. It was distinctly proved that some of the assertions of the hostile witnesses were not merely incredible, they were impossible. The House, however, when put to the vote sustained the Bill of Pains and Penalties by an inconsiderable majority which at the next stage of the proceedings was so much less that the Government—not daring to face the people, all but up in arms for Caroline—withdrew the Bill. This step, though hailed as a triumph by the populace, was of all measures the most disappointing and disarming to the Princess. As long as a battle was to be fought she could fight it inch by inch, she could hope for an overthrow of some part of the charges, she might even plead for a new trial; but this surrender of the Bill by its promoters was a fatal compromise. It left matters no better but rather worse than they had been. It declared her neither innocent nor guilty, her rights were still denied to her, her reputation instead of being cleared was worse sullied than before. Lady Charlotte Bury had a glimpse of Caroline leaving the House after she had been made acquainted with the withdrawal of the Bill, and could not forget the "dazed look" with which, clutching the banister, she descended the stair, seeing nothing.

After the first blow the Princess rallied; she continued to sign herself "Caroline Regina"; she claimed the grant of a house in accordance with her rank; she insisted on her coronation taking place at the same time as that of the King. She refused to touch the

£30,000 income settled upon her unless her name was inserted in the liturgy; but her poverty soon forced her to yield on this point. She gave intimation that she intended to go in state to St. Paul's to return thanks for her deliverance from the machinations of her enemies. She did go on November 29th in a white velvet pelisse, in such state as her means would permit, in a procession of the friendly Members of Parliament, the Corporation, and many of the citizens of London, the representatives of the trades and a large assortment of the rabble. Personally she was attended by some of the gentlemen of her former suite and by Lady Anne Hamilton.

The clergy of St. Paul's, ranged between two fires— the will of the King and the will of the people—admitted her, but only promiscuously as it were, with the rest of the heterogeneous throng. They held no special service for her; they even omitted the clause in the service which may state the name of the man or the woman who requests the thanks of the congregation for special mercies.

Caroline held large receptions at Hammersmith, to which a concourse of extraordinary guests resorted. In addition to the wives of City magnates favourable to her cause there were hosts of the humbler tradesmen's wives totally unaccustomed to the circumstances in which the women found themselves. According to Lady Brownlow they flaunted in silks and satins procured for them by the leaders of the Princess's party, who desired that her adherents in passing through the streets should make as fine a show as possible; but the bearing of the wearers was not in keeping with their finery: they lolled against the cushions, stared about them, and thrust "their red elbows" out of the windows of the hackney coaches. Lady Brownlow quotes a rumour that Caroline was sometimes too intoxicated to receive her company otherwise than stretched upon a sofa. But it is necessary to remember that Lady Brownlow was an ardent Tory, one to whom the King was the King, who could do no wrong—at least, who was not answerable to any fellow-creature for his actions—while his wife was a foolish, disreputable woman of whom the worst might easily be believed. Though Caroline was notoriously self-indulgent in her recklessness, a prey to every foible of the moment, from no other source do we learn that she was degradingly intemperate. On the other hand, the unfortunate woman's strong peculiarities and wild eccentricities were exactly the foundation on which a charge of drunkenness would be built.

On every side, apart from the flattery of the mob, Caroline was met with obstacles, slights, and indignities. The King refused to set aside a palace for her. He would not consent to her coronation either when his own—for which the most elaborate preparations were in train—was being celebrated, or afterwards; and as a Queen-Consort of England can only be crowned when the reigning sovereign chooses she was legally without any power to enforce her demand. She established herself in Cambridge House, Hammersmith, in tolerable quietness till May, 1821.

In the meantime a new family connection in the person of the Duchess of Kent, sister of Caroline's son-in-law Prince Leopold and of her ally in Switzerland, Juliana, wife of the Grand Duke Constantine of Russia, had taken up her residence in Kensington Palace. She was a second time a widow, the mother of a fatherless baby girl in whose interest the Duchess must walk warily. She could not but regard with fear and trembling the proximity of Caroline. To a sensible, punctilious woman, the Princess of Wales, or as she was now generally called whether crowned or uncrowned "Queen Caroline," was, if nothing worse, a royal randy unapproachable in rowdiness, outraging propriety the one moment and clamouring for her dues the next.

Caroline and her councillors agitated in vain for the concession of permission for her to be present at the coronation of George IV. The rite was to be performed with much splendour and all the old picturesque customs —the procession from the Abbey to the Hall, the throwing down of the gauntlet by the King's champion, the royal banquet, etc., etc. Certainly there was a reasonable apprehension of a violent interruption to the proceedings and a public scandal, and the King had to be dosed with sal volatile to steady his nerves before setting out.

Caroline would not relinquish her purpose of going to Westminster for the occasion, though her health was beginning to suffer from the life of unceasing strife and contest which she had led for many months. As early as six o'clock in the morning she drove through the already crowded streets; according to one account she was loudly cheered, according to another she was hooted and bidden go home as a disturber of the public peace. She was in a carriage and six accompanied by Lord and Lady Hood and Lady Anne Hamilton. Arrived at the Abbey amid a circle of excited spectators, she tried door after door, seeking to procure admittance. There were those in the interior of the building who declared they heard the ominous knocking which shifted from one quarter to another. Nemesis was very near George at that moment. The skeleton in his house in the shape of his wife was threatening to illustrate the "*Mene, mene, tekel, upharsin*" on his palace walls.

The uniform answer to Caroline's application was that the officials had their orders; nobody could enter the Abbey without presenting such a ticket as Caroline did not possess. "This is your Queen," said Lord

Hood. "Yes, I am your Queen," repeated the poor soul piteously; "will you not admit me?" But the door-keepers knew too well the injunctions laid upon them and were inflexible.

Caroline was in hysterical tears and laughter. Lord Hood had a ticket which he offered to her, but it would only admit one, and even she shrank from encountering alone the ordeal which awaited her.

At last the poor Queen turned away and re-entered her carriage. That repulse which convinced her of the futility of the struggle was her death-blow. "She seems to have lost her head," wrote Lady Brownlow. "When going through the Horse Guards the officer on guard ordered the men to present arms; she jumped up in her carriage and called out, 'I am the Queen! you dare not stop me!' Later in the day she was seen at a back window of Curzon House talking with two gentlemen and gesticulating like a fury."

The King was crowned with great magnificence, presided at the coronation banquet and immediately afterwards set out on a state visit to Ireland, where he was the centre of fresh honours and rejoicings. The Queen returned sick and sorry to her house at Hammersmith. One more effort she made to cast off the pall which was closing in round her. She appeared again at Drury Lane Theatre, and then she was seen no more abroad in the surging mäelstrom of friends and enemies which had fought for and against her. The bone of contention over which the nation had so long wrangled was removed at once and for ever. On August 2nd Caroline's medical attendants issued a bulletin to the effect that she was suffering from internal inflammation. The disease lasted only five more days and was accompanied with great suffering, which she bore courageously and patiently. Indeed, the dignity which she could exercise on occasions stood her in good stead on her death-bed. If she had only lived as she died posterity would have had a different record of her history. She cherished no hope of her recovery and expressed herself as not only resigned but willing to leave a world in which her misfortunes had been many. She arranged her affairs as far as her illness permitted her, directing that the free-spoken diary which she had kept in her earlier years at Kensington and Blackheath should be burnt; she signed her will and turned her face to the wall. After two hours of unconsciousness she died, on the morning of August 7th, 1821, at the age of fifty-three years. Lord and Lady Hood and Lady Anne Hamilton were with her to the end.

The previous night had been one of wild tempest, thunder and lightning, wind and rain. The news had reached London that Queen Caroline lay dying. A party of Methodists who had been among her followers hired a boat and, rowing up the Thames as near as they could reach to the house she occupied, sang hymns in the fitful darkness and raging tempest, fondly trusting that the sound might reach the fast dulling ears and carry with it a sense of the rowers' sympathy and of the divine mercy. It was such a gale as that which blew on the night when Oliver Cromwell died, and it burst open doors and windows in the dying woman's house.

The King was still at sea when he learnt the news of the death of his wife. He had the decency to leave the deck and remain in private for the next few hours.[1]

A galling encumbrance was lifted from his path, and he and his ministers for him were in haste to get rid of Caroline's lifeless remains. Caroline herself had left a request that her body should not be embalmed and that it should be conveyed without delay to Brunswick.

[1] There was no public mourning for the Queen, though the royal family made the concession of wearing black.

But the speed of the Government in complying with the direction was so unprecedented and unseemly that the dead Princess's executors protested over her coffin at the insult thus gratuitously inflicted on her. The envenomed dispute was fated to be continued throughout the ceremony of her funeral, till the lifeless body had for ever quitted the shores of that England where Caroline had met no welcome, found no peace, and out of which her cold clay was hustled at last with as little respect as if she had been proved to be the criminal she was accused of being.

The Government's wary determination was that there should be no public demonstration at the funeral, and for that reason that the small *cortège*, guarded by soldiers, should pass along by-ways and through suburbs —not by the main thoroughfares of London—until it should arrive at Romford, where the coffin would rest for the night before going on to Harwich, from which it was to be embarked for Brunswick.

But the populace were neither to be balked of a spectacle nor to have their heroine shorn of any distinction which they could procure for her. It was as if Caroline's stormy career was to be stormy to the last; even her breathless body was to give ground for disorder and riot. Amidst torrents of rain the melancholy procession started from Hammersmith and got as far as Church Street, Kensington. There the cavalcade was stopped in an attempt to go up Bayswater Road by a furious crowd collected in thousands, who, in spite of the Life Guards, called out for the occasion, tore up the road and rendered it impassable, so that the leaders of the funeral party had no resource save to take the high road to London, amidst shouts of triumph from their opponents. Another encounter between the mob and the military escort took place at the Kensington Gate of Hyde Park, where amidst hoarse cries of " The City, the City," the funeral was again turned back from traversing the Edgware Road. A third obstruction was raised farther along the route, when the Guards fired, two persons were killed and several wounded. The people were quelled for the moment, but at Tottenham Court Road the struggle was renewed so successfully that the funeral was forced down Drury Lane and into the Strand. When the hearse passed under Temple Bar its rude escort raised " a wild hurrah ! " in token that they had carried their point and won the day.

Out in the open country it is said another funeral train crossed Caroline's ; it was that of her ancient enemy the banker Childe's heiress, Sarah, Countess of Jersey.

At Harwich a frigate, two sloops of war, three brigs, and a schooner were awaiting their consignment. The coffin was taken by a barge to the schooner and by the schooner to the frigate, the captain of which (Captain Doyle) was the midshipman who had handed Caroline a rope to help her to gain the deck of the *Jupiter*, on which she had stood an ill-fated bride.

The little company of mourners consisted of Lord and Lady Hood, Lady Anne Hamilton, Mr. Austin ("Willikin" the adopted child, grown to manhood, to whom Caroline had left the bulk of such worldly goods as she possessed),[1] Dr. Lushington (one of her legal advisers), his wife, and Count Vassali. The progress of the funeral up the Elbe and the Schwinde to Stade was very much the course Caroline had followed when she came to England twenty-seven years before. Arrived in Brunswick her poor remains were treated with affection and respect by her country people, many of whom must have remembered the comely, open-hearted, openhanded girl who had gone about freely among them. One of the resting-places had been at Zell, where

He died soon afterwards.

Caroline's coffin had lain for a night on the tomb of a Princess as wilful and unfortunate as Caroline—her aunt, her mother's sister Caroline Matilda of England, Queen of Christian VII. of Denmark.

The last resting-place of all that was mortal of Caroline was in the vault beneath the Church of St. Blaize, Brunswick, between the coffins of her father who fell at Jena and her brother who fell at Quatre Bras. Dr. Doran vouched for the fact that there is still to be seen on Caroline's coffin the marks of the nails which had fastened on the plate that was removed in the course of the journey between London and Brunswick. The inscription on the plate had been according to Caroline's injunctions: "Here lies Caroline of Brunswick, the injured Queen of England." The second plate substituted for the first bore only the style and titles of the deceased.

There is no match to be found for Caroline among the royal ladies of Hanover, with the single exception of Sophia, the wife of George I. Even Sophia, if she was more criminal than Caroline, was not so outrageously deficient in all dignity, delicacy, and common sense. Without being wicked Caroline, in her boisterous self-assertion, reckless bravado, and utter disregard of appearances and consequences, was a scandal to the right-judging public, even when a portion of it recognising her wrongs figured as her partisans. She was a sore trial to all connected with her who were capable of measuring and condemning her senseless outrages of propriety, her grievous sins against good taste, her egregious vanity, bounce, and bluster, together with her senseless, hopeless struggle with the overwhelming power and authority of her foes (chief among whom was her unworthy husband).

The Electress Sophia was wise and virtuous. Caroline, the beautiful, witty wife of George II., though a coarse-spoken representative of a coarse generation and curiously callous on many points which are to us of the first importance, which we still view as sacred, even when their sweetness is turned to bitterness, was in the main a good and dutiful woman—a devoted, all-indulgent wife, an affectionate mother of those children who were not, like her son Fritz, her unnatural enemies. Augusta of Saxe-Coburg, her daughter-in-law, if narrow-minded and harsh-tempered, was a good submissive wife to the most trying of princely mates and a good mother to a family of unruly children. Charlotte of Mecklenburg-Strelitz was good throughout, an example of solid worth, generous dignity, and active benevolence to her subjects, of whom only the lawless and dissolute held her in small esteem. The younger Caroline's sisters-in-law (save only the Duchess of Cumberland), the Duchesses of York, Clarence, Kent, and Cambridge, were honourable women. The mouth-pieces of the nation described them satirically to begin with as "amiable ladies who spoke very little English," but ere long treated them with cordial respect, and finally with loyal affection. They might have served as examples to their feather-brained, coarse-grained sister-in-law who was their senior, who looked forward to being their Queen. But Caroline was incorrigible and fulfilled her sorry destiny. The pity of it was, when we come to regard the evidence calmly and dispassionately, that Caroline, with all her faults and extravagances, was good-natured, kind-hearted, and generous, guilty only of supreme imprudence and wanton indiscretion, and of the additional offence, for which she was not altogether to blame, of receiving the rampant idolatry of the mob, which provoked cooler-headed, more reasonable lookers-on to recoil from the idol and her cause. Never was the force of the command which bids men and women avoid the very appearance of evil more strikingly illustrated than in the life of Caroline of Brunswick, who in her audacity and wrong-headedness positively courted calumny, and laid herself out with the malicious short-sighted glee of a perverse child to be misjudged and defamed.

VI.

ADELAIDE OF SAXE-MEININGEN, WIFE OF WILLIAM IV.

AUTHORITIES

Dr. Doran, Lady Brownlow, Lady Bedingfield, Mrs. Crawford, etc.

ADELAIDE OF SAXE-MEININGEN, QUEEN OF WILLIAM IV. (SOON AFTER HER HUSBAND'S DEATH).

CHAPTER I.

THE DUCHESS.

Adelaide of Saxe-Meiningen was the eldest child, born in 1792, after ten years of marriage, of Duke George of Saxe-Meiningen and his Duchess (Princess Louise of Hohenlohe-Langenburg). Duke George was an honest patriotic German of somewhat cultivated tastes. He showed his patriotism by gallantly holding his little duchy against French invasion, and his culture, such as it was, by seeking the friendship of Schiller, Jean Paul Richter, etc. His genial German affinities came out in his friendly relations with his burgher subjects and with the country people around his little capital.

He had his mother buried in the town churchyard, saying she was worthy to lie among her subjects. He died after a short illness in 1803, leaving the widow guardian to his only son Bernard, a child of three, and to his two daughters, the Princesses Adelaide and Ida, of whom Adelaide was then a young girl of eleven years of age. "Altenstein, the simple and unpretending home of Queen Adelaide's childhood," was visited in later days by Lady Brownlow in the suite of the Queen. Lady Brownlow remarks on the extraordinary plainness and simplicity of the furniture and appointments of that summer palace of a German Prince, at which an English eye, accustomed to any ordinary squire's house, would have been astonished ; and on the bedroom with its uncarpeted floor, and two small beds with white dimity curtains, which had been shared by the Queen and the Duchess Ida her sister till they married. A fine English maid would have turned up her nose at them.[1]

The widowed Duchess of Saxe-Meiningen was an able and sensible woman who was qualified in conjunction with her councillors to maintain the courageous and prudent policy of her husband which saved his duchy from French devastation. Such a woman was likely to rear her daughters with good judgment. It is said that it was Queen Charlotte who selected Princess Adelaide, a womanly Princess of twenty-six years of age, as a fitting wife for the Duke of Clarence at the time when the death of Princess Charlotte and the absence of heirs to the throne in the third generation caused the nearly simultaneous marriages of three of Charlotte's younger sons, the Dukes of Clarence, Kent, and Cambridge. Of these three, the Duke of Clarence stood nearest to the throne, coming next in age to the now childless Prince Regent and the equally childless Duke of York. No doubt Charlotte, like the wise woman she was, gave due weight to the Duke of Clarence's comparative nearness to the throne. After the terrible fiasco of the marriage of George, Prince of Wales, and Princess Caroline of Brunswick it was doubly necessary that the future Queen should be an upright, reasonable, well-disposed young woman. It was these qualities in Princess Adelaide which decided Queen Charlotte, for the selected bride was not beautiful, not even pretty. Neither was she accomplished. She was not a fine musician like the Duchess of Kent, and her attempts at art were of the flimsiest description, even in that generation when what were classed as "feminine accomplishments" were superficial to the last degree. Princess Adelaide had ordinary features,

[1] Article in *Temple Bar* on "Slight Reminiscences of a Septuagenarian," by Lady Brownlow.

a bad skin and complexion which some of her detractors called "scorbuticness" and others a "gingerbread complexion," weak eyes, and hair of that trying shade of yellow which is more akin to lemon than to gold colour; yet the whole was redeemed by the pleasant, friendly expression of the face. She was very fond of what was then called "carpet work," in which she was a model of industry. She was an adept in the construction of the needle-cases, card-racks, watch-pockets, etc., which figured at bazaars and were the usual stock of "the repositories" for the work of poor ladies.[1]

What was of much more consequence than beauty or trifling accomplishments, Adelaide was thoroughly well-principled, affectionate, sweet-tempered, not difficult to please, not exacting in her requirements, brought up as she had been, in the land of sauer-kraut and lager-beer, among bluff German Princes and officials whose morals and manners alike left a good deal to be desired. She was willing to make the best of things and to condone and ignore much that a more fastidious woman, perhaps a woman of higher standards and ideals and more delicate, sensitive instincts, could hardly have endured.

The bridegroom was over fifty, a weather-beaten sailor, not destitute of kindness of heart, but the least well-mannered of the family, priding himself as he did on what was then considered the bluntness and roughness characteristic of a sailor. His previous life had

[1] She was mistress of "scumbling," Padua work, Berlin wool tapestry, etching, flower-painting (such as it was in amateur hands), and knitted window-curtains, etc. "There was at the house of a rich Quaker lady where I was often taken as a child quite a collection of artistic knick-knacks made by Queen Adelaide and her sister Ida, Duchess of Saxe-Weimar, for fancy fairs." Adelaide decorated a pair of letter-racks with likenesses in water-colours of some beautiful children. "The royal womanly hands were never idle with their owner's will."—*Emily Crawford in the "Contemporary."*

been lax in virtue and dissipated after the fashion of his elder brothers' lives. It must have revolted an innocent young Princess if she had not in accordance with the precepts of her education and her generation resolutely shut her eyes and turned her back to it.

The Duke of Clarence is supposed to have simply acquiesced in his mother's choice for him. He made no attempt to see and make the acquaintance of his bride, as the Dukes of Kent and Cambridge did in reference to their brides, and when Parliament refused to grant him the £10,000 annual addition to his income which was asked for him and insisted that he should be satisfied with the supplementary thousands bestowed on his younger brothers on their marriages, he flatly refused for a time to go on with the contract. The bride may not have realised the uncomplimentary indifference and resistance of her bridegroom; anyhow she arrived in London with her mother on a July evening in 1818. The two ladies took up their quarters at Grillon's Hotel, Albemarle Street, for Adelaide also had to face the discouraging reception accorded repeatedly to foreign brides entering the House of Hanover. Nobody awaited her, nobody received her. The Duke of Clarence was out of town, the Prince Regent was at dinner at Carlton House, the old Queen was in one of the last stages of her illness, the Princesses waiting on her were not expected to come forward on the occasion. The two Princes, the Regent and the Duke of Clarence, were sent for, and both these stout, elderly gentlemen had the grace to obey the call, and to hurry to welcome the stranded Duchess and her daughter. No offence was taken and no bad impression made. The Duke of Clarence was nothing if he was not hearty and hilarious, in the style of the stage Jack Tar, and he was pleased by the unaffected gentleness and good humour of his future wife. The Prince Regent could, when he chose, be the most gracious and agreeable of hosts. The little party fraternised admirably, and sat talking and laughing, advancing in common liking, till far into the night.

The marriage, as has been said, was a double marriage, the Duke of Kent—who had gone to Germany for his Duchess, marrying her there according to the Lutheran form—was to be married by the Archbishop of Canterbury from the service of the Church of England at the same time and place that the knot was tied between the Duke of Clarence and Princess Adelaide. The two marriages were celebrated at the old country palace of Kew under the roof with Queen Charlotte, but not in her presence, since she was too ill for the effort and could but have a brief glimpse of her daughter-in-law before the Duke and Duchess of Kent returned to Kensington Palace and the Duke and Duchess of Clarence, after waiting to drink tea on the lawn, started for St. James's Palace, followed by the company's cheers led by no less a person than the Prince Regent, the sound of the rejoicing rising to the old Queen's sick-room.

The Duke and Duchess of Clarence repaired soon afterwards to Hanover, where the Duke acted as the Prince Regent's representative.

The details of the last parting between the young Duchess and Queen Charlotte were told with simple good feeling by Queen Adelaide to her friend and lady of the bedchamber, Lady Bedingfield, in whose diary (included in *The Jerningham Letters*) we have a good picture of the Court of King William and his Queen. The old Queen had always been good to the unassuming, amiable young Duchess, who on going to bid her mother-in-law good-bye would fain have thanked her for her goodness, only the Duchess knew the Queen did not like to speak of her health or to take leave of anybody. After the Duchess had gone she stole back, fearing that she would never see the Queen again, and opened the door softly that she might look on her once more. The Queen heard (and doubtless understood); she recalled the Duchess, but merely spoke on indifferent subjects, pretending not to notice the younger woman's sorrow. The Queen did not survive the parting many weeks.

In the meantime the Court and fashionable gossip was all about the marriage of the Princess Elizabeth, the mature bride of forty-eight summers, a clever, high-spirited woman. She had latterly felt galled by the somewhat rigid yoke under which Queen Charlotte kept her daughters to the last; and without question the Princess dreaded beforehand, as her mother also feared it, the fate likely to be that of the unmarried Princesses left in a manner dependent on their elder brother, the Prince Regent. Therefore Princess Elizabeth, who had been one of the handsomest as she was the most gifted of the sisters in the days when Louis Philippe of Orleans was faithless to her, who was now as big for a woman as her brothers were for men, was resolute in marrying late in life. Report had it that she even entertained a romantic attachment for her rather uncouth elderly bridegroom, the Landgrave of Hesse-Homburg, " blushing rosy red" when he entered the room. The English public exaggerated his uncouthness and made game of it. They were not then in a particularly suave humour with regard to the predominance of the German element at Court. As for the poor Homburg Prince there was no end to the amusing, palpably in-vented or distorted stories told of him. It was said meaningly of the man who walked stockingless in his military boots that the servants had to immerse him several times in a warm bath. Not smoking but snuff-taking was then the accepted practice of the majority of the gentlemen of England, and the gossip that the German Prince smoked "four pipes a day" was listened to with hearty disapprobation, followed by proportionate approval when it was alleged that the English courtiers among whom he was established for the time, had kept him for the three days previous to his marriage without suffering him to smoke. When he and the Princess drove out to spend their honeymoon at Frogmore, where Princess Elizabeth and Mary Moser[1] had painted a room with garlands of roses and lilies in the old happy days when the King was sane, and the Queen, unburdened with years, cares, and sorrows, was less stringent in her demands on the absolute submission of her daughters, the unlucky foreigner, unable to bear the motion of an English carriage, was forced to leave his new-made wife within, and to take a seat without on the box beside the coachman. In spite of the sarcasms Princess Elizabeth did not tire of her bargain; she was as loyal to him as her mother was to King George. She was happy, loved, and honoured in his beautiful castle of Homburg, from which she re-visited England when her brother William was King, and where her younger sister Princess Augusta—an adventurous maiden Princess for those days—visited the Landgrave and Landgravine on her way to see the Princess Royal, the Dowager-Queen of Würtemberg. The two sisters returned together to Homburg, and three English Princesses sojourned for several happy months in 1823 in the old castle.

Five years before, at Hanover in 1819, three months previous to the birth of Princess Victoria at Kensington Palace, another baby Princess was born, the child of the Duke and Duchess of Clarence. She only survived a few hours. In the end of 1820 a second Clarence Princess was born. She was christened "Elizabeth," and her parents

[1] A contemporary of Angelica Kauffman's famous for flower painting.

fondly hoped she would live to be another "Good Queen Bess"—with a difference. But she died at the age of three months. At the request of the sorrowing Duke and Duchess the sculptor Chantrey reproduced in marble the sleeping figure of the little child.

When the Duke and Duchess of Clarence returned to England they had apartments in St. James's Palace, while their country-house, where they stayed principally, was Bushey Park. There probably Adelaide's happiest years were spent. She helped the Duke to keep their household expenses within the limits of his income, and at the same time she induced him to go hand-in-hand with her in generosity to their poorer neighbours. She was content to live quietly with her elderly husband. She showed much friendship and sympathy for her sister-in-law the widowed Duchess of Kent, who was staying with her baby at Kensington Palace. When the Clarences were at St. James's the Duchess went almost every day to Kensington to console and encourage her friend and country-woman and to fondle the child which was to take the place of her own dead children. Adelaide, like the Duchess of Kent, seems to have kept aloof (and who need wonder at the attitude even in a simple-minded, kind-hearted woman!) from the miserable Queen Caroline, then fighting desperately for her rights, and on the eve of passing before a higher tribunal.

At Bushey the Duchess of Clarence was able to receive long visits from her sister, Princess Ida, Duchess of Saxe-Weimar. (Lady Brownlow thus describes their brother Duke Bernard of Saxe-Weimar: "The Duke was a prodigious man, six feet four at least in height, and large in proportion; all was round about him, round body, legs and arms, a round face, a small button of a nose and a small mouth; he appeared to me the *beau idéal* of a Brobdignag Cupid.")

One of the Duchess of Saxe-Weimar's children, Prince Edward of Saxe-Weimar, was born at Bushey, and became as a son to the childless Duchess of Clarence He grew up in England, was naturalised, and has long served in the English Army.

CHAPTER II.

THE QUEEN.

ON June 24th, 1830, nearly twelve years after her marriage, when Adelaide was thirty-eight years of age, she became Queen-Consort by the death of George IV. and the succession to the throne of his next surviving brother the Duke of Clarence as William IV. It is said she burst into tears when the news was announced to her and gave the prayer-book she held in her hand as a remembrance of the day to the messenger who brought the tidings. Certainly, the duties and obligations laid upon her by King William's accession were heavy and irksome to a woman of quiet habits, simple tastes, and somewhat delicate health. Though she discharged the obligations with cheerful conscientiousness she aged manifestly under the burden. Happily for her, William, whose earlier years had hardly promised such a consummation, was, to his lasting credit, a faithful and kind husband to her. Apparently he never ceased to marvel, with respect and admiration, at his wife's virtues, and to praise them whenever he had the opportunity. Parliament settled on her a hundred thousand a year, with Marlborough House and Bushey Park for residences if she survived her husband. The King himself was the happy bearer of the information, which he gladly confirmed by promptly appointing her perpetual Ranger of the Park. Many stories (highly welcome to those of the nation who had loved to hear of the honest attachment between King George and

Queen Charlotte and of the peaceful domesticity of their lives) were in circulation of the somewhat similar frank heartiness and unaffected simplicity of the old sailor King and his Queen and their *ménage*.

The joint coronation took place on September 8th, 1831. There was much excitement in connection with the bringing forward of the Reform Bill, and considerable distress from the ravages of cholera throughout the country, and the King and Queen were anxious that the ceremonial in which they were to play their part should be as unpretending and inexpensive as possible—a great contrast to the coronation of George IV. We have a graphic description of the scene from Lady Brownlow, who was already appointed a lady-in-waiting. Before her marriage, when as Lady Emma Mount Edgcumbe she had resided with her father at Twickenham, a friendship had sprung up between her and the Duchess of Clarence at Bushey. Lady Brownlow writes: " Whether the irritable state of the public feeling, or a desire for economy actuated the King and his ministers, I know not, but the coronation was very different from the last. No assembling in Westminster Hall of King, Lords, and Commons, to form a procession to the Abbey ; no banquet, no great officers of state riding up the Hall to see the dishes placed on the King's table ; no champion of England on horseback armed *cap-à-pie*, throwing his gauntlet and defying any who denied the right of the King to the throne ; all these interesting old customs were omitted, the religious ceremony in the Abbey being the only one performed as on former occasions. In this there was, indeed, an improvement in the general effect, for as a Queen also was to be crowned all the peeresses wore their robes and put on their coronets when the Queen's crown was placed on her head by the Archbishop. Then my duties as Lady-in-waiting were to be performed. With my coronet tottering unfastened on my head, I had to wipe her Majesty's forehead after the anointing, first with a piece of cotton wool, then with a piece of cambric; after which I fastened the crown by inserting four long diamond-headed pins into holes made for them. The cotton wool and cambric I carried in a little white velvet and gold purse-like bag hanging to my girdle; and the pins were stuck in my dress; so I had all ready and there was no bustle; yet I never felt so nervous in my life, for I knew that thousands of eyes were observing me."

Dr. Doran gives the Queen's dress "a gold gauze over a white satin petticoat, with a diamond stomacher, a purple velvet train lined with white satin having a rich border of gold and ermine."

The crown was made up at Adelaide's own expense of the jewels already in her possession. It was a small coronet composed of diamonds and pearls. Dr. Doran states it was too small, and had it not been for the presence of mind of two of the ladies-in-waiting (who resolve themselves into one, Lady Brownlow, prepared for the emergency) it would have fallen from the head on which the Archbishop of Canterbury had merely rested it. The knob of hair worn on the top of the head was there in order that the crown might be drawn firmly over it.

Lady Brownlow proceeds to describe the homage of the Lords—"a very impressive part of the ceremony. When the Duke of Wellington in his turn ascended the steps and knelt before the King to do his homage, there arose a simultaneous cheer from all parts of the Abbey. It was perhaps wrong, but the effect was electric and thrilling at this irrepressible outburst of feeling as the hero of a hundred fights, the true patriot, the loyal and devoted subject, took the oath of allegiance to his Sovereign." The Duke of Wellington was a personal friend of the great Tory lady, and she held him in the highest esteem. She did not extend her favour to Lord Brougham, for whom she had an aversion equal to that she had entertained for Queen Caroline. When fresh cheers were raised for various Whig leaders among the peers, she did not hesitate to attribute the ovation to Brougham; she declared he acted as fugle-man to the applauders. She called his appearance ludicrous in the extreme. " His ugly features, his twitching nose, his chancellor's wig hanging on each side of his face, surmounted by his coronet, made him resemble the old lion in the royal arms, and it was impossible to look at him without laughing. Even my good Queen, whose feelings of devotion were very strong, confessed to me afterwards that she was so struck with the glimpse she had of his absurd ugliness that she could scarcely refrain from laughing and therefore never ventured to look in his direction again. The ceremony being ended, their Majesties returned to the palace in the same order in which they came, the King and Queen in the state coach attended by the Duchess of Gordon, acting Mistress of the Robes, and myself as lady-in-waiting. The procession was, I believe, a grand one; but I saw nothing of it, and it was considered a poor substitute for that to and from Westminster Hall and the Abbey, with the revival of old feudal customs. In short, John Bull was discontented, though grudging expense and calling for economy, and called this ' a *half-crown*ation.' In the evening there was a great dinner at St James's Palace, and my lot was to be handed in by Prince Talleyrand the French Ambassador![1] Princess Victoria was not present at the coronation, the delicacy of her health being given as the excuse for her absence."

[1] At the first great drawing-room after the coronation the Queen told Lady Bedingfield she had to put something round her knees to lessen the fatigue of bending them so often.

The ferment in the country continued. William had been reckoned on the Whig side, and when he hesitated in the promotion of Liberal measures in the reform of election to Parliament above all, it was supposed that the Queen, born and brought up in a country which had suffered severely from the consequences of the French Revolution, was influencing her husband against what she might consider revolutionary politics. This was loudly said and largely believed of the modest, retiring woman, who had a difficulty in asserting herself and did not know where to stop when the question was of being kind and obliging, instead of standing firm in opposition to the pressure brought to bear on her, the woman who spent so much of her time plying her needle. A tide of unpopularity set in against the gentle, friendly Queen.[1] Occasionally the Princesses, those daughters of George III., the Duchess of Gloucester and the Princesses Augusta and Sophia, who remained in the country were associated with Adelaide in the popular dislike, because they too were supposed to influence their brother, the King. At other times poor Adelaide was singled out in party speeches by the press as forming the most undesirable contrast, in her interference in public affairs, to Queen Charlotte, who had never meddled in politics which were altogether beyond her sphere. Queen Adelaide was written and spoken of as "the foreign woman whom the nation may have too easily adopted." There was an open comparison made between her position and that of Marie Antoinette, and threats uttered of a like destruction which would befall Adelaide if she persisted in her supposed opposition to a great and necessary reform. So fierce was the tempest that leaders on both sides, able and experienced men, dreaded a revolution. " A hooting, yelling mob followed the most obnoxious

[1] The Tories did something to provoke it by loudly calling her *their Queen*.

member of the royal family—the Duke of Cumberland—when he drove down Constitution Hill one morning. There were nightly disturbances with volleys of stones, brought into the streets in carts for the purpose, flung at the windows of the principal Tories. The windows of the Duke of Wellington at Apsley House were shattered, and he caused iron shutters to be fixed to the windows."

On George III.'s birthday, June 4th, the Reform Bill passed and London was illuminated in spite of the authorities, the populace smashing the windows of all the houses which did not " light up." Lady Brownlow describes the progress of the Queen from the " ancient Concert Rooms" to which she had gone that evening. Lady Brownlow had previously dined with her Majesty at Clarence House. "The King had a dinner for gentlemen only at St. James's, at which my father and Lord Brownlow had the honour of being present. As I attended the Queen downstairs to her carriage, Sir Herbert Taylor came out of the King's room, and I said to him, 'So there are to be illuminations to-night.' 'Oh no,' he replied; 'the King has spoken to Lord Melbourne, who has promised to check on the part of the Government anything of the sort.' 'That is all very fine,' was my answer, 'but depend upon it there will be illuminations, for I have seen preparations at the Lord Chancellor's [Brougham's] and other houses.' Sir Herbert shook his head and I wagged mine, being perfectly convinced that I was right; and so events proved that I was. Well, we proceeded to Hanover Square, the Landgravine of Hesse-Homburg (Princess Elizabeth) in the carriage with the Queen, and myself in attendance, the rest of the suite following in another carriage. On these occasions the Queen had no escort; but a guard of honour was stationed at the Rooms. All went harmoniously inside, and we supposed the same was the case outside, till the officer on guard came into the royal box to inform her Majesty that the mob were breaking the windows of the houses not lighted up ; and the names of two or three of the King's guests were mentioned whose windows had already been broken. This was not a pleasant hearing ; but still less pleasant was what awaited us as her Majesty drove down Regent Street on her return to the palace. Both sides of the street were blazing with illuminations and transparencies, the intervening space filled with a frenzied mob shouting 'Reform for ever!' and waving their greasy hats into the Queen's carriage, which was forced to go at a foot's pace. The Landgravine, opposite to whom I sat, was grinding her teeth and stamping on my feet with rage ; and I confess I was equally angry, and also alarmed for the Queen, who was not then popular, and I felt that a few disloyal and exciting words might change the mood of the frantic people around, to whose tender mercies she was left, for not a policeman was to be seen. Most thankful was I when we reached St. James's in safety. There we found the King much disturbed and displeased ; and with reason, for not only had the ministers broken faith with him in not trying to check the illuminations, but the Admiralty was lighted up behind its gates, and Lansdowne House in its garden. The unaccountable absence of the police was explained by the fact that they had all been confined to their stations, to be ready when wanted."

1833 was not better than its predecessor so far as the relations of the King and Queen to the country were concerned. On the grand stand at Ascot the King was struck on the forehead with a stone thrown by a man in the crowd. A week later Queen Adelaide was treated with marked rudeness at a review in Hyde Park. "The King looked old and infirm, the Queen depressed and apprehensive."

During the same season an ominous visitor passed through London. The Duchesse d'Angoulême, "the daughter of sorrows," whose father, mother, and aunt had been guillotined, was a second time a fugitive from France, which had finally cast out the main line of the Bourbons. Queen Adelaide went to greet her and was not cheered by her story.

On the night of the Queen's birthday there was such a dense fog in London that the usual illumination was "blotted out."

At a small card-party at the Pavilion, Brighton, the Queen was playing whist with Mr. Greenwood, the army agent, against the King and Sir Herbert Taylor, when Mr. Greenwood, seized with illness, was carried into the next room and died in a quarter of an hour, the company receiving a painful shock.

In 1834 the storm had blown past and matters began to mend. The Queen visited her relations in Germany, and on her return met a hearty welcome from the people, who began to see how foolishly and cruelly she had been calumniated. Adelaide and the King resumed the even tenor of their way which had been practised at Bushey Park, as Duke and Duchess of Clarence, before the business of the State troubled them. They fed thousands of the poor in Windsor Park and looked on at the feasting. They shopped together like ordinary mortals. When the Queen attended a Brighton fancy fair and saw an infirm old lady drop her reticule, her Majesty, before she could be stopped, stooped and picked it up. The couple went visiting freely among their subjects—especially at Brighton among the families of the old admirals who had been William's shipmates. The King and Queen were fond of Brighton and the sea. They were the last sovereigns to reside for any length of time at the monstrosity of a Pavilion which George IV. erected for a marine palace. William and Adelaide still gave balls and dinners there.

It is difficult to abide by the *juste milieu*. Kindly, not over-particular, good-natured Queen Adelaide erred in receiving at her Court on the most familiar terms the numerous handsome, but with the exception of Lord Adolphus, rowdy sons and daughters of William and the popular actress in comedy, Mrs. Jordan. These ladies and gentlemen had by the King's decree been ennobled; the eldest son was created Earl of Munster, the younger brothers and sisters took the name of Fitz-Clarence and were promoted to the rank of the sons and daughters of Dukes. Relying on their father's affection and on the Queen's indulgence, they swarmed about Windsor and the Pavilion, out-talked everybody, and helped to lend to the royal household a loud, free-and-easy character which was far from a desirable attribute for such a circle. It was with reason that the Duchess of Kent kept her young daughter, Princess Victoria, as much as possible away from Court. The King and Queen, remembering the old friendly relations, were hurt and offended. On one of the few occasions when the Duchess and her daughter were present at a royal banquet the King, in making a speech, gave way to his temper and so far forgot himself as to publicly reproach the Duchess of Kent for withdrawing the heir to the throne from his control and notice. The poor Duchess, thus assailed, gave way and wept, the girl Princess joining in her mother's tears, while Queen Adelaide was greatly distressed, and the rest of the company were covered with confusion.

Nowhere have we so lifelike a picture of Windsor in its lights and shades in King William and Queen Adelaide's days as in the diary of Lady Bedingfield, one of Queen Adelaide's bedchamber women and eventually a lady-in-waiting till the Queen's death. The diary—

or rather what survives of it—has been preserved among the *Jerningham Letters*, Lady Bedingfield being by birth a Jerningham. The intimacy between the Queen and Lady Bedingfield began earlier and was even closer than that between the Queen and Lady Brownlow. It affords one of the many proofs of the amiable and constant nature of the Queen. Lady Bedingfield with her husband and family had gone abroad to retrench, and, as they were Roman Catholics of an old Norfolk family, to educate and establish in foreign service some sons of the house. The Bedingfields spent several years in Ghent, where they became well acquainted with the Duchess Ida of Saxe-Weimar and through her with her elder sister the Duchess of Clarence. By the time the Duchess became Queen Lady Bedingfield had returned to England and was a widow with her family scattered and her income small. Adelaide immediately appointed her former friend one of the women of her bedchamber. The appointment was not calculated to be popular on account of the lady's religion—in fact, she passed the time when she was not in waiting on the Queen as parlour-boarder in a convent at Hammersmith.

Between court and convent was a unique division of life in England for centuries past ; but it did not hinder the appointment or bring it to a close, neither did it spoil the wits or the affections of such an excellent and brightly intelligent woman as Lady Bedingfield.

The Queen sent for Lady Bedingfield as the appropriate person to go and meet the Duchess of Saxe-Weimar, who was coming on a visit with six of her children and was expected that morning at Tower Stairs. Before giving Lady Bedingfield her instructions the Queen kissed her and seated her on the ottoman beside herself. By a mistake Lady Bedingfield was kept waiting for an hour at Buckingham Palace and then found that Lord Howe and Lady Mayo had set out without her; but she was determined to obey the Queen's orders. A footman brought her a crust of bread at her request and a coach-and-four arrived for her to follow the others. She rushed out calling to some one who spoke to her from behind, "I can't stay," and then found, to her dismay, it was the Queen following her, laughing. Preceded by a man on horseback the royal carriage-and-four trotted rapidly along Pall Mall, all eyes curiously inspecting the occupant, people standing on tip-toe to see the amused Lady Bedingfield. Surrounded by Beef-eaters and Guards she entered the gate of the Tower with its historical and tragic memories, to discover that Captain Fitz-Clarence's yacht with the Duchess and family had arrived and that Lord Howe and Lady Mayo had gone on board. Lady Bedingfield resolved to do likewise, and was not to be prevented, she confesses, by Lord Howe, who had returned and told her the Duchess was coming on shore and it was not worth while for her to be rowed to the ship. When he saw she would do it he good-naturedly escorted her in a boat; midway he cried out in distress that he saw the barge coming and that he ought to be at the Tower Stairs to receive the Duchess. Nimbly the boat was turned, and rowed back so rapidly that the Tower Stairs were reached in time. The Duchess's only anxiety was to see her lame daughter land. The Princess was raised in a chair on the bargemen's shoulders and put into a chariot with her mother; a procession of eight royal carriages came next, making a grand show as they turned the corners of the streets.

At the Court ball on the birthday of the Duchess of Gloucester the Queen wore a magnificent coronet of diamonds and carried a nosegay of diamonds (in the style of Queen Charlotte). Lady Bedingfield had to put off her widow's weeds and wear white according to etiquette on royal birthdays.

At the Queen's request Lady Bedingfield went to the Pavilion, Brighton, to preside for a time over the establishment of the young invalid Princess of Saxe-Weimar, on whom sea baths were tried in order in restore to her the power of walking. On the last birthday she had sat down, which the uninitiated viewed as a great liberty; but in reality all that the poor Princess, who was wasting away, could do, was to walk one or two steps, and that only occasionally. Lady Bedingfield had to write every night to report progress to the Queen; but instead of recovering Princess Louisa took chicken-pox! Then Lady Bedingfield had the opportunity of remarking how the fear of infection for their children kept away the King's daughter Lady Sophia Sidney and another lady, and how that fear vanished on the arrival of the King, Queen, and Court at the Pavilion. The royal party consisted of the King and Queen, the Princess Augusta, the Duke and Duchess of Gloucester, Prince George of Cambridge, Princess Louisa of Saxe-Weimar, four of the King's daughters (Lady Erroll, Lady Sophia Sidney, Lady Augusta Erskine, and Lady Mary Fox—all well married), Mademoiselle D'Este (daughter of the Duke of Sussex and Lady Augusta Murray and afterwards Lady Truro), with the ladies and gentlemen in attendance.

The King was like a bluff old admiral who looked up other admirals and summoned them and their womankind unceremoniously to dine or to spend a social evening at the Pavilion. On such occasions the Queen and the ladies worked (by invitation) at her table. Princess Augusta often played on the piano all the evening. She could play any old or new air that might be asked for. The gentlemen walked about the room and conversed. There was not more than one card-table. The King would get Lord Mayo, who had neither voice nor ear, to sing Irish songs. It was one of his Majesty's practical jokes.

When the guests were at table the signal for their rising and retiring was the King's saying the word "Doors" audibly.

Princess Augusta always came from Frogmore to Windsor to dinner when the Court was there. Princess Sophia never appeared in public and looked melancholy. The Queen was very attentive to her when she came to Windsor and sought to entertain her. Perhaps the boisterousness of the Fitz-Clarences was too much for the Princess, as in the instance when Lady Bedingfield remarks that "Lady Sophia Sidney sat by the King and talked a great deal, as she generally does." The talk was apt to be neither instructive nor decorous. It was gossip of the most careless description, out of which small scandals affecting even the blameless Queen arose. Lord and Lady Bingham and Lord and Lady Falkland were members of the household. Lord Bingham was supposed to admire Lady Falkland and Lord Falkland to admire Lady Bingham, and if Lady Falkland and Lord Bingham tarried behind the others at the card-table, or Lady Bingham and Lord Falkland lingered in the music-room the incidents awoke titters and mischievous comments. The King was so fond of a bad joke and had so little sense of propriety as to observe aloud at table that Lady Bingham had changed her seat in order to be with Lord Falkland. Queen Adelaide herself was infected by the prevailing levity and indiscretion when she kept telling Prince George of Cambridge, in the hearing of the Court, that the little Queen of Portugal had fixed upon him for her husband and was come to fetch him. They were but boy and girl of fourteen, and in their case the jest was innocent enough, except for the position of the lady who uttered the jest, and the example she set to the frivolous and coarse jesters around her, who were capable of taking the most extraordinary liberties in her company. The Queen told Lady Bedingfield when driving with her one day in her pony phaeton to the Chinese Lodge near Virginia Water, and when talking of Lady Bingham's beauty and folly, various anecdotes of the "odd ways" of Lady Bingham's sister Lady Howe.

The King and Queen, and Lord and Lady Howe had made a journey in the same carriage, when Lady Howe, feeling tired, had put up her feet on Lord Howe's knee, to his great embarrassment. Not content with this freedom she put her feet out of one of the carriage windows, and at Lord Howe's signs of distress asked calmly, "What do you mean by shaking your head?"

At another time, when placing tickets with prices on articles to be sent to a bazaar, in the company of the Queen and Lord Howe, Lady Howe fancied a pair of slippers. Her husband said he would buy them for her if they fitted her; on which she not only tried on the slippers on the spot, she put her foot on the table to show how well the slippers fitted. After these performances the *gaucherie* of a maid-of-honour who was in the custom of coolly appropriating her neighbours' seats, without asking their permission, sounds light by comparison.

We cannot be astonished at the Duchess of Kent's reluctance to take Princess Victoria to Court, except at rare intervals and for short visits. The King and Queen were wounded, and the regret was reciprocal, for the Duchess of Kent was warm-hearted and the Princess was fond of her indulgent aunt and cordial uncle; but the circumstances of the case rendered it very unadvisable that Princess Victoria should be brought into close and prolonged contact with the somewhat rollicking Court circle. It is reported that the Duchess of Kent had a special distrust of the ten Fitz-Clarences, who were the moving powers in their father's palaces, and to whose predominance the Queen made no objection, having the daughters constantly about her. She embroidered frocks for their children, painted their likenesses, and supplied them with pocket-money—as if they had been her own grandchildren.

At the juvenile ball at St. James's when Prince Albert and his brother were visiting their aunt at Kensington and were present at the ball with their cousin Princess Victoria, the Duchess would not bring them up to the Queen (on such occasions the royal family sat on an elevated row of chairs under a canopy), retired at an early hour with her daughter and nephews from the ball, and would not consent to their visiting Windsor.

Queen Adelaide was so intent on her needlework that she carried it even to the tent at Epsom on the race-days. One would have thought that her "drawing-book," in which she was in the habit of drawing with those diligent fingers such likenesses as struck her and as she could take, would have been a more natural accompaniment at Epsom.

On the anniversary of the coronation in 1833 a great dinner for ninety guests was served at St. George's Hall. When the King returned thanks for the terms in which the Queen's health was drunk he delivered an affectionate eulogium on her character. There were one hundred and thirty-five lamps in the dining-room and one hundred and twenty-four wax lights on the table at the banquet. After it the King gave every lady present a little Chinese bottle, the Queen distributing the bottles in the corridor before luncheon next day.

Lady Bedingfield gives an amusing account of that

visit of the young Queen of Portugal to Windsor which has been mentioned by so many chroniclers. Four carriages and a guard of honour were sent to meet the Queen and her party. Guards were stationed in the Park. The household was assembled in the corridor, getting cold and tired with the long delay; a regiment of Foot Guards with their band was drawn up in the court. Prince George of Cambridge came running, out of breath, to say he had seen carriages coming. The ladies hurried to the bottom of the stairs, the Queen stood at the top, with her lady-in-waiting, Lady Mayo, behind her. The band struck up "God save the King," and King William and all his gentlemen went down to the entrance hall to receive the visitors. He gave an arm to each princess (the Queen and her mother) and brought them upstairs to the Queen. She embraced them and put Dona Maria's arm within her own, while the King with the elder Princess led the procession to the great drawing-room. The Queen then presented the visitors to the ladies of her household. The two Portuguese ladies and the three Portuguese gentlemen were presented also. The last appeared old, bent, and ugly. The guests were then conducted to their apartments. The dinner hour was seven, and the Queen sent Lord Denbigh beforehand from her private drawing-room to see if the royal ladies were ready, as she meant to come and fetch them. In spite of the message there was an unaccountable delay, till at last the Queen went to Dona Maria's room and found that the luggage had only just then arrived. Her Majesty, who was accompanied by Princess Augusta, the six ladies of the household, and the Lord Chamberlain, lingered in the corridor, remarking on the busts and pictures, for the purpose of giving the strangers more time. At last Dona Maria's door was thrown open, and there, facing the Queen, stood the young girl bolt upright, with her lady-in-waiting, "equally tall, stout, straight and grave behind her."

Dona Maria's step-mother, who was with her, had French blood in her veins, as she was the grand-daughter of the Empress Josephine. She was graceful and mistress of the situation, with beautiful blue eyes, black eyelashes, and marked black brows.

The young Queen was as tall as her step-mother and much stouter. Her features were "small and childish, with fat cheeks squeezing up her mouth;" she had no colour, and was not a blonde though with light eyes and hair. According to Lady Bedingfield Dona Maria "had no expression whatever." Other observers thought the shy, reserved girl haughty and inclined to be sulky when anything put her out. The dinner, at which the young Queen sat between the King and Queen, was in St. George's Hall. The dinner-service was splendid, "all vermeil." The health of Dona Maria was drunk standing. In the evening the Queen and her ladies worked as usual.

The visitors breakfasted in their own rooms, the King and Queen with the household, as was their wont, where the conversation seemed to flow unchecked, and any lady who liked discussed the unfortunate foreigners with the greatest freedom. The King said he had never seen so uninteresting a girl as Dona Maria. The boy Prince George compared her to "an immense doll." The good-natured Queen considered her features regular, and thought she might improve. Lady Sophia Sidney, with her fine lady airs and her flippant sarcasms, was tolerably certain to have her "say."

In the course of the morning the company set out in five carriages-and-four, and many gentlemen on horseback, to see the park and Virginia Water. Rain began to fall, and the carriages had to be closed, with the air so overcoming Lady Mayo that she could not shake off the sleep which had beset her from the time that she was in one of the boats on the water. The spectacle of the nodding lady broke down the gravity of the young Queen who had been so sharply criticised at breakfast. But her gaiety was not more agreeable than her gravity; her manner was uncouth, her voice unpleasant, and she seems to have been seized with an inclination to romp; while the person she chose to " pull about" was the elderly Princess Augusta, of all people.

On the Queen of Portugal's departure Queen Adelaide conducted her to the door at the foot of the stairs. The visitors went to Lalham, a house at which the Queen of Portugal had stayed when in England before, and there Dona Maria showed girlish delight at finding the place unaltered, and that the tree which she had planted had grown. She graciously sent back sprigs of it to all the ladies (of whose censure she was unconscious).

Lady Bedingfield went in the suite with the King and Queen to Kew to a farewell dinner given to the Duke and Duchess of Cumberland before they left for Germany.

The Duchess of Cumberland came out to meet the Queen, holding the arm of her "beautiful blind boy," when the party were shown into a square room, plainly furnished, hung round with pictures. Prince George of Cumberland was not yet fifteen. He was tall and thin, with a round fresh face in which the eyes were partly closed. He wore the dress of the period—dark coloured pantaloons, a waistcoat buttoned to the chin, a black silk neckerchief with a cambric frill appearing above it, boots, and military spurs. He was " a fine-looking, spirited lad, unsubdued by his infirmity." He said he could not do without his tutor Mr. Jelf, and "Do you know he is so kind as to say he cannot do without me?" Prince George of Cambridge was with the King and Queen, and his blind cousin recognising him by his voice pretended to kneel down and kiss his hand.

The Queen showed Lady Bedingfield the little old palace of which all the royal family were fond, because so much of their youth had been spent there. Adelaide took her friend to the room in which the Queen was married, and pointed out where the royal family had stood on the occasion that July afternoon sixteen years before. Another room visited was that in which Queen Charlotte breathed her last, with the chair on which was pinned the paper containing the information, "Queen Charlotte died in this chair."

The company dined at Cumberland Lodge, which was modern and fashionably fitted up. The King gave the health of the Duke and Duchess in such terms that even the Duke was moved. Poor Duke! Nobody liked him, with his odd, abrupt manners and fierce countenance. He was "teasing and disagreeable." When he was at Windsor he professed a great fancy for Lady Bedingfield, which he illustrated by sitting next her and cracking the strangest jokes, which she could not comprehend. Somewhere, however, he had a heart which was bound up in his unfortunate son.

The Queen also showed Lady Bedingfield over the charming old home of Bushey, in which her Majesty delighted, she herself acting the part of cicerone in the shrubbery and grounds. Kew and Bushey were home-like; "Golden Windsor" was too magnificent. When there were only sixteen people at dinner the Queen was pleased, for then the couple and their household were like a private family, and the King himself led Adelaide to the table.[1]

In 1837 the King's favourite daughter, Lady de L'Isle,

---

[1] The Queen presided over the building and decorating of a small house called "Adelaide Lodge" in Windsor Park, a memorial of her.

whom he had recently appointed to the sinecure involved in being nominally housekeeper of Kensington Palace, died. Grief for her loss hastened the break-up of her father's constitution. Without any more special malady than an attack of hay fever, he gradually sank, lovingly waited upon by his faithful Queen. When she burst into tears on the eve of his death, he strove to speak cheerfully to her, "begging her to be of good heart" and to "bear up, bear up." He died at last in a peaceful sleep with his hand resting, where it had lain for hours, on Adelaide's shoulder.

The King was seventy-two and Queen Adelaide forty-five years of age.

On July 8th she was present at his funeral, occupying the royal closet during the service. Dr. Doran states that she was the only English Queen who paid this mark of respect to her dead King.

Most people are familiar with the anecdote indicative of Queen Victoria's good feeling and good taste which belongs to this time. Queen Victoria in writing a letter of affectionate condolence to her aunt addressed it to the "Queen of England." Her Majesty was reminded that she was now Queen of England. "Yes," answered the Queen, "but I am not going to be the first person to recall that fact to her Majesty's recollection."

In August, 1837, Adelaide left Windsor and repaired to her own house of Bushey Park. Her health, never very robust, soon began to fail. Her chest was weak and she sank into the condition of a chronic invalid who pursued in vain a sad search for a climate which might be of permanent benefit to her physically. She lived, however, for twelve years longer, spending a winter at St. Leonard's, another in Malta, where she caused an English church to be built at her expense. She rented Canford Hall, Witley Court, and Cassiobury, in turn.

Ten years after King William's death the Queen-Dowager was able to pay a last visit to her friends in Germany. On her return to England she sailed as a forlorn hope to Madeira. In spite of her weak and suffering condition her genuine sympathy for those around her whether in sorrow or in joy did not fail. A sailor on board the *Howe*, the vessel in which she sailed, over-balanced himself in trying to catch a bird which had alighted on the rigging, and fell overboard. The Queen's interest survived the details of the rescue and busied itself with the man's future welfare.

On nearing the coast of Portugal an impromptu ball took place on board, and there was merry dancing both on the main and quarter decks. The sick Queen lay below, unable to be present; but she would not throw cold water on the festivity, to whose echoes she listened with patient indulgence. She landed at Lisbon, where she was met by the King-Consort of Portugal. She returned, as probably she had not dreamed she would do, the long past visit to Windsor, when Adelaide was its royal mistress, in the days of comparative health and happiness, of the shy girl Queen, Dona Maria, who had been twice married since then and was the mother of many children.

Madeira was of little service in staying the progress of the Queen's fatal disease. She returned to England, tarried for a time at her beloved Bushey, and then went for the last change to Bentley Priory near Stanmore. There her complaint reached its final stage. Her niece Queen Victoria, hearing how grievously ill Queen Adelaide was, went with Prince Albert, on November 22nd, 1849, to visit her aunt.[1]

---

[1] At Queen Victoria's marriage, after the ceremony, when, according to etiquette, the Queen-Dowager, who was present, ought to have come forward with her congratulations, the younger woman anticipated the movement by passing quickly to the elder and claiming her embrace. On the birth of the Princess Royal one of the first messages announcing the joyful event was sent to the Queen-Dowager.

Eight days afterwards death released the kindly spirit from the worn-out body. Queen Adelaide's attached ladies and some of her nearest kindred had been much with her during those last sad years. In addition to her nephew Prince Edward, a niece, Princess Ida of Saxe-Weimar, resided frequently in England towards the end, which came when Queen Adelaide was in her fifty-eighth year. It was thirty-one years since the arrival in England of the bride of William, Duke of Clarence.

In her will the good Queen declared that she died in all humility, "knowing well that we are all alike before the throne of God." She requested that she might be conveyed to her grave "without pomp or state." She desired that she might not be dissected or embalmed, that her body might not lie in state, but that it might be buried by daylight as privately and quietly as possible. She, the widow of the sailor King, wished that her coffin might be carried by sailors to its resting-place in St. George's Chapel. Her relations and friends, the ladies and gentlemen of her household, her dressers, etc., etc., might if they chose follow her to the grave. She died in peace and wished "to be carried to the tomb in peace and far from the vanities and pomp of this world." She desired "to give as little trouble as possible."

In a sense this was her aim throughout her life—an aim which was full of simple dignity and genuine modesty. Probably one of the last of her acts was done still with the view of saving trouble, and under the idea that it might be wrong in her (where others were concerned) to dictate even the circumstances of her funeral, and that exception might be taken to the terms of her bequests of her worldly goods to members of her kindred. For very shortly before her death she sought in a few lines to cancel this will, and to substitute for it the brief direction to divide the means she died possessed of between her brother Duke Bernard of Saxe-Meiningen and her sister the Duchess of Saxe-Weimar. But as the memorandum was without attestation it did not hold good in point of law, and the original will was carried out.

The funeral was conducted according to the request of the dead Queen. An ordinary hearse, with nothing distinctive save the Queen's arms on the pall, conveyed the body. Three mourning coaches followed, and a small escort of cavalry completed the cavalcade, on which the Harrow boys and the country people all along the route gazed with awed interest. At the entrance to St. George's Chapel ten sailors stood ready to propel the platform on which the coffin rested to the mouth of the vault into which it was in due time lowered, with all honour, but without ostentation.

A good wife, sister, daughter, and friend, a conscientious and faithful benefactress of the poor, a reverent and devout Christian; in the integrity, sweetness and kindliness of a most womanly nature Adelaide of Saxe-Meiningen has rarely been surpassed among the Queen-Consorts of England. Slander assailed her, as whom will slander not assail when goodness provokes its poisoned sting? But false and base insinuations quickly die a natural death when neither arrogance nor folly exists to afford the evil weeds nourishment.

www.ingramcontent.com/pod-product-compliance
Lightning Source LLC
Chambersburg PA
CBHW020234240426
43672CB00006B/524